Wisdom@Work

Wisdom@Work

[THE MAKING OF A MODERN ELDER]

Chip Conley

CURRENCY
NEW YORK

All rights reserved.
Published in the United States by Currency, an imprint of the Crown Publishing Group, a division of Penguin Random House LLC, New York.
currencybooks.com

CURRENCY and its colophon are trademarks of Penguin Random House LLC.

Grateful acknowledgment is made to the following for permission to reprint previously published materials:
Doubleday, an imprint of the Knopf Doubleday Publishing Group, a division of Penguin Random House LLC: "For a New Beginning" from TO BLESS THE SPACE BETWEEN US: A BOOK OF BLESSINGS by John O'Donohue, copyright © 2008 by John O'Donohue. Used by permission of Doubleday, an imprint of the Knopf Doubleday Publishing Group, a division of Penguin Random House LLC. All rights reserved.
Pantheon Books, an imprint of the Knopf Doubleday Publishing Group, a division of Penguin Random House LLC: "There is something I don't know" from KNOTS by R. D. Laing, copyright © 1970 by R. D. Laing. Used by permission of Pantheon Books, an imprint of the Knopf Doubleday Publishing Group, a division of Penguin Random House LLC. All rights reserved.

Currency books are available at special discounts for bulk purchases for sales promotions or corporate use. Special editions, including personalized covers, excerpts of existing books, or books with corporate logos, can be created in large quantities for special needs. For more information, contact Premium Sales at (212) 572-2232 or email specialmarkets@penguinrandomhouse.com.

Library of Congress Cataloging-in-Publication Data
Names: Conley, Chip, author.
Title: Wisdom@work : the making of a modern elder / Chip Conley.
Description: First edition. | New York : Currency, [2018] |
Includes bibliographical references and index.
Identifiers: LCCN 2017052982 | ISBN 9780525572909
Subjects: LCSH: Older people—Employment. | Mentoring. |
Organizational learning. | Wisdom. | Career development.
Classification: LCC HD6279 .C66 2018 | DDC 658.4/071240846—dc23
LC record available at https://lccn.loc.gov/2017052982

ISBN 978-0-525-57290-9
Ebook ISBN 978-0-525-57318-0

Printed in the United States of America

Book design by Lauren Dong
Jacket design by Darren Haggar
Jacket illustration by Oliver Munday

10 9 8 7 6 5 4

First Edition

*To the Airbnb founders—Brian, Joe, and Nate
Without your trusted invitation, I wouldn't have discovered
these truths.*

*And thank you to my fellow Airbnb employees—
Great dance partners in the tango between my mentor and
intern identities.*

Contents

Foreword

by

Brian Chesky, cofounder and CEO of Airbnb

To understand Chip Conley and his role as a Modern Elder at Airbnb, I need to first share with you the story of our company's humble beginnings.

In October 2007, Joe Gebbia and I were roommates at our Rausch Street apartment in San Francisco. Our rent had gone up, and we were on the brink of losing our place. It was around that time that there was a design conference in San Francisco, and we noticed that all the hotels were sold out. So we thought, why not create a bed-and-breakfast for the conference out of the empty space in our apartment?

With three spare air-mattresses from our closet, we decided to offer conference attendees a place to stay, plus breakfast. Along with Nathan Blecharczyk, our third cofounder, we created a website, Airbedandbreakfast.com—and what the world now knows as Airbnb. We certainly never imagined what that idea would become.

By the time of this book's publication, Airbnb will have had more than 250 million guest arrivals, across more than 191 countries. Our community now offers over four million homes—that's more space than the top five global hotel chains combined. And in every single one of them, travelers from every corner of the planet can feel like they can belong anywhere.

"Belong anywhere" is a powerfully designed paradox—and it's the mission that drives us at Airbnb. To belong is a universal need, and the simplest way to understand belonging is to think of feeling accepted. "Anywhere" actually means two things. The obvious meaning is that belonging can be offered anywhere—as in the more than 65,000 cities, villages, and tribes around the world where you can find an Airbnb host. But "anywhere" also has a deeper meaning. The best way to think of anywhere is where you are "out of your element"—it's a place you've never been before. And our belief is that when you belong outside of your element, you become your best self.

That's the transformative power of travel, and it's why Airbnb exists.

But back in 2013, when I first met Chip, Airbnb was still just getting started. Though we had nearly four million guests staying in homes around the world, most people saw us as strictly a technology company. But Joe, Nate, and I knew we had more to offer. We knew that we weren't just in the business of home sharing. We envisioned a community that helped people with not only where you stay, but what you do—and whom you do it with—while you're there. In other words, a complete end-to-end trip. What we were actually selling was *hospitality*. The only problem was we didn't yet fully understand how hospitality worked.

So I did what I always do when I want to learn. I try to find the top expert in the field, and ask if they would be willing to give me advice.

When we first started to build out Airbnb's international presence, I turned to Facebook COO Sheryl Sandberg for wisdom. For product design, Apple SVP Jony Ive provided invaluable insights. When I wanted to think through corporate culture, CIA director George Tenet took my call and offered his counsel.

And when it came to the global authority on hospitality and service with a heart, I kept hearing over and over again that the person to call was Chip Conley.

I'd heard that Chip was a boutique hotel disruptor who oversaw the creation and management of more than fifty boutique hotels during his twenty-four years as CEO of Joie de Vivre Hospitality, a company he started when he was about the same age as we were when we founded Airbnb. Chip and I first met when he came to a fireside chat with our employees at our headquarters in early 2013. And from how he's translated Maslow's hierarchy of needs into a hierarchy of hospitality, to his deep understanding of Joseph Campbell's revolutionary approach to storytelling, I knew his knowledge would be invaluable.

So after a dinner at his home, I successfully persuaded Chip to become a part-time adviser to Airbnb. And before long, I offered him the role of Head of Global Hospitality and Strategy. I knew that he could help us transform our company into the international hospitality brand I had envisioned. But even more than this, we shared the belief that we could harness the power of millions of micro-entrepreneurs to learn how to be hosts and establish new standards for hospitality.

Truth be told, early on, we actually considered hospitality a "dirty word" at Airbnb. Hospitality was what the hotel industry did, where guests are called "sir" and "ma'am," and everything is a transaction, not an interaction.

Chip helped us understand that Airbnb could do hospitality differently. Our hosts call guests by their names. The houses and empty spaces guests stay in don't create belonging, people do. By inviting guests into their homes, Airbnb hosts personify true hospitality by getting to know their guests, learning their stories, and maybe even becoming their lifelong friends.

Chip also introduced Joe, Nate, and me to the power of what Dr. Carol Dweck from Stanford calls a "growth mindset." It's a way of seeing the world through a lens of curiosity—where risk and imagination combine to open up new possibilities. It's no coincidence that one of Airbnb's core values is "embrace the adventure." In contrast, too many of us are often hobbled by a fixed mindset, which limits our ability to change and our understanding of how to solve problems. But Chip invited us to see that experiencing a sense of wonder and surprise will always be a fundamental part of what travelers seek—and taught us how to approach hospitality with expansive and timeless curiosity.

But perhaps most important, Chip consistently demonstrated the reciprocal power of a Modern Elder. He affirmed that we all have a story to share and something to learn from one another. That if we take time to connect, we can learn anywhere and from anyone. And for me, there's nothing more important or that speaks more clearly to Airbnb's mission than the lesson that we can all belong anywhere, as well.

Your decision to read this book is no different from me picking up the phone and calling a colleague or trusted adviser, as I have done many times in the past. Chip will be your guide in learning how to cultivate a beginner's mind with the ability to learn and grow *and* be the sage counselor who draws on a lifetime of experience.

He'll show you that wisdom has very little to do with age and everything to do with approach. He'll teach you that when you open your eyes, ears, and heart, you'll find that everybody has a story worth hearing.

And that if you're paying close enough attention, someday your story could help others write their own.

[1]

Your Vintage Is Growing in Value

"It is not by muscle, speed, or physical dexterity that great things are achieved, but by reflection, force of character, and judgment; in these qualities old age is usually not only not poorer, but it is even richer."

—CICERO (106–43 BC)

———

"What the hell are you doing?!"

Bert Jacobs, all six feet five inches of him, barked at me as I was about to take the stage in Tulum, Mexico, in May 2016. My friend Bert, whom I often ran into at entrepreneurial speaking gigs, cofounded the clothing lifestyle company Life is Good. We were two of the older speakers at the idealistic, entrepreneurial global tribe event called Summit. At fifty-five, I was probably two dozen years older than the average attendee, and Bert was just four years behind me. After more than three years in the trenches with the millennial founders of Airbnb, helping them guide their rocket ship, this was my first "coming out" speech about what it means to be a "Modern Elder" in today's youth-obsessed world.

Bert's blunt question—part offended, part perplexed—serves as a litmus test for our grand ambivalence with age. At a time when Botox is becoming as popular in Silicon Valley as it is in Hollywood, why was I willingly prancing onstage calling attention to myself as the oldster in the crowd? And I got the sense that beneath the surface of Bert's semirhetorical question lurked another, more pressing one: What the hell is going on with our relationship with age?

Just before my fiftieth birthday, I sold my baby. Not exactly. But that's sort of what it felt like to part ways with the boutique hotel company that I founded and ran for two dozen years. The Great Recession had taken its toll on my financial and emotional well-being, and it was clear I was ready for a change. In my early fifties and nowhere near ready to retire, I found myself temporarily adrift. That is, until Brian Chesky, the young CEO of Airbnb, came calling and thus began my odyssey into a new world, which reacquainted me with the wisdom I'd accumulated in my years on this planet. But it also reminded me how raw and curious I could be as well.

I'll tell you more about that story later, along with stories of many inspiring people who are not only surviving, but thriving, in the later years of their working life. Like a schoolteacher who reinvented herself as an entrepreneur and started a booming travel agency in her late forties. Or a software engineer in his early fifties who went from writing computer code to counseling colleagues as he became a Silicon Valley leadership coach. Or a former Merrill Lynch exec who found inspiration for the memoir he was struggling to write at age seventy by becoming a summer intern surrounded by college students at a pharmaceutical giant.

You don't have to be on the other side of fifty to find this book relevant. The age at which we're feeling self-consciously "old" is creeping into some people's thirties, with power cascading to the young in so many companies. At a time when "software is eating the world," tech is disrupting not just taxis and hotels, but virtually all industries, the result being that more and more companies are relentlessly pursuing young hires and putting high DQ (digital intelligence) above all other skills. The problem is that many of these young digital leaders are being thrust into positions of power—often running companies or departments that are scaling quickly—with little experience or guidance.

Yet, at exactly the same time, there exists a generation of older workers with invaluable skills—high EQ (emotional intelligence), good judgment born out of decades of experience, specialized knowledge, and a vast network of contacts—who could pair with these ambitious millennials to create businesses that are built to endure. Ironically, the more technology becomes ubiquitous, the *less* DQ is actually a differentiator. While coding skills may become commoditized, the one thing that can never be automated or left to artificial intelligence is the human element of business. You may not be a software developer, but you are a soft skills developer—and soft skills are the ones that will matter most in the organization of the future.

Whether this is the second, third, or fourth act of your working life, the principles and practices in this book will show you how to leverage your skills and experience to stay not just relevant, but indispensable in the modern workplace. The world needs your wisdom now more than ever.

WHAT'S YOUR VINTAGE?

Yesterday I woke up with a fifty-seven-year-old man in my bed and, more painfully, he showed up looking back at me in my bathroom mirror (à la Gloria Steinem). I may feel seventeen, but catching a glimpse of my badly lit fifty-seven-year-old image, whether in the mirror or in some friend's photo on Facebook, is awful-tasting truth serum. Yet, oddly, my fifties have been my favorite decade. I'm enjoying the "Indian summer" of my life: young enough to take up surfing, old enough to know what's important in life.

Dr. Laura Carstensen, founding director of the Stanford Center on Longevity, has shown that people prioritize the present when time horizons are constrained. Accordingly, she's surprisingly found that people in their seventies are often happier and more content with life than those in their fifties, forties, or even thirties. By midlife, we may have slayed some of our internal dragons and healed many of our youthful wounds. All kinds of happiness surveys demonstrate a U-curve of adult satisfaction with younger adults starting out pretty excited by life. Then happiness starts to dip in one's late twenties and thirties when the mash-up of responsibilities associated with friends, family, infants, finances, and finding time for oneself takes its toll. It can hit its low point in our forties when midlife disappointment may lead, for some, to new sports cars and wrecked marriages.

And, then, you're in your fifties and miraculously, the grand reset of expectations you experienced during the prior decade, a reprioritization of what's important, leads you to feeling a little better about life. You're finally getting to enjoy all the confidence, courage, and crazy sense of humor you've accumulated along the way. An inner calm has started to emerge after decades of frenzied juggling. You feel an increasing capacity to be true to yourself. So it's great to be this age! But, just as this U-curve points us back in the right direction, we're faced with a tiny voice in our heads (echoing financier Bernard Baruch) saying, "Old age is always fifteen years older than I am." Hence, Bert's reaction. We've never been so young *and* so old.

We can distract ourselves from the mirror and "untag" ourselves in Facebook photos, but society has an uncanny way of reminding us of our age. A growing number of people fear being increasingly invisible. Others feel like an old carton of milk, with an expiration date mistakenly stamped on their wrinkled foreheads. One paradox of our time is that baby boomers enjoy better health than ever, remain vibrant and stay in the workplace longer, but feel less and less relevant. They worry, justifiably, that bosses or potential employers may see their experience (and the clocked years that come with it) as more of a liability than an asset. Especially in the tech industry, where I somewhat accidentally found myself launching a second act in my own career.

But we workers "of a certain age" are in fact less like a carton of spoiled milk and more like a bottle of fine wine of an especially valuable vintage. Especially in the digital era. And especially in the tech sector, which has become as famous for youth as for innovation, and as notorious for toxic company cultures and human resource headaches as for reckless twentysomething CEOs—and where companies and investors are finally waking up and realizing they could use a little "wisdom insurance": the humility, emotional intelligence, and wisdom that comes with age. In this book, I will argue that those of us with a little aging patina *do* have something to offer. Especially now.

We may live ten years longer than our parents and may even work twenty years longer, yet power is moving to those ten years younger. That can lead to a decades-long "irrelevancy gap" for those in my age range if we don't rethink our role. To avoid the fate of "boomer angst," we'd be wise to learn how to store the wine so it doesn't go bad. What makes a wine good is not only its age, but also the way you store it, the way you serve it, and the reason for raising a glass.

ARE OLDER PEOPLE NEEDED
IN THE DIGITAL ERA?

Recently, my iPhone went haywire. It lost an hour, so for a couple of days my phone was an hour younger than the time on my MacBook Air. This technical snafu didn't just affect me—thousands of iPhone users were missing flights and appointments as a result of this software glitch. I chalked this up to further evidence that the digital gods at Apple, with a median employee age of thirty-one, are orchestrating our lives in more and more ways. I searched for an answer in the place I always go, Google (median employee age of thirty), to see how

I could hack a solution and age my phone by an hour, but turning the damn thing on and off didn't solve things. So I retreated to another familiar spot, Facebook (median employee age of twenty-eight), to ask for help from my posse.

While the median age of employees in the United States is forty-two, that number is more than a decade younger among our tech titans. And a *Harvard Business Review* study showed that the average age of founders of unicorns (young, private companies with more than $1 billion in valuation) is thirty-one, and the average age of their CEOs is forty-one, as compared to the average age of an S&P 500 company CEO, which is fifty-two. So power in business hasn't just lost an hour, it's lost a decade or two. Sixty may be the new forty physically, but when it comes to power, thirty is the new fifty!

In many cultures, passing wisdom was once a prized tribal tradition, but today many of us fear it might be as popular as passing gas. In a pre-Gutenberg world, elders were keepers of their culture and agents of its survival and communication through myths, stories, and songs passed from one generation to the next. In an economy that was slow to change, the practical experience and institutional knowledge of the old remained continuously relevant to the young.

The acceleration of innovation made the elder less relevant. Literacy meant society was no longer solely dependent upon the memory and oral traditions of elders to share wisdom. Moving from an agricultural to an industrial economy meant age-old traditions of farming were replaced by the technological efficiencies of the machine age. Plus, young people started moving away from their parents to the city, and in the second half of the nineteenth century, a flood of young Europeans immigrated to the United States, forging a life on their own without the wisdom of their parents to guide their path.

The brisk march of progress from the industrial to the tech era has created a strong bias toward digital natives who understand gadgets and gigabytes better than those of us who didn't grow up "byting" from the Apple in childhood. And there's a growing anxiety in the boardroom about keeping up, as change in the digital world is happening so fast that most companies report that their DQ is actually declining. CEOs are kept awake at night by the worry that their competitors are younger and digitally smarter. According to PricewaterhouseCoopers (PwC), the grass is greener on the other side as the percentage of companies that feel they are doing a great job of harnessing and profiting from technology dropped from 67 percent to 52 percent between 2016 and 2017, creating even more of a frenzy to hire young talent favoring the generation that seemed to have emerged from the womb with an iPad in hand and a Snapchat account.

And yet, so many of us feel like we're growing whole rather than growing old. Is there a way for us to be integrated into cultivating young brains like farmer elders of the past were able to cultivate young grains? What if there was a new, modern archetype of elderhood, one that was worn as a badge of honor, not cloaked in shame? What if we could tap into our know-how and know-who to be an asset in the workplace rather than a liability? With more generations in the workplace than ever before, elders have so much to offer those younger than them, including introductions to those who can cultivate and harvest their skills.

Maybe eldership offers a higher form of leadership. Gray heads are generally wiser than green ones. What if Modern Elders were the secret ingredient for the visionary businesses of tomorrow?

MODERN AGE WISDOM

Not every aged wine is a spectacular vintage. Similarly, just because you're older, it doesn't necessarily mean you're wiser. Paul Baltes and Ursula Staudinger of the Max Planck Institute for Human Development did a comprehensive study and found the average correlation between age and wisdom is roughly zero from ages twenty-five to seventy-five. While this may be disappointing on the surface, the researchers did find that many people cultivate something even more valuable: a skill for *gathering wisdom* as they age.

Dr. Darrell Worthy, who led a group of University of Texas psychologists in a series of experiments on wisdom, found older people were far better at making choices that led to long-term gains. Younger adults made faster choices that led to more immediate rewards, while older adults were more adept at making strategic choices that took the future into account. Gandhi once wrote, "There is more to life than simply increasing its speed." Maybe the Modern Elder can be the designated driver in a world where the accelerator pedal is pushed to its limit.

Professor Robert Sutton suggests that the hallmark of wisdom is an alchemy of confidence and doubt, and knowing when to up the ante of one versus the other. Scholar Copthorne Macdonald has listed forty-eight characteristics of wisdom that can help create a framework for making the best choices. Wise people tend to acknowledge their fallibility, are reflective and empathetic, and have sound judgment, but these characteristics alone don't define wisdom.

If there's one quality I believe defines wisdom in the workplace more than any other, it is the capacity for holistic or systems thinking that allows one to get the "gist" of something by synthesizing a wide variety of information quickly. Part of this is aided by the skill of pattern recognition that helps you come to hunches faster that account for the bigger picture. And this is where age gives us the indisputable upper hand: the longer you've been on this planet, the more patterns you've seen and can recognize.

And this capacity for seeing the big picture can foster novel thinking. In his book, *The Mature Mind: The Positive Power of the Aging Brain*, psychiatrist Gene D. Cohen explains that older people, with the advantage of years of experience, have a vast storehouse of solutions embedded in their maturing brains that allows them to synthesize more information and potentially offer more solutions. Just take Dr. John Goodenough (his real name!) who, at fifty-seven, coinvented the lithium-ion battery, which shrank power into the smallest possible size. And then, thirty-seven years later, he became a late-life celeb when he filed for a patent application on a new kind of battery that might put an end to petroleum-fueled vehicles. Imagine that: ninety-four and his synapses are still synthesizing!

There's no question the media has created a mythic ideal of the youthful, hoodie-wearing genius leading the march of progress to a glorious digitally utopian future. But are these renegades supposed to be doing this alone? Can they? If the fate of Travis Kalanick, former CEO at Uber ousted by his board after a series of very naive leadership mistakes, is any lesson, maybe there's a symbiotic relationship that can exist between the digital natives and their elders.

We celebrate these young leaders—those who disrupt industries and show great promise due to their tech prowess, energy, speed, and stamina. What these young tech entrepreneurs lack in experience, we tell ourselves, they must make up in digital savvy and chutzpah. But, summing up what she's seen demonstrated by the leadership challenges at many of the "unicorns," strategic futurist Nancy Giordano suggests that a faster and more intuitive grasp of technology does not guarantee maturity. "With little training, we expect young digital leaders to miraculously embody the relationship wisdoms we elders had twice as long to learn, with significant guidance and formal training," she explains.

Maybe the elders' role is to accelerate this process of self-awareness in younger generations, as power is being thrust on them so quickly, before they are fully "baked." Rather than older generations being less valuable due to lack of specialized knowledge with an ever-increasing speed of obsolescence, maybe older generations are more valuable because they can help balance that narrow specialty thinking with the ability to see the bigger picture.

This concept of intergenerational reciprocity emerges at a perfect moment in our history. For the first time, we have five generations together in the workplace: the silent generation (in their mid to late seventies), baby boomers, Gen X, millennials, and Gen Z. The natural order at work has typically been predicated by a hierarchy, or a food chain, that places older, experienced people above the younger newcomers. But there's been a gradual shift of power from old to young that didn't just start with elderly greeters flanking the front doors of your local Walmart while thirty-year-old managers ran the store.

Generally speaking, people sixty-five and older spent the middle to latter part of the twentieth century putting their feet up as the average retirement age declined. But for three decades, we've seen a rising percentage of older people participating in the workplace. As reported by the *New York Times,* more than half of American baby boomers plan to work past age sixty-five or not retire at all, and the number of workers in the sixty-five and older demographic is expected to increase at a faster rate than any other age groups. In 2025, we will likely have three times as many sixty-five-year-olds working in this country than we did thirty years earlier, and the number of workers age seventy-five and older is expected to increase by an unprecedented 6.4 percent annually through 2024. Take note brave, new world: the wisdom of older people is one of the few natural resources globally that is increasing, not declining!

This unprecedented age diversity in the workplace can be confusing, as we may have drastically different value systems and work styles at play. But it can also be a wellspring of opportunity that the world has never experienced. When generations were siloed, both older and younger workers were like hermetically sealed containers with their wisdom trapped inside, but breaking down these walls, there is just so much that we can all learn from one another. Wisdom isn't rare, but it can be hard to access, like diamonds, unless you've developed the tools needed to dig for it.

This is happening in an era when automation is changing the landscape. Tech innovation of the past often eliminated repetitive factory jobs and, theoretically, led to better ones (only, the dirty little secret was these new jobs require different training that society didn't properly offer the displaced workers, hence our recent political upheaval). But, in the era of artificial intelligence, jobs will be taken over by machines faster as machine learning allows computers to teach themselves how to progressively serve our needs better. If millennials don't make us redundant, robots and artificial intelligence will. So people are living longer and needing to work longer. Automation is taking more jobs. And there are more generations in the workplace at the same time. Ouch! This sounds like it's going to get more painful, along with a lot of generational finger-pointing.

And yet, this is the perfect time for elders to make a comeback, thanks to their ability to synthesize wise, empathetic solutions that no robot could ever imagine. In an era of machine intelligence, emotional intelligence and empathy—something older people have in spades—are more valuable than ever. The more high-tech we become, the more high touch we desire. A decade ago, hoteliers predicted that the friendly concierge would disappear from the hotel lobby due to the access of information on the Internet. Similarly, travel agents were considered extinct in the era of Expedia, but consumers have flocked to travel counselors more recently because they appreciate the nuanced, personal advice from a wise professional who knows them. So not only is the supply of elder wisdom in the world increasing, but the value of that wisdom is increasing in tandem.

RECLAIMING "ELDER"

In the past, when people lied about their age, it was often to portray themselves as older than they were. Being an elder gave you clout, gravitas, power. Today, people lie in the opposite direction for fear of ageism. And for good reason. Call someone elderly today and it's like you're suggesting they had a personal relationship with Moses or Abe Lincoln.

It's time to liberate the term "elder" from the word "elderly." "Elderly" refers solely to years lived on the planet. "Elder" refers to what one has done with those years. Many people age without synthesizing wisdom from their experience. But elders reflect on what they've learned and incorporate it into the legacy they offer younger generations. The elderly are older and often dependent upon society and, yet, separated from the young. On the other hand, society has historically been dependent upon our elders, who have been of service to the young. Moreover, today, the average age for someone moving into a nursing home is eighty-one (compared to sixty-five in the 1950s), so there are a lot of people who qualify as elders, but are not yet elderly.

What was that? Am I hearing something? "I don't want to be an 'elder,'" you might be muttering resentfully. "I'm not old, crotchety, or wrinkled enough." Suspend judgment (a skill that elders have nurtured) for a moment and read on.

This won't be the first time a demographic group has taken back a term, turning a pejorative into a symbol of pride. "Yankee" was a derogatory term of the Brits to describe the New World upstarts, but it was soon adopted by New Englanders themselves (and many a baseball fan, centuries later). Similarly, Malcolm X and other leaders helped our country's African American population embrace the word "black" in the 1960s even though it was a word many racists had used to describe them. Southern comedians like Jeff Foxworthy have taken back "redneck" as a proud word that defines their identity. And when you were a kid on the playground a generation ago, you didn't want to be called "queer," but LGBTQ folks have reappropriated that slang and made it cool. Own the word, it gives you power.

So how do we take back the term elder, and create a modern definition as someone who has great wisdom to offer, especially during a time when wisdom is ever more valuable? As the geriatrician and author Dr. Bill Thomas said to me, "We see a child and know that this person is living in childhood. We see adults and know that they are living in adulthood. What is missing is the experience of seeing an elder and knowing that person has outgrown adulthood and is living in elderhood." Let's make it a 'hood that's not scary. Just as a child peers into adulthood with intrigue, wouldn't it be miraculous if an adult peered into elderhood with excitement?

Sad but true, the one ritual you can bet on—that defines this unnamed era that is expanding in length—is receiving your AARP card by mail right before your fiftieth birthday. Every fifty-year-old ought to also receive a two-sentence letter to help set the stage for his or her next chapter. This letter should read: "You may live another fifty years. If you knew you would live to the age of one hundred, what new talent, skill, or interest would you pursue today in order to become a master?"

As I will describe in chapter 2, through no plans of my own, I stumbled upon a job in my fifties at Airbnb, where I was surrounded with people who were half my age, and maybe twice as smart as me. It was disorienting, as there is no modern-day manual for the afternoon and evening of one's life. Unprepared, many people face their Modern Elder years with a sense of anxiety. They fear that their skills are extinct, relics of a bygone era. But what many don't realize is that the Modern Elder hasn't just acquired more skills by virtue of being older, but also has achieved the skill of *mastery*, which can be applied to learning new things. Modern Elders can move from being the wisdom keepers of the past to the wisdom seekers of the future. Aging with vitality exists when you create the perfect alchemy of wisdom and innocence.

What I truly needed when I joined Airbnb was a "consciousness raising" manifesto to help me understand the new rules of the road, as well as some tips to amplify what I might have to offer this new, younger workplace.

So, rather than stick my head in the sand or spout millennial stereotype slurs (I heard a few from my boomer friends when I joined Airbnb), I'm now offering the manifesto that I wish I'd had. And along the way, I'm introducing a new framework for wisdom at work and in life, one that's particularly relevant to those in the second half of their life. But this book isn't just for those pushing fifty or older; it's valuable for those in their twenties, and thirties, and forties who want both a road map for their future as well as a better sense of how they can tap into the wisdom of those who are a generation or two older than them.

As deeply divided as we are politically and culturally today, the eventual arrival of elderhood is a condition that unites us all. If you're thirty and reading this, it applies to you, too, as elderhood is the only demographic that all of us—if we are lucky—shift into someday. My friend Ken Dychtwald, founder and CEO of Age Wave and one of the nation's leading experts on the longevity revolution, wrote a book in 1989 in which he suggested of the future workplace: "mature men and women who will be retained and whose compensation will be based not on the number of hours they work but on their experience, contacts and wisdom." He called these people "wisdom workers," and went on to say, ". . . I am convinced that many corporate blunders and well-intentioned misdirections could be avoided if there were a better blend of the energy and ambition of youth and the vision and seasoned experience of age."

Thirty years later, maybe it's finally time for us to be more intentional about our "wisdom worker" status. Maybe it's time to distinguish and define the era between "middle aged" and "elderly" as one of mature idealism. For many of us, the baseball game of our career will likely go into extra innings. So maybe it's time to get excited about the fact that most sporting matches get more interesting in their last half or quarter. By the same token, theatergoers sit on the edge of their seat during the last act of a play when everything finally starts to make sense. And marathon runners get an endorphin high as they reach the final miles of their event. Could it be that life gets more interesting, not less, closer to the end?

As Ken recently suggested to me, "If you can cause maturity to become aspirational again, you've changed the world."

WHO IS A MODERN ELDER?

Thinking about America's modern version of a tribal council of elders calls to mind images of the Supreme Court, but there are many more than nine wise elders in a country of 325 million people. Internationally, one might think of "The Elders," a prestigious group established by entrepreneur Richard Branson and musician Peter Gabriel based on the idea that in today's increasingly interdependent world—a global village—many communities look to their elders for guidance. The group launched in 2007 with Nelson Mandela, Graça Machel, Jimmy Carter, and other humanitarian world leaders committed to using their collective experience and influence to help tackle some of the most pressing problems facing the world today.

But you don't have to be the recipient of a Nobel Peace Prize or sit on the highest court in the land to qualify as a Modern Elder. And, unlike in some tribal traditions, you don't have to be a man to be an elder. One of Airbnb's most valuable elders is the intensely loyal, infinitely wise, and brilliantly intuitive Belinda Johnson, Airbnb's chief operating officer (fifteen years Brian's senior), who joined the company a couple of years before I did and has been wisely advising Brian longer and more comprehensively than I have. Whether it's Sheryl Sandberg, the COO, as the elder to Mark Zuckerberg at Facebook or Ruth Porat, the CFO at Google/Alphabet (and in that same role at Morgan Stanley), who is fifteen years senior to CEO and cofounder

Larry Page (two examples of many), when you review the five qualities below that define a Modern Elder, you realize they are gender
neutral.

A Modern Elder doesn't have to be older than some specific age
or in a senior position in a company, but the person does have to be
older and wiser than those around them. That could mean the elder
is forty and surrounded by twenty-five-year-olds, or a sixty-year-old
surrounded by 40-year-olds, but whatever their biological age, Modern Elders are somehow able to marry an air of gravitas with a spirit
of humility.

Most Modern Elders I know are over the age of fifty and exhibit
wisdom in the following ways:

1. **Good Judgment.** The more we have seen and experienced, the
better we can handle problems as they come along in stride. The
older we are, the more proficient we may be at "environmen-
tal mastery," or the ability to create or choose environments
where we thrive. Will Rogers wrote, "Good judgment comes
from experience and a lot of that comes from bad judgment."
My skinned knee from the past can help prevent you from falling and skinning yours today. Modern Elders have a long-term
perspective based upon the wisdom they've gathered over the
years. To a young person, it's invaluable having an experienced
guide to warn them about what invisible rocks are downstream
as they make their way through the whitewater.

2. **Unvarnished Insight.** One of the chief assets gained by experience is a clearness of view, an intuitive insight. A Modern
Elder can cut through the clutter quickly to find the core issue
that needs attention, whether in a job interview or a strategic discussion. This phenomenal editing skill gives the elder a
certain gravitas such that everyone in the room hangs on this

person's next sentence. And because many elders have ceased to try to impress or prove themselves, there's a certain unvarnished yet polished authenticity to the observations of a wise elder. Youth is the time for harvesting and accumulating raw ingredients, while elderhood is the process of distilling those ingredients to bring out their best flavors and then blending those flavors together in a perfectly orchestrated meal.

3. **Emotional Intelligence.** Wisdom isn't just about what comes out of your mouth, but what you understand based upon listening from your ears and heart. Ninety-two-year-old Brother David Steindl-Rast, whose TED video on how happiness is synonymous with gratitude is legendary, told me, "Yes, I'd agree that the first task of an elder is to listen with genuine interest to younger people: how much we might be able to give them will depend on how well we have been listening." As the old saying goes, "Knowledge speaks, but wisdom listens." Modern Elders are self-aware, patient empaths who are good at both understanding and managing their own emotions, and tuning in to the emotions of others. I received one of the highest compliments of my time at Airbnb from a twenty-one-year-old employee named Hugh Berryman. He said, "When it comes to how generations think, it's almost like an old-fashioned radio. Metaphorically and literally, young people resonate with the frequency at one part of the radio dial and then as you move up in age, you can more easily tune in to other frequencies on the dial. Chip, you have the empathic capacity to tune in to virtually any frequency on the dial."

4. **Holistic Thinking.** In middle age, the brain has lost a step, so memory and speed decline. But the ability to connect the dots, to synthesize and get the gist of something, grows into

late adulthood. Part of this crystallized intelligence is due to the fact that an older brain has the capacity to traverse from one side to the other more adeptly. Psychiatrist Gene Cohen describes this as "moving to all-wheel drive," which helps us to see the whole as opposed to just the varied parts. And because the elder brain more calmly manages emotions, it can dispassionately recognize patterns more easily.

5. **Stewardship.** The older you are, the more you recognize your small place on the planet. But the more you also want to put your lifetime of experience and perspective to work to positively impact future generations. Robert Bly said an elder is someone who knows when it's time to give rather than to take and they often get their inspiration from seeking wonder in the woods. Joseph Meeker wrote "Wilderness is to nature as wisdom is to consciousness." The legacy of Modern Elders is the love they invest in both neighbor and nature.

As we age, we are called to become more and more human. This doesn't mean an elder shows up only as a wise, old wizard like Gandalf or Obi-Wan Kenobi. In fact, Modern Elders experience an emancipation from others' expectations that allows us to transcend needless conventions, which means we may appear more youthful and innocent. "Neoteny" is a quality of being that allows certain adults to seem childlike and leads people to remark about how these elders seem so young at heart and timeless.

As Walt Disney put it, "People who have worked with me say I am 'innocence in action.' They say I have the innocence and unselfconsciousness of a child. Maybe I have. I still look at the world with uncontaminated wonder."

HOW DO YOU BECOME A MODERN ELDER?

"In spite of illness, in spite even of the arch-enemy, sorrow, one can remain alive long past the usual date of disintegration if one is unafraid of change, insatiable in intellectual curiosity, interested in big things, and happy in small ways."

—EDITH WHARTON

That question may be why you're reading this book. And I'm a big believer in managing people's expectations, so here's what to expect . . .

First, in chapter 2, I will tell you more about my story as a reluctant disruptor at Airbnb and my early education as a Modern Elder. The chapter is entitled "Am I a 'Mentern'?" because I believe Modern Elders are interns as much as they are mentors. But let's recognize that my story of being a former CEO jumping on the Airbnb rocket ship is unusual so that's why I offer dozens of other Modern Elder stories in the book as well. Whether it's my story or one of the other Modern Elders in the book, the sentiments and initiation to this era of life are universal. They apply to anyone who knows they have something valuable to offer companies and employers; they just don't know quite what to do with it.

Next, in chapter 3, you'll learn more about the obsolete aging paradigm we've been living with, and how to free yourself from this outdated three-stage model of working life. Then, we dive into how anyone can reinvent themselves as a Modern Elder by becoming "unafraid of change, insatiable in intellectual curiosity, interested in big things, and happy in small ways."

While her quote is from a century ago, Pulitzer Prize–winning novelist Edith Wharton effectively sums up the four abilities that I define as my four lessons: evolve, learn, collaborate, counsel. In chapter 4, we'll explore Lesson 1, which may be the most difficult but critical of the four steps to becoming a Modern Elder: our ability to evolve. If we're too wedded to the past and to the costume of a traditional elder—making wise pronouncements from the pulpit—we aren't likely to grow much of a congregation. I'll show you how to shed all those old costumes to don a new one and grow into a new, fresh, and relevant reputation or personal brand. If I can evolve from being a brick-and-mortar hotelier to becoming a Silicon Valley start-up exec, you can move through your own fear of change too.

In chapter 5, you'll learn the value of adopting a beginner's mind and how to use this fresh perspective to increase your ability to learn (Lesson 2). Modern Elders are both student and sage, mentor and intern, and have a thirst for mastery. I'll show why questions hold more power than answers in the modern world and help you to be catalytically curious so that your inquiring mind becomes one of your greatest assets.

In chapter 6, we look at Lesson 3, leveraging our ability to collaborate and make something bigger. There's empirical evidence that older workers have more aptitude for collaboration, and for fostering team effectiveness. We'll also talk more about the intergenerational transfer of wisdom and consider what implicit trade agreement you can offer your younger colleagues. In my case, it was offering my EQ (emotional intelligence) for their DQ (digital intelligence) and we were both better for it.

In chapter 7, I'll share with you why I get such joy out of growing my ability to give counsel, Lesson 4—and help you do the same. One by-product of being seen as the elder at work is becoming the confidant of younger employees who want to bathe in your fountain of wisdom and are likely to be more candid with you as they don't see you as a competitive threat. Quite the opposite; by tapping into your know-who (your network), and your know-how (your library of wisdom), they see your presence as Miracle-Gro for their careers. Some of my happiest moments at Airbnb were the one-on-ones I had with young leaders who were getting wiser every day.

At the end of chapters 4 through 7, you'll find a few prescriptive tips and practices to help you put each lesson into action. I call these ModEl Practices, for two reasons: because, yes, Modern Elder can be shortened to ModEl, and also because that's what you are if you're an elder, a role model.

Chapter 8 focuses on putting all the puzzle pieces together. How do we take these four abilities and help you rewire who you are to catch your second (or third) wind in the workplace? Since older people tend to be good at synthesizing, you'll appreciate how I stitch together what you've learned to make this actionable. Together we'll look at a few stories of elders who've done so in the nonprofit sector, in the arts, as teachers or coaches, and as entrepreneurs. You'll also learn about the Modern Elder Academy for those of you looking for a place and a process for pressing the reset button at midlife.

Chapter 9 is the call to action for CEOs and HR departments around the world. I will debunk a number of myths about older workers as well as give organizational leaders suggestions for how to create a habitat that fosters the conditions for elders, and all generations, to thrive. I'll also outline why I think it's competitively smart for companies to develop a strategy to attract and retain Modern Elders—especially at a time when we're facing shortages of labor and talent and your customers' average age is probably rising (given the aging of the population). There's a big upside for a company in getting this right.

Then we wrap up with chapter 10 on what it means to leave a legacy in the workplace and beyond, and how to channel your beginner's mind and love of mastery to stay actively engaged by life as long as possible.

In the appendix, you'll find my ten favorite quotes, books, articles, films, speeches/videos, websites/blogs, academic papers, and organizations relevant to being a Modern Elder. I felt this would be much more valuable to you than a series of footnotes. You'll also find my eight prescriptive action steps to becoming a Modern Elder.

If you take away just one lesson from this book, I hope it's this: Just as your hearing is starting to occasionally be suspect, listening is more important than it's been in decades. And the people you need to listen to look nothing like the people you've listened to before. First, it was your parents and grandparents, then your teachers and coaches, your doctors and your bosses and peers. These were the faces of authority, and they were always older or your own age. We're not really wired to listen to and learn from young faces—but that's exactly what we need to do in order to reap the rewards of being a Modern Elder. Learn, grow, teach, and then learn again. That's what we have to offer ourselves and the world.

IS LIFE GOOD?

Back to Bert and the story of my "coming out" as a Modern Elder at the Tulum Summit. I wasn't clear about Bert's intent with his blunt question, but it was clear he had some complicated feelings about his age, especially among all the young start-up folks at this Summit event. Excuse the self-referential expression, but Bert may have had a "chip" on his shoulder based upon his own perspective on aging. Ironically, he's one of the more youthful entrepreneurs I know over the age of fifty. He and his brother bootstrapped Life is Good from selling T-shirts out of the back of their car for five years out of college, and never really lost that scrappy, working-for-beer-money mentality even as they grew the lifestyle brand into a company generating more than $100 million annually twenty-two years later. Bert—with his boundless energy and his incalculable wisdom—in many ways embodies the very best of what it means to be a Modern Elder.

As I rushed onstage, I told Bert, "Listen to what I say and then, after my speech, tell me if you're still upset by the fact that I'm outing myself as an elder."

Postspeech, Bert came up and hugged me with tears in his eyes and said, "Now I get it!" And, in fact, he's gone on to incorporate many of the practices in this book in his role as the CEO, or "chief executive optimist of life," for Life is Good. As you read this book, I hope you get it too. Many people suggest this midlife period is a time of crisis. I believe you're in the midst of your "midlife awakening."

Life IS good, and it may be getting even better!

[2]

Am I a "Mentern"?

"Musicians don't retire. They stop when there's no more music left inside of them."

—ROBERT DE NIRO IN *THE INTERN*

"How would you like to democratize the hospitality business?"

Grabbing a snack at one of the San Francisco tech crowd's favorite haunts, I was face-to-face with Airbnb CEO Brian Chesky's charismatic vision. It was March 2013, and I'd been advised that Brian had a Steve Jobs type of intensity: he was whip-smart, asked a million questions, and wanted to change the world. He was not your average, young tech CEO. He wanted to solve global problems as much as he wanted to create a successful business. I was just home from a five-week odyssey to Asia, experiencing five festivals including Kumbh Mela, the massive one-hundred-million-person Hindu pilgrimage. So I was a little jet-lag-confused even before Brian offered that provocative proposition.

How do you answer that question when you've spent more than a quarter century as a hotelier?

In 1987, I started my own boutique hotel company. I was in my midtwenties and got a little too clever calling it Joie de Vivre. I liked the fact that this French phrase for "joy of life" also defined our mission statement. How many companies have a mission statement that's also the name of the company? Well, my friend Bert Jacobs, whom I mentioned in chapter 1, pulled off this feat with Life is Good, but most people can at least pronounce, spell, and understand the meaning of his company name. As for Joie de Vivre, I joked that the brand was popular with intellectuals and Francophiles. Fortunately, there were lots of customers who fit our psychographic, and the company eventually grew into the second-largest boutique hotel company in the US with fifty-two boutique hotels in California, each one with its own unique character and spirit.

Then, twenty-four years later, in 2010, I sold it. Why? You'll read more about my story throughout the book, but let's just say that something deep inside me told me it was time for a change. You may have heard that same internal voice. It's easy to ignore it or silence it, for a time, but then it grows louder, especially in the middle of the night. Once I finally gave in to that voice telling me to sell the company, I knew my next path would be offbeat. I was in my early fifties and knew I still had some music inside me, but I just wasn't sure where to share it. I had recently founded Fest300—a website dedicated to profiling the world's three hundred best festivals—and was sharing a little bit of my "music" with my small start-up team. But this felt more like a passion project than a new career.

As I was pondering my next step, Brian—who'd read my book *PEAK*—reached out to me and asked if I would give a speech on hospitality innovation at his small, fast-growing tech start-up. He introduced me to his cofounders, Joe Gebbia and Nate Blecharczyk, as well as the head of "Product" (a word I didn't fully understand, Luddite that I was), Joebot (Joe Zadeh). Nice bunch of guys. And they truly aspired to grow the company into a hospitality giant.

Sounded good. But I was an "old school" hotel guy, and not even sure exactly what Airbnb was (I asked a millennial friend of mine if it was a subsidiary of Couchsurfing). For that matter, I didn't even have an Uber or Lyft app on my phone in early 2013, and I'd never heard of the term "the sharing economy." Science fiction writer William Gibson wrote, "The future is here. It's just not evenly distributed yet." That aptly describes this old dog pondering a new trick when Brian asked me to come on board as the company's Head of Global Hospitality and Strategy.

Initially, I was excited about the global reach of the company and the opportunity to democratize hospitality. But I was also more than a little intimidated. At fifty-two years old, I'd never worked in a tech company, where one's value can be defined by the maxim, "I code, therefore I am." Let's face it, I didn't read or write code. I was nearly twice the age of the average Airbnb employee and, after two dozen years running my own company, I'd be reporting to a smart guy who was twenty-one years my junior. What would it feel like getting my first performance review from a boss young enough to be my son who I was also supposed to mentor?

I asked a few hotelier friends whether they thought I should join Airbnb. One hotel exec mused, alluding to the film *Field of Dreams*, "If you build it, they will NOT come, but they WILL laugh! There's a tiny market of people who want to stay in someone else's home." But I did have a few tech-minded friends who told me Airbnb was a rocket ship ready to launch. And, my gut told me that home sharing might just be scaling the experientially minded "live like a local" ethos that boutique hotels had pioneered for the previous quarter century. At the end of the day, it wasn't the financial upside that intrigued me as much as it was the prospect of sharing the same air with this young and curious rebel CEO who was the son of two social workers. I seem to have a strong instinct for the fresh scent of possibility, and I sensed a blooming bud of potential in Brian. His humble roots, visionary aspirations, and deep desire to create a more connected world lifted the spirits of all around him. Intuitively, I felt we had something to learn from each other.

So I told Brian I was in. The night before my start date, April 22, 2013, we decided to work out the final details at a dinner at my home. While we didn't arm-wrestle that night, we came close. I was to be his in-house mentor and adviser to him and his executive team. I agreed to give him fifteen hours of my time each week.

In my first week, I sat in on a series of meetings just to acclimate myself. In one meeting of engineers, the bespectacled twenty-five-year-old wizard leading the meeting looked straight at me (I guess I was fresh meat) and posed an existential tech question, "If you shipped a feature and no one used it, did it really ship?" I had taken a philosophy class or two in college so I got the gist, but given that I had not taken any computer science classes, the specific meaning was lost on me. I gave him a blank stare. Bewildered, I realized I was in "deep ship" as I didn't even know what it meant to "ship a feature."

After my first week on the job, my fog of confusion only thickened. Brian had asked me to be his mentor, but I also felt like an intern. *Could I simultaneously be both?* I asked myself. *Am I a "mentern"?* Like a unique, older breed of unicorn? I later discovered a wonderful word—"liminality"—that describes the ambiguity and disorientation one feels in the midst of transforming one's identity (I'll discuss more about it in chapter 4). My word for it? "Gooey." Like what happens to the caterpillar in the middle of its metamorphosis into a butterfly. Airbnb was my chrysalis.

We all have fish-out-of-water experiences, which can make us feel a little over the hill. It could be when your kids are talking about a new social media platform or some new musician you're not familiar with, things you can afford to ignore or shrug off without any real consequences. But when this happens in the workplace, we have two choices: either we hole up in the safe cocoon of the familiar and resist learning from those younger than us, or we embrace an evolution. Yes, an evolution might cause some initial discomfort. But it's far better than the alternative.

THE RELUCTANT DISRUPTOR

Soon after I joined Airbnb, Brian asked me to address an all-hands employee meeting to talk about what it means to become a hospitality company. Having been a disruptor in the hospitality industry once before, as a rebel boutique hotelier in the mid-1980s (not long after Brian was born), I knew that being a "disruptor" didn't mean we should be disrespectful. In fact, quite the opposite; we'd have a lot of people to win over in the next few years.

"First they ignore you. Then they ridicule you. Then they fight you. And then you win." I used this quote, commonly attributed to Gandhi, in my speech because it inspired me and conveyed a sense of where we were headed. I suggested that the process of moving people from "ignore" to "win" wasn't going to be easy, so our attitude better be hospitable. Now, of course, we weren't fighting for our lives, but we were facing a whole lot of opposition. I recounted the wide variety of groups that might be included in this Gandhian arc: convention meeting planners, destination marketing organizations (known as DMOs), corporate travel managers, landlords and real estate developers, and, of course, hoteliers and politicians. We needed to prove we added value to a community. Another win for us was to be regulated and taxed. I know that sounds strange. But it's also what gave this movement and our company legitimacy. The quote's disruptive words became one of our rallying cries.

Sometimes we sounded that cry at eleven at night in the offices. Tech never sleeps. Especially when you're a global hospitality company with guests using your product (both the online and the physical one) twenty-four hours a day, nearly everywhere. Brian and I met for lunch near our new Dublin, Ireland, operation just a few weeks after I'd started. I was meaning to talk with him about this supposed fifteen-hour-a-week gig. It was turning out to be more like fifteen hours a day.

But before I could bring that up, Brian was already asking if I could take the lead in setting up an internal learning and development function (with longtime employee Lisa Dubost). Since we had many twenty-eight-year-old managers leading twenty-four-year-old direct reports, it was apparent that the company needed to offer these first-time managers some guidance. Any delusions I still harbored of this being a part-time job went out the window that day. So, after a pint of Guinness, I was signed up to be a full-time leader for Airbnb with the title Head of Global Hospitality and Strategy, with a few other roles thrown in for good measure.

Honest truth? I loved learning. So much. And, while there was so much I didn't know, it was clear that what I *did* know was needed. We kept my Airbnb involvement quiet publicly until September. This meant I got to have one last boondoggle before the press and my hotel industry cronies were going to ramp up the inquiries about why on earth I'd joined this young and unconventional company. Being a board member of the celebrated arts festival Burning Man, I promptly headed out to the Nevada desert in an RV with some friends just before Labor Day.

While on the playa, as we call it, I had a meal with the young cofounder of Couchsurfing, Casey Fenton, who gave me the lay of the home-sharing land. Another night, amid the dust in the desert, I sat down to dinner with a group of dressed-down businesspeople and struck up a conversation with a friendly guy from Austin, Texas. He told me he was the founder of HomeAway, the home-sharing public company that also owned VRBO (Vacation Rentals By Owner). I was aware that Brian Sharples's company was worth more than $4 billion on the public NASDAQ stock exchange, maybe double Airbnb's private market valuation, and that they were our biggest competition in those early days. Before he started divulging too many details about his business, I told him that I'd recently joined Airbnb and saw Brian Sharples's eyes become saucers. At the time, I read this coincidence—me running into our biggest competitors in this unlikely setting—as a message from the universe that I'd chosen the right path. But maybe the larger lesson is simply that it's amazing who you can meet at Burning Man.

In the fall of 2013, I cautiously asked my smart, young boss to give me some feedback on how I was doing, knowing this review might feel a little awkward coming from someone so much younger than me. Brian was effusive in his praise. But he also said I seemed "reluctant" and he wanted to see how we could evaporate my sense of hesitation.

Some of my reluctance had to do with the fact that the part-time gig I'd signed up for was now taking up all my time. And I was trying to quickly edit the rest of my life to make way for Airbnb's full-time dominance of my calendar. But I had to acknowledge that the bulk of my reluctance was due to being unsure whether my skills and advice were relevant to this new era of business disruptors. As one of my direct reports said to me a few weeks into my new job, "How can you be so wise and so clueless at the same time?" She had a point. I was clueless with a capital Q when it came to my lack of tech fluency. I had never used a Google doc. I thought MVP (minimum viable product in start-up tech talk) was a great athlete and that "blue flame" was the fire on a gas stove (in Silicon Valley, it's code for a young entrepreneur who's burning hot). Clearly, I didn't get the lingo. Brian assured me that what I lacked in digital fluency, I made up for in strategic thinking, emotional intelligence, and leadership guidance, and he encouraged me to double-down on my commitment to this new path. I'm glad I took the advice of my young boss.

WHEN IN DOUBT, FIND A ROLE MODEL

As I settled in for the long haul in this new role, I searched for books that could educate me or some kind of rite of passage that might define the dawning of this new era in my life. Finding no resources, I started searching for a role model, someone who had experience in the trenches as the wise counselor to younger tech CEOs. Six months into the job, I was a little less dizzy from the teeter-totter of being both a mentor and intern, but I was still looking for guidance on how I could be a humanist in the land of numbers. One man's name popped up, over and over. Bill Campbell. He was the original "CEO whisperer."

Journalist Ken Auletta wrote a glowing piece about Bill in *The New Yorker* (the link is in the appendix) that described the man perfectly: "His various titles—Columbia football coach, Apple executive, co-founder of Go Corp., Intuit C.E.O., chairman of Apple, chairman of the Columbia University board—do not convey his influence. In the world capital of engineering, where per-capita income can seem inversely related to social skills, Campbell was the man who taught founders to look up from their computer screens. He was known as 'the Coach,' the experienced executive who brought a touch of humanity to the Valley as he quietly instructed Steve Jobs, Jeff Bezos, Larry Page, Sergey Brin, Marc Andreessen, Ben Horowitz, the founders of Twitter, Sheryl Sandberg, and countless other entrepreneurs on the human dimensions of management, on the importance of listening to employees and customers, of partnering with others." While Bill's own career was impressive, what made him a legend was how he provided jet fuel for the careers and talents of those who built the tech world as we know it today. As Steve Jobs commented in the media, "There's something deeply human about him."

Not knowing him at all (though I was told that, like me, he was fond of giving bear hugs to his fellow business associates), I tried to get a hold of Bill a couple of times in the fall of 2013. I didn't hear back from him so I started reading everything I could about "the Coach" and, when in doubt, my mindset shifted to "What Would Bill Do?" His example led me to schedule longer weekend meetings with Brian Chesky because our weekday time in the office was often brief and interrupted by urgent issues of the moment. Bill was well known for taking long, ambling walks with Steve Jobs on Sundays in the Valley foothills or around downtown Palo Alto. So Brian and I would dive deep for a few hours on the weekend in my backyard cottage whenever we were both in town.

Bill was also fond of saying, "Your title makes you a manager, your people make you a leader." As a practitioner of prowess and process, Bill believed in helping people live up to their true potential. I like to believe I was channeling Bill when I came up with my favorite question to ask my direct reports back at Joie de Vivre and then at Airbnb, "How can I support you to do the best work of your life here?" This question not only gave those who worked for me the sense that I wanted them to succeed, it also put some responsibility in their laps to help fashion a working relationship that would encourage them to make suggestions on how to improve their performance, rather than play the role of victim if they felt stymied in their career.

During my time at Airbnb, I enjoyed taking on junior managers who had hit a career cul-de-sac and helping them to reclaim their mojo. I would give them a full-body listen, filter that through decades of experience, ask a few leading questions, and often help them find an answer that was deeply buried in their consciousness. I would offer them advice and direction much in the way that most great athletes and musicians have a coach who helps guide them to be their best. I was learning the less there is of me, the more room there is for the person I was mentoring.

MORE THAN A MENTOR

Some of the most legendary leaders in business today have benefited from the counsel of a wise mentor. With the company he founded in his college dorm room, Michael Dell wisely pulled into board service such older advisers as Teledyne cofounder George Kozmetsky and former AMR CEO Don Carty, who served as vice chairman. Facebook founder Mark Zuckerberg similarly tapped the wisdom of elder statesmen like Donald Graham of the Washington Post Company, Netflix founder and CEO Reed Hastings, and PayPal cofounder Peter Thiel as board advisers.

This kind of role is different from the relationship an entrepreneur may have with their investor or venture capitalist. Just because someone has invested in a company, it doesn't mean they've invested in the young founder. Truth is, some venture capitalists on the boards of rising young tech companies have scarcely more operating experience than the founder. And, while many young entrepreneurs may find their investors to be a great source of wisdom, often this relationship trends toward the tactical and transactional, with the investor more focused on optimizing returns as quickly as possible than on building a legacy in the leader they are advising or patiently grooming a great leader who can develop a great company.

As I studied this further and had now become a sixty-hour-a-week insider, I learned there are typically three kinds of roles an outsider can play in helping an entrepreneurial leader, although these are often blended. An *adviser* offers domain expertise to assist with quite specific decision-making. A *coach* helps you build your tactical leadership skills. And a *mentor*—the most rare of the three—helps you make the best decisions for you and helps you to become a better person in the context of your work. Quite often, a mentor is a mirror as he or she (ideally) has an almost alchemical connection with you that can help you see yourself better. But because mentors can, theoretically, be the same age as or even younger than their mentees, I soon realized that none of these words perfectly defined the relationship I was developing with Brian, which is how I stumbled upon the word "elder."

If a mentor is a mirror, I believe an *elder* is an editor. Elders may be advisers, coaches, and mentors as well, but their unique value is in their ability to truly get inside the mind of those they advise. Because of their vast experience, they are able to see in their students what they have already been able to overcome themselves, as well as the characteristics and challenges that make each student unique. The elder naturally distinguishes between what's worth sweating about and what's not. The student is a storehouse of something the elder is quite familiar with, but some rearranging is necessary for it to make sense to the student.

Since most elders are older, midlife or beyond, they have some understanding of the sheer weight of accumulation—friends, marriage, kids, jobs, outside obligations, material possessions. So they know that the sagging happiness that can accompany middle age (as defined by the "U-curve" of happiness mentioned at the start of this book) cannot be solved by more accumulation of responsibilities, but rather through prioritization and ruthless editing. Simplicity can be like a religion for those in the later chapters of life. It's also a great metaphor for effective strategic thinking in business.

Ironically, one of Airbnb's early six core values was "Simplify" and, yet, the 2013 strategic initiatives that I encountered when I joined were so wide and disparate, almost no one in the company could recite what was truly important to us from an operating perspective. Plus, as a new "sharing economy" darling, we were being presented with opportunities to expand into all kinds of new businesses—outside travel—in which we could create an online marketplace.

This prompted me to lead a three-day strategic retreat, soon after Burning Man 2013, in New York City with the founders and senior leadership team. We were going to consider twenty-three different potential initiatives for 2014, but we were going to force ourselves to only select four. We also studied the principles in my book *Peak: How Great Companies Get Their Mojo from Maslow*. I didn't yet have a word like "elder" to describe my evolving role at Airbnb at that time. But I've come to see that great elders are as much editors as sculptors who, like Michelangelo, chip away at the rock to find the piece of art to be revealed inside—whether that's the unique gifts of a young CEO or the unique value proposition of a company.

You can see how in some ways a mentor is responsible for inviting the genius out of the person. And once this genius is released, it requires maintenance, sustenance, and growth. This is where the elder's job begins. A mentor complements the elder. The mentor helps mirror, while the elder shapes this genius into its most essential form. The more time I spent with Brian, the more jazzed I was about this elder role. Philosopher Arthur Schopenhauer reputedly wrote, "Talent hits a target that no one else can hit; genius hits a target that no one else can see." Brian was a genius in the making.

Bill Campbell did return my call in early 2014. But ironically I was tied up in an Airbnb meeting and wasn't able to take it. Sadly, we never did speak before he passed away in 2016. But, while I didn't take the call, it was Bill Campbell who inspired me to follow my calling. Studying Bill helped me to see my calling was to be a Modern Elder who helped Brian as well as dozens of other young leaders in the company to maximize their potential and, consequently, the company's potential to make a difference in the world.

CREATING AN EFFECTIVE TEACHER-
STUDENT RELATIONSHIP

I was fortunate. Twice. First that Brian Chesky invited me to have this relationship with him, and second that he had a voracious appetite for learning from those older than him. That's not always the case.

Twenty years ago, I was on the other side of this equation. I hired Jack Kenny, who had been president of Hotel Group of America, to be my chief operating officer and president of Joie de Vivre while I was CEO. Jack was fifteen years my senior, helping to guide a young, confident buck who'd founded his own company at age twenty-six and now, ten years later, needed some senior leadership as the company had grown so quickly. Ostensibly, Jack and Chip were the mirror image of Chip and Brian.

As the junior person in this equation, I learned a bushelful from Jack. Perhaps most significant for my future role as a Modern Elder at Airbnb was the fact he did his best to intern publicly and mentor privately. He would often ask a relatively obvious question that helped assure everyone was on the same page. And instead of counseling me or someone in a meeting in front of everyone else so they might feel like they were being scolded publicly by their father, he would pull the person aside after the meeting and ask, "May I share an observation about how you could have been even more effective in that meeting?" He would also often ask me "What are you pretending not to know?" when he knew I needed to make a difficult decision. A lesser person might have tried to solve the problem for me, but Jack was masterful at guiding his young CEO to the wise answer without letting his own ego get in the way.

Jack's sense of humor and his accessibility drew people to him. If you were in a room with Jack, you knew you'd have a good time— even if you were talking about very sober subjects. I greatly relied upon and never questioned Jack's confidentiality. As a youngish CEO, I had my faults and there weren't many people I could talk with about them. Jack was always a steward for me to become more effective. He never betrayed private conversations and was very open to sharing his own vulnerability as a welcome mat for me to be more honest about my opportunities for improvement. Jack wisened me up.

Sallie Krawcheck has exemplified the art of mentoring privately and interning publicly—all while leading some high-profile businesses in turmoil. She was charged with turning around Merrill Lynch's wealth management business after Bank of America acquired it during the subprime crisis, and she rehabilitated Citigroup's research business after a scandal. Sallie has some insightful perspectives on how to create symbiotic teacher-student relationships. She believes we need to move from mentors to sponsors because a sponsor advocates on your behalf.

Sallie says, "All the important decisions about your career are made when you're not in the room. People decide to hire you, fire you, promote you, fund you, send you on the overseas assignment, all when you're not there. So how do you ensure that you have someone in the room fighting for you? I would strongly argue that you need to have in place your Personal Board of Directors. Those are your mentors, your sponsors, your confidants, the people you can turn to when you're thinking about a career transition—for the kind of advice your boyfriend, your parents, and your best friend from college just can't give you."

Sallie now is the CEO and cofounder of Ellevest, a digital investment platform that is reimagining investing for women. She also speaks to women's groups around the country, acting as a mentor, elder, and friend to a wide variety of women who are looking for wise counsel in the workplace. After she left Bank of America and felt like she was in a liminal space not fully clear on what was next, she started mentoring a handful of women entrepreneurs in New York.

She writes in her book, *Own It: The Power of Women at Work*, "The surprise was that, without my even knowing what the words meant, they quickly 'reverse mentored' me. So, while I was making connections for them and guiding them in some corporate introductions, for example, I was learning from them about entrepreneurialism and social media and what was on the minds of women their age."

Similarly, the CEO of New York City–based SoulCycle, Melanie Whelan, couldn't be more excited about her new millennial mentor. Melanie told me that Liv, her reverse mentor, has a whole different perspective that helps her stay current, on everything from new tools for digital influencing to what's becoming hip in terms of new exercise regimes to new health-minded apps to download.

Brian reverse-mentored me in all kinds of ways. Just two months after I joined the company, we moved our San Francisco headquarters to 888 Brannan Street, ironically, a building my first boss out of business school previously owned. Airbnb had spent a small fortune designing a twenty-first-century vertical campus that rivaled the fancy corporate campuses down in the Valley as we were competing for these same tech employees. But currently we were occupying only a small percentage of this large building with options to take over the rest of the building over the next couple of years. I pulled Brian aside after one of our senior leadership meetings to warn him that some of our leaders (all of them typically a little older) were worried about the financial commitment we'd made; and understandably so, as both the upscale nature of the offices and the sheer size felt disproportionate to where we were in the early summer of 2013. But as he did so many times, Brian assured me that our growth trajectory necessitated this and, of course, he proved to be right as we now occupy virtually the whole 888 Brannan address as well as three other large buildings in the area. My brick-and-mortar thinking had underestimated the rampant scalability of a tech company. Whether it was the pace of growth of a "unicorn," cultural trends of millennials, or how to size up the needs of Silicon Valley investors, Brian taught me as much as I taught him.

The philosopher Martin Buber says elders become advocates for the young, but they are rewarded in return: "The teacher helps his disciples find themselves, and in hours of desolation the disciples help their teacher find himself again. The teacher kindles the souls of his disciples and they surround him, his life with the flame he has rekindled. The disciple asks, and by his manner of asking, unconsciously evokes a reply, which his teacher's spirit would not have produced without the stimulus of the question."

In any workplace, as an older employee, just showing a genuine interest in what younger people are doing can create an intergenerational bridge. Letting someone younger teach you something opens a conversation and shows that you have humility, an interest in learning, and respect for that younger person. You also might be surprised by how many people see you as a role model. As author and book critic Meredith Maran—someone who reentered the traditional workplace in her early sixties—writes in her brilliant book *The New Old Me: My Late-Life Reinvention*, a thirty-seven-year-old coworker calls her "FM," for "Future Me." You don't have to be a rock star CEO to be able to offer those younger than you a path to which they can aspire.

WISDOM VERSUS GENIUS

When I joined Airbnb, a thoughtful friend of mine mused that the world is rich in genius but poor in wisdom, and maybe the Airbnb young ones wouldn't mind a little bit of that scarce resource. But others privately positioned this as an EQ versus IQ face-off: me in a death match with the brainiacs of the Valley.

I've come to learn a couple of things since then. First of all, not all older people are wise and not all younger people are brilliant. I've met quite a few very wise young adults as well as some foolhardy people in the later decades of their life, so let's be careful with our age-related stereotypes.

Second, it doesn't have to be "versus"; it can be "Wisdom AND Genius." These aren't sibling rivals. They're kissing cousins. And the roles can be symbiotic, as Robert Pogue Harrison suggests in his book *Juvenescence*: "Wisdom could hardly meet this [*sic*] challenge if it were not in some sense ingenious, nor could genius build upon its past achievements if it were not in some sense wise. In sum, there is a wisdom at the heart of genius that enables genius to reap the rewards of its history without having continually to reinvent the wheel, just as there is a genius at the heart of wisdom that allows wisdom to creatively transform and rejuvenate the past, while giving a measure of continuity to the otherwise discrete history of genius."

A fundamental challenge that we will explore in chapter 9 is that genius is more measurable—for example, there are standardized tests of intelligence, but not of wisdom—and so companies and employers often don't know when they have true wisdom in their midst. But as I pointed out in my TED talk in 2010 about measuring what's truly valuable in life, just because wisdom is harder to evaluate or quantify doesn't mean it's not of great value.

Years ago, a young Sheryl Sandberg sat down with new Google CEO Eric Schmidt and showed him a spreadsheet that laid out why the offer to join Google as a senior leader didn't make sense for her, based upon the smart career criteria she'd developed. Eric looked her in the eye and said, "Get on a rocket ship. When companies are growing quickly and they are having a lot of impact, careers take care of themselves. And when companies aren't growing quickly or their missions don't matter as much, that's when stagnation and politics come in. If you're offered a seat on a rocket ship, don't ask what seat. Just get on."

For me, it's been quite a humbling and exhilarating journey on

Airbnb's rocket ship. I thought I would run my company, Joie de Vivre, for the rest of my life. But, at nearly age fifty, burned out by the Great Recession, with no idea what would come next after I sold the company at the bottom of the market, Airbnb's young CEO came calling. Sometimes you have to make space in your life to see what will emerge. In this book, you will learn how to evolve and rewire yourself for the next exhilarating and rewarding chapter in your life.

But first, let's explore some of the structural social scripts you'll have to rewrite as you're finding your calling in the latter half of your career.

[3]

Raw, Cooked, Burned, Repeat

*"My life may be summed up in three phases. I was raw. I became
cooked. Then I burned."*

—JALĀL AD-DĪN MUHAMMAD RŪMĪ, OTHERWISE
KNOWN AS RUMI (1207–1273)

———

*"Is it just my imagination or is life getting faster
and longer at the same time?"*

One of my college classmates asked me this question about life's
time clock after I gave a speech on Modern Elders at our thirty-
fifth reunion. It was an astute observation. Sufi poet and philosopher
Rumi wrote *"I was raw. I became cooked. Then I burned"* 750 years
ago, but digital life seems to have accelerated our cooking time since
Rumi's era. Back in 1900, US life expectancy was forty-seven years
old. A hundred years later, in 2000, it was seventy-seven. Who knows,
maybe it'll be 107 by the year 2100. And, at age fifty-seven, I may be
less than halfway through the adult part of my life. I may cook for a
very long time! You may, as well.

Rumi, as it so happens, was no stranger to the value of an elder.
He was an Islamic cleric before he met the mystic Shams-i Tabrizi,
a generation older than him. Through a deep intellectual and spiritual partnership, Shams helped Rumi to find his inner poet. Rumi

wouldn't be the most widely read poet in America if it hadn't been for Shams, as he'd never written a poem prior to their meeting.

Of course, there are countless examples throughout history of older mentors who helped nurture a young genius. Ralph Waldo Emerson mentored Henry David Thoreau. Maya Angelou did the same for Oprah Winfrey. Warren Buffett: Bill Gates. Steve Jobs: Mark Zuckerberg. We know what a mentor relationship looks like as, historically, wisdom flowed downhill. But, today, for the first time, we are seeing the power of an intergenerational transfer of wisdom that flows in both directions. This offers the elder the opportunity to be raw again by being receptive to learning in a new way.

While each generation tends to think itself wiser than the one immediately preceding it, all generations can learn something from each other. Yet, today, the older half of the population is feeling increasingly less relevant, while the younger half is increasingly more powerful, and yet lacking in formal modes of support and guidance. Many of us boomers had decades to become fully baked leaders, whereas millennials have had to microwave their leadership skills as power is granted to them so quickly today due to our growing digital reliance.

And, yet, wise old souls—our elders—with so much to teach these would-be protégés, have been disappearing from our workplaces with increasing speed. It's like a neutron bomb dropped on our shiny, open-air offices and wiped out everyone over forty. Maybe we as a society were too busy playing with our new toys—Internet, iPhones, Instagram—to notice that the elders had been purged. Yet those in their fifties (and older), who may have shared their wisdom with their children during adulthood, were now ready to share that wisdom at work during elderhood. But if you're not working, there's no one to share it with. So, while some in Silicon Valley are on a quest to create technology that can help make death optional, many others think to themselves, *If you're irrelevant after forty, who'd want to live forever?*

As Jo Ann Jenkins, CEO of AARP, writes in her book *Disrupt Aging,* "We added more years to average life expectancy in the last century than in all previous history combined. . . . For the first time in history long life isn't a rarity. Over half of the people born today will live to be 100." Ponder that for a moment. A baby born in the US today will most likely live till at least 2118. And medical advances in our lifetime could add a generation to our life. Former president Bill Clinton has suggested biology will be to the twenty-first century what physics was to the last century.

So we'll live to one hundred, but can we afford it? Probably not. Economist John Shoven says, "You can't finance a 30-year retirement with a 40-year career." The math doesn't work for the retiree nor the government. Since 1955, the overall amount of time people spend in retirement has increased by 50 percent. When Otto von Bismarck brought in the first formal pensions in the 1880s, payable from age seventy (later reduced to sixty-five), life expectancy in Prussia was forty-five. In fact, back in 1880 in the US, nearly half of all eighty-year-olds were engaged in some form of work (mostly farming) and 80 percent of those between sixty-five and seventy-four were in some form of employment. But let's recognize that in 1935, when Social Security started in the US, a small percentage of the citizenry actually made it to the stated retirement age of sixty-five.

Today in the developed world, 90 percent of the population lives to celebrate their sixty-fifth birthday, mostly in good health, yet that date is still seen as the starting point of old age. It's above my pay grade to propose a retirement system redesign, but one thing is obviously clear: the expectation that full-time retirement will start in one's early- to midsixties is likely to be a thing of the past, or a privilege of the wealthy. And that has many of us a little on edge.

How can we make a longer life a blessing, not a curse?

RETHINKING THE THREE-STAGE LIFE

"When work for most people meant manual labor, there was no need to worry about the second half of your life. You simply kept on doing what you had always done. And if you were lucky enough to survive 40 years of hard work in the mill or on the railroad, you were quite happy to spend the rest of your life doing nothing. Today, however, most work is knowledge work, and knowledge workers are not 'finished' after 40 years on the job, they are merely bored."

—PETER DRUCKER

The age-old, three-stage life cycle—education, work, retirement (raw, cooked, burned)—is deeply ingrained in our institutions and psyches. Changing it won't happen overnight, especially when "employers can smell fifty," as actor Steve Martin exclaimed in the film *Bowfinger*. Being too young to retire but too old to find a job is a modern problem that's ripe for disruption.

As Laura Carstensen suggests, "The young study, the middle-aged work, the old rest or volunteer. We're supposed to do things one at a time and in order. There is very little overlap between life stages and, as a result, not only do members of different generations have limited interactions with one another, which fosters misunderstanding and unease, but it's hard for anyone—of any age—to find a holistic balance between family, work, community and educational opportunities." It's time to retire the three-stage life since life stages are just a social construction that today fosters ageism, the squandering of wisdom, and a diminished sense of meaning and fulfillment in the latter half of life. Fortunately, there is another way that isn't such a linear conveyor belt to a cliff.

One of my favorite books I've read while researching *Wisdom@*

Work is *The 100-Year Life: Living and Working in an Age of Longevity,* by Lynda Gratton and Andrew Scott, professors at London Business School. And, fortunately, I've gotten to spend some time with Andrew exploring this subject in more depth.

They write about a more fluid, multistage life—with transitions and breaks in between: less of a lifelong "raw, cooked, burned" and more of a concentrated series of cycles. These multistage lives are more of a smorgasbord and less of a progression of appetizer, entrée, dessert, but as such, it requires building new habits to accommodate the many more transitions you will likely experience. It is a radically different way of thinking of the trajectory of one's life. At its best, it offers us an opportunity to explore who we are and arrive at a way of living that is nearer to our personal values with the knowledge that we will constantly evolve who we are and what we know to adapt our skills to our changing interests and the changing marketplace.

Some older people lament millennials' breaking from the traditional values built on the three-stage life. Maybe millennials can see the future better than we can and realize that being "outwardly mobile"—traveling the world as "digital nomads" with a smartphone as a compass and without the weight of owning a home or car—is more valuable today than being "upwardly mobile" on the old-school corporate ladder. No wonder dozens of millennial-focused programs like Remote Year, We Roam, and Outsite are surfing this wave of young people shifting their "odyssey period" to ten to fifteen years postcollege as opposed to ten to fifteen months in previous generations for those who took a singular "gap year." Maybe this is why millennials are living with their parents more often as well as waiting to get married and have children as young people are extending their process of entering adulthood.

Although this kind of change may sound daunting to those of us in older generations, in the twentieth century we've already seen major shifts in the social constructions around life stages with the advent of the concepts of a teenager and a retiree. Pre-1900, society didn't create institutions for or didn't even recognize these new stages of life. But maybe we're at the dawning of an age-agnostic era in which your identity is defined more by *how* you're pursuing your life at this moment than by your chronological age. Why should colleges be exclusively full of young adults a half-dozen years past puberty? Why can't people in their fifties pursue a "gap year"? Should we be surprised when we show up at a hotel and see a friendly seventy-five-year-old smiling at us from behind the front desk, ready to check us in?

Gratton and Scott expand upon this new age: "Conventionally, living for longer is seen as being older for longer. There is evidence that this convention will be reversed and people will be younger for longer. . . . The last time stages emerged—teenagers and retirees—these were age-located stages. You have to be young to be a teenager and old to be a retiree. What is fascinating about these new emerging stages is that they contain many features that are age-agnostic."

My friend Gina Pell, forty-nine[*], coined the term "Perennials" in 2016 to define the idea that people may be in their prime much longer, in ways that defy traditional expectations about age. As Gina, an Internet entrepreneur, explains, "Perennials are ever-blooming, relevant people of all ages who know what's happening in the world, stay current with technology and have friends of all ages. We get involved, stay curious, mentor others, and are passionate, compassionate, creative, confident, collaborative, global-minded risk takers." This kind of antigenerational thinking will become more and more prevalent as we have five generations in the workplace and need to find the common language to create bridges to one another.

Boomer Paul Bennett, chief creative officer at the design firm

---

[*] All references to the current age of individuals interviewed for this book refer to their age at the time of writing.

IDEO, told me, "Life has historically been viewed as a mountain. The first half of your life you're climbing, attempting to be all you can be. The second half of your life you're descending, realizing all the things you won't be. But what if that top of the mountain lets you take flight at your peak and allows curiosity to be the fuel that spurs you on? So many people don't come to grips with their own definition of aging. Many have an unconscious voice in their head saying, 'I don't want that to be me' when thinking of older people." Maybe life is just a series of peaks and valleys, but as you get older you appreciate the scenery a little more and can guide others along the way.

A LATER CAREER ON "SLOW SIMMER"

I was first introduced to Karen Wickre about the time she wrote a splendid online article about how to get into tech when you're not an obvious fit. Karen doesn't fit the part and acknowledges there are five demographic reasons why she could have self-selected out of the tech world: she's a woman, now sixty-six years old, with a liberal arts background (dual degrees), a lesbian, and single. Karen was a bookish kid, loving art and ideas over math and science, so she is definitely not the poster child we imagine for HBO's hit series *Silicon Valley*.

Karen spent more than fifteen years at Google and Twitter in mid-level manager jobs and more than thirty years in tech overall. She sees her working career as the development of competencies rather than an accumulation of job titles; since graduating from college in 1973, Karen has held seventeen full-time jobs and that doesn't count the variety of consulting gigs and several years of freelance writing she has done along the way. She credits her positive attitude, EQ (emotional intelligence), flexibility, and skill as a "seasoned word wrangler" (writer and editor) with allowing her to create a multidecade career path in a field that might be foreign to most liberal arts grads.

While she doesn't fit the typical tech demographic, she's the "every person" who helps make sense of the complicated world of tech for the rest of us.

Her parents, both from working-class backgrounds, successfully moved into white-collar, middle-class jobs and owned a home in the Washington, DC, suburbs. But like most upwardly mobile Americans of their generation, they aspired for more for their kids, including a college education. Her father was a radio engineer, the hot technology of the 1920s–1950s, who became a civilian employee of the navy, but later in life always cursed the college-educated peers who surpassed him in his career. Her mother worked for thirty-five years for the same trade association and counseled Karen as she was leaving college that it was important for her to get a stable, long-term job with one company after she graduated. And her mom, who saw her way out of the working-class world with secretarial school, insisted that Karen take typing in high school. "Something to fall back on," she told her, even as she hoped for more for her daughter. Being a very fast touch typist, it turns out, is probably the single skill Karen has used most consistently for the last fifty years.

Karen's break into tech happened in 1985. She was running a struggling nonprofit in San Francisco, and a new board member, a burgeoning media mogul cutting his teeth in the new category of personal computer magazines for consumers, saw her talent and wanted her to join him at his new publications, *PC World* and *Macworld*. She knew nothing about computers, but the mogul recognized her capacity for empathy and her ability to translate complex ideas into something anyone could understand. Figuratively speaking, Karen's mastery was being a translator, who in 1995 wrote one of the first consumer guides to the web.

In 2002, she was hired at Google, which was still in its early days, as a writing contractor, and, after fifteen months of proving herself, joined the communications team as a full-time employee, growing into a senior media liaison role during her nine years there. She had seven managers in those nine years, with every one of them younger than her—sometimes by as much as almost thirty years. Since Karen was already steeped in the technology business, and had more general work experience than her peers, most of her managers valued her and didn't condescend. Except, that is, for one striking instance when an ambitious newcomer about twenty years younger briefly became her manager. She knew that he had pressed to become a director, and one step toward promotion was to have managed people. Since she was aware of the power politics at play, she tried to make it work. But some tough run-ins, and way too much micromanagement, forced her to confront him by saying, "I know you don't like this tension any more than I do, and I know you have other aspirations. If you understand how to work with me, you'll get there faster. Let me tell you how." After that, he dropped the gruff boss act, rotated to a new role, and even after several years of working separately he often came to her and asked for her advice and expertise. Even though he never acknowledged his poor behavior, he clearly took her words to heart and it's just one more small example of how the generations can learn from each other.

She left to join Twitter to become their editorial director as she wanted to learn more about social media even though she was sixty years old. And, more recently, she decided it was time to recast her work life such that she no longer needed to manage people and could make a living well into her late seventies, through a hodgepodge of freelance and part-time work since she's spent more than thirty years building a network within the Valley.

This "portfolio" approach to one's work has gotten a lot of press recently due to the explosion of the "gig economy," and the growing number of people bringing in additional streams of income by driving for Uber or renting out a backyard cottage on Airbnb as a host.

According to PwC, a quarter of all workers in the sharing economy are fifty-five or older. More than half of workers over fifty-five have said they'd like to have a flexible, gradual transition to retirement, but most employers don't offer that. So older workers leave to take on work as part-time lawyers, accountants, or teachers, or they become entrepreneurs.

A recent *Economist* issue about the "young old" profiles the New York–based company WAHVE (short for Work At Home Vintage Experts) that provides work for hundreds of former finance and insurance professionals, mostly in their sixties and seventies. "Carriers and brokers have huge talent problems; it takes years to train an underwriter," says Sharon Emek, the firm's seventy-one-year-old founder. She realized boomers were retiring from the workforce but didn't want to stop working; so now they are "pre-tiring." And, the Kauffman Foundation reports today that those between fifty-five and sixty-five are now 65 percent more likely to found a new company than those between twenty and thirty-four.

Karen Wickre, on the other hand, doesn't necessarily consider herself an entrepreneur. She's just a brilliant networker who knows how to "translate." Modern Elders aren't just editors, they're also master translators due to their finely attuned understanding of people and their communication styles. Due to her accumulated network and her translation skills, this means in Karen's late sixties, she can be a board member for a variety of nonprofit organizations she believes in, an advice columnist for a tech magazine, an editorial strategist, a consultant, and a book writer. Karen says, "It all represents an inadvertent career path my mom and dad could scarcely imagine, but it's one built by hand that serves me well." And it's one that will become more and more familiar with boomers and Gen Xers in the next few years.

CREATING NEW RITES OF PASSAGE

Karen is a role model because she's spent a lifetime reinventing herself, so her transition to juggling many gigs hasn't required an adjustment. But, for many of us, the process of career transition in midlife or beyond can create a state of discomfort and insecurity, especially if you feel like you're moving in the wrong direction, like oddly transitioning from a butterfly into a caterpillar. This is in part because society does little to prepare us for career transitions that deviate from the expected script of "learn, earn, retire."

Societies have historically celebrated the movement of an individual from one part of life to another by creating festivities or formalities that mark that rite of passage, whether it be birth, puberty, marriage, having children, or death. The intent is to strip the person from their most recent role and prepare them for their new role and status.

Yet rites of passage are almost nonexistent in the workplace. Yes, some companies celebrate employee anniversary dates and, in the past, you earned a gold watch or some other reminder that your time has expired when you hit sixty-five. Even before this dawning of a "young old" person in the workplace, there was a need to create some recognition that we do not fulfill the potential of life's development stages by just gradually drifting through our career. You could imagine a first-time manager going through some simple ritual that gave her the psychological and spiritual support to understand her new role with more clarity, or a sixty-five-year-old leaving a company to pursue a master's degree marking her transition with a commencement ceremony. I wish I had had access to some kind of catalyzing rite of passage that helped me understand my burgeoning role as a Modern Elder at Airbnb in my early days.

My hope is that this book will serve as literary rite of passage for those wanting to embrace their Modern Elder role. More than a hundred years ago, anthropologist Arnold van Gennep studied many indigenous societies and distinguished three key phases in a typical rite-of-passage ceremony: (a) "severance" from the past; (b) a "threshold" that is the uncomfortable space of being in between two phases of your life; and (c) the "incorporation" of reentering the community in a new role. So many cultural cornerstones—from the author Joseph Campbell's work on "the hero's journey" narrative pattern to the *Star Wars* movies, and, for that matter, most great films—track this arc that van Gennep developed in the early twentieth century. Yet the reality is that most adults today have no conscious recognition of moving through these thresholds, which is why so many people in the second half of life feel incomplete and unprepared.

My friend Marianna Leuschel is a lovely outlier, though. When she was winding down her successful design and consulting firm in her late fifties, she knew she needed to make a clear break from the past and transition into that uncomfortable place of the unknown. She decided to have a Closing Ceremony at a bucolic cemetery where she rented the beautiful memorial services space. She asked every one of the people that had worked for her over the twenty years as well as friends and family to come celebrate. She said something brief about each person and how they had touched her along the way, starting with her first employee and ending with her mother (the instigator of her creative life). She hoped that the community created through the work of her small studio would continue to live on, in some form, and that it would always be a part of her. And it has. After a sabbatical that had no determined end date, she's going back to the part of her job she enjoyed the most—helping clients with brand strategy and storytelling work—without the worries of running a moderate-sized design studio.

Not all of us are as creative as Marianna in crafting our transition ritual. So to guide you through your hero's journey, I offer you the lessons of the next four chapters. People in indigenous societies have been following this path for tens of thousands of years; it's time we explore how to formalize it in the workplace, beyond celebratory cakes and proverbial gold watches.

My Lesson 1 (chapter 4), in which I talk about how to evolve or edit your identity, addresses the severance part of this rite. In a vision quest, this is when you're sent out into the wilderness nearly naked. In the context of work, this could be when you make a dramatic shift in your career or employment status (which can indeed sometimes feel a lot like being sent naked into the wild). If you don't get this severance part right, it is very hard for you to pass through the next part of your rite of passage. A vessel cannot be filled unless it is first emptied.

Lessons 2 and 3 (chapters 5 and 6), in which you learn to adopt a beginner's mind and maximize your collaboration skills are when you are in the threshold world forging a new way of being in a new habitat. In my case, discarding the role of having to be wiser because I was older allowed me to be both a mentor and intern at the same time. And, like a little kid, I was often filled with the mystery of life— with wonder and awe—and felt more gratitude than I'd ever imagined, after feeling so stupid in my first few months as a tech neophyte when I was evolving out of my past identity. There is nothing more life-affirming in midlife than to be reacquainted with that old childhood friend named Curiosity. And, in this new habitat, I saw that some of my gathered wisdom—like my emotional intelligence and ability to collaborate—were particularly valuable.

Your reincorporation at the other end of this journey occurs with Lesson 4 (chapter 7), when you become the wise counselor in your organization. As my collaborative spirit became more evident in team meetings, I was approached by more and more employees— across virtually all departments of the company—seeking my confidential advice. By the time you've finished chapter 7, you will know your new role as an elder is to serve. This path has marked indigenous societies throughout the history of man, but it's time we explore how to formalize it in the workplace.

Psychologist Erik Erikson suggested that adulthood is defined in part as facing the crisis of generativity versus the despair of believing we have nothing to offer. If you follow these lessons and put yourself in a habitat that can see the value you are creating, there's no doubt you'll feel not only relevant but indispensable in your role as a Modern Elder for many years to come. And better yet, you'll get the sense you're creating a legacy based upon how you've influenced people and the organization as a whole.

RETIRING AGEISM

"We've allowed a youth-centered culture to leave us so estranged from our future selves that, when asked about the years beyond 50, 60, or 70 . . . many people can only see a blank screen, or one on which they project disease and dependency. This incomplete social map makes the last third of life unknown country. . . . We may not yet have maps for this new country, but parallels with other movements can give us a compass. . . . first, rising up from invisibility by declaring the existence of a group with shared experiences; then taking the power to name and define the group; then a long process of 'coming out' by individuals who identify with it; then inventing new words to describe previously unnamed experiences."

—GLORIA STEINEM

While it's encouraging that the tyranny of the three-stage life is loosening its grip on us, creating more of an age-agnostic workplace, the reality is ageism is an ugly fact in today's jobs marketplace. Author Ted Fishman has called it "global age arbitrage," in which older engineers (and other workers) with what are perceived to be more costly benefits are traded in for younger ones. Although the Age Discrimination Employment Act of 1967 prohibits discrimination against people forty and older, a recent survey by AARP showed that two-thirds of workers between the ages of forty-five and seventy-four said they have seen or experienced ageism. And, during the past decade, Silicon Valley's 150 biggest tech companies faced more age bias cases than racial bias or gender bias.

We can now add "facial discrimination" to racial discrimination as a societal ill in much of the developed world. One of the oddities of age versus disease is that illness warns us of its presence, so we likely feel it personally before others notice it. But my advancing age is more apparent to others than it is to me. And, yet, we often assume age and disease are congruent. What if we substituted the word "growth" for "aging" with the knowledge that it was a progressive, lifelong process rather than something that attacks you later in life? I wish retiring ageism was that easy.

Ageism affects us all, though some older workers feel the pain more than others. Some, refusing to go quietly into the night, choose to start their own companies when they feel invisible looking for a job after age fifty. But, for others, age discrimination in employment has a far more severe effect. It makes less difference in the lives of people who have a nest egg, can start a business, or can pick up some consulting assignments. But Voltaire had it right when he commented that equality before the law means that the rich and poor are equally forbidden to sleep under a bridge at night. Clearly, both equality and age discrimination are applied differently to some groups as compared to others.

Women disproportionately feel the effects of ageism. Yvonne Sonsino, innovation leader and partner at Mercer, the world's largest human resources consulting firm, and the author of *The New Rules of Living Longer: How to Survive Your Longer Life*, says, "Women live longer, tend to be paid less, are more likely to work part-time and more likely to have career gaps. As a result, the value of their pensions may be reduced by 40 percent compared to a man doing the same job." A Federal Reserve Board of San Francisco study found that the callback rate for older women for jobs they're qualified for is also substantially worse than for older men, as Hollywood has taught us that older men are considered "distinguished" while older women are "just old."

A British study warns that businesses are creating a "forgotten generation" of older workers who, despite their experience and knowledge, do not feel their voice is being heard at work—less than a fifth (17 percent) of those over fifty-five believe that their company values their opinion at the workplace, compared with over a third (37 percent) of those under twenty-five. This takes a toll on one's psyche, and maybe even one's health, as research suggests that negative stereotypes about aging may well shorten the lives of older people. Professor Dr. Becca Levy found that older people with a positive perception of aging lived seven and a half years longer than those with a negative perception of aging: a bigger increase in lifespan than associated with either exercising or not smoking. So if you enjoy the prospect of growing older, you live longer.

Ageism moves in both directions though. Watching the Uber leadership meltdown, a boomer friend said to me, "When did the young Turks become young jerks? Odd that puberty has an 'Uber' embedded in the middle of the word." But let's also recognize that some of Uber's challenges aren't specifically due to millennial senior leadership; the majority of Uber's senior leaders during Travis Kalanick's time as CEO were older than millennials.

When a company grows as quickly as many of the Valley's unicorns have, you scale the business much faster than you do your people and processes. The manager who ran a division when you had five hundred employees companywide may not be the right fit for when you have twenty-five hundred employees just three years later. But, of course, it helps to have an experienced leader on the team who can anticipate the icebergs on the horizon due to hyperaccelerated growth. We've never seen companies grow this far across the globe this quickly, so this is one more argument for why seasoned leadership should be paired with young founders and CEOs.

I can't tell you how many times people have called me "the grown-up supervision" or "the adult in the room," as if the millennial cofounders of Airbnb and their peers are infants. And then there was the text I received welcoming me to my first week at Airbnb from an older hotelier: "Good for you, Chip. Help the youngsters change the world, but make sure you change their diapers. LOL." I'm sort of surprised this guy knew what LOL means (to me, it means Lame Old Loser).

Then there was the infantilizing July 2017 *New York Times* op-ed on the young bros of business, which started this way: "I've been thinking about dog collars, the ones that deliver electric shocks to keep dogs from straying out of their yards. Why not use them to correct the behavior of our bad boys of tech and finance?" The piece then went on to deride Facebook's old engineering motto, by pointing out that "move fast and break things" is something that toddlers, not young CEOs, do.

It's time to stop with the generational name-calling and recognize we all have something to learn from one another. Never before have we seen the kind of workplace where brilliant thirty-year-olds can tutor wise elders twice their age about the future of technology, while the sixty-year-old can offer emotional, leadership, and general life advice to the talented, accelerated young exec. This is a golden opportunity, right under our noses. We'd be wise to seize it.

RAW AGAIN

Peter Kent, sixty-four, failed at retiring twice before. He'd spent the past thirty years helping lead ten start-ups and turnarounds, with his biggest success being Automated Trading Desk (ATD), which he joined at age forty-nine when the company's average age was twenty-seven and the CEO was fifteen years his junior. ATD changed the way Wall Street trading operated, moving it from a manual to a primarily automated system. Investors often brought him into companies to serve as their "adult supervision," a phrase that makes him cringe due to the disrespect it shows young founders. He sees his role more as a translator of youthful vision into operational excellence.

This time, he received the call from Alan Guarino, vice chairman of the global executive search firm Korn Ferry. He patiently listened as Alan told him about Joanna Riley, thirty-five, an entrepreneur and mentor for young women in technology, and the CEO and cofounder of 1-Page, a tech company transforming the way companies find their best next hires using artificial intelligence. She founded the company based upon the thesis of a book authored by her father, which argued that job seekers should be evaluated on what they can do, as opposed to their previous accomplishments, experience, age, or gender. In 2014, she led 1-Page to a successful IPO on the Australian stock exchange and the stock price had recently risen to nearly thirty times its original value. But it was also clear the company was in a fragile state. Peter just didn't realize how fragile.

Joanna's process for finding a seasoned COO/CFO had been painful and laborious, as it seemed like all the candidates went to the same school of hyperaggressive financial projections. Each impressive candidate, all of them younger than Peter, were super-salespeople brimming with optimism about 1-Page, but Joanna was unconvinced. Peter was different. He controlled the interview.

"He asked me what I believe in fundamentally. He taught me a few things, not just about business, but about leadership, and, ironically, he was supposed to be the one being interviewed. He had a presence and authority that had nothing to do with selling me on who he was. I asked him to do a 'Lunch and Learn' talk with my team and, as they were asking him questions and not knowing he might become my 'right-hand man,' he said, 'If you don't have true alignment of your team, you're assured of failing' and I realized in that moment, we didn't have internal alignment as a ballast on the high seas. Little did I know how essential that would soon be."

Peter was hired and the day he joined the company, whose stock price was starting to go into free fall, he and Joanna learned that activist investors were launching a takeover attempt through a proxy battle to secure power away from the current board of directors. With no time to waste, Peter accelerated his process of learning, asking Joanna and the leadership team individually to "teach me about your business." Listening and absorbing, Peter built a deep relationship with Joanna quickly, and not long after he joined, Joanna decided to elevate Peter to her role, CEO, and she became president. They jointly made the difficult but necessary decision that they needed to cut their operating costs by 40 percent. Peter, who could see the storm clouds forming on the horizon, also suggested 100 percent transparency with the employees because trust would be their number one asset in what was likely to be a topsy-turvy time.

In fact, the stock price, which had once seen the fastest rise in Australian stock market history, now experienced the fastest fall and the activist investors got a foothold on the board. This is the point in the story where most people in his position would have jumped ship, but Peter stayed for two reasons. He was looking for a business with a brilliant plan that could disrupt an industry and believed 1-Page could potentially do that for global recruiting. And he was looking to partner with a young, creative talent who complemented his skill set.

With Joanna's savvy in sales, product, and vision and Peter's expertise in finance, technology, and operations, the two of them forged an unstoppable if unexpected partnership that transcended age and gender.

While I'd had conversations by phone and email with them, my first face-to-face meeting with them started in a fashion that left no doubt as to how connected they were. I called Joanna on her cell phone because I'd arrived at our designated meeting place but didn't see them. To my surprise it was Peter who answered Joanna's cell phone, mentioning that she was finishing a lunch meeting, and that they'd be ready for me soon. When we sat down, it was clear that these two—who had only been leading the company together for six months—had forged a bond that was life-altering for both of them.

They told me about how the activist investors had wrestled control away from them and even put out public misinformation that Peter had left the company. And how 1-Page's stock trading had been suspended on the Australian exchange because it had become so volatile. And, yet, Peter and Joanna had only experienced two disagreements in this half year of high-stakes finance mud wrestling.

In the end, their bets on each other paid off. Peter helped steer the company through this difficult time as 1-Page morphed from a public to a private company with a new corporate brand and friendlier investors. And, after hostilities from earlier investors had negatively affected employees, Peter and Joanna—whose transparency helped create trust—were able to rehire most of the key staff at their new company, Censia, that is now growing and expanding.

Now, after having spent a half year in a foxhole, this unlikely partnership—a millennial founder and her boomer cofounder with nearly thirty years separating them—is plotting their company's future together. Joanna is often shocked that Peter is still by her side. Joanna says, "I'm fortunate to have realized at a young age how much there is to learn from those older than me. It was my father's idea that led me to starting 1-Page and he taught me to find mentors when I was in my teen years. I know my vision and enthusiasm helped the company get this far, but without Peter joining me and living this trial by fire, I'm not sure we'd still be in business."

Peter tells me he feels raw again each time he joins a new company, and this was particularly true for his experience jumping into business with Joanna: "What a gift it is to take a lifetime of learning and be able to apply it to such a brilliant young leader with a spectacular business concept. While I joined partly because of the financial opportunity, I stay because of how psychologically rewarding it is to invest in a talent like Joanna who isn't just a phenomenal learner, but she's constantly teaching me as well. I'm not sure I'll ever retire."

In hearing their story, it's impossible not to be reminded of Shams and Rumi, who created a trusted connection even against a backdrop of a community that desperately tried to separate them. Shams's effect on Rumi helped him to see the poetic wisdom in everyday life. Rumi pondered the wonder of flowers, love, water. He saw water as shapeless, as it takes the shape of the vessel in which it is contained. If water is poured out of the vessel, it evaporates and returns to its source. Similarly, when breath no longer exists in one's body, the soul departs and returns to its source. And one could say wisdom is like water. It adapts to the environment, is life-affirming, and yet can disappear into the collective consciousness when its work is done.

Rumi was a wise man and defined our three-stage life long ago, but maybe it's time for Modern Elders to add to Rumi's three phases of life. Maybe there's a fourth ... I was raw, I became cooked, I burned. And, then, *I became raw again.* Let me introduce you to the four lessons that will help you to become raw again. It all starts with changing your costume.

[4]

Lesson 1: EVOLVE

"I think as one grows older, one is appallingly exposed to wearing life instead of living it. Habit, physical deterioration and a slower digestion of our experiences, all tend to make one look on one's dear life as a garment, a dressing gown, a raincoat, a uniform, buttoned on with recurrent daily (tasks). . . . for myself I found one remedy, and that is to undertake something difficult, something new, to re-root myself in my own true faculties. . . . for in such moments, life is not just a thing one wears, it is a thing one does and is."

—WILLIAM MAXWELL'S "THE LETTERS OF SYLVIA
TOWNSEND WARNER"

———

"How can you turn your fear into curiosity?"

My father asked me this wise question in 2013 while we hiked up a mountain together—not far from his Silicon Valley senior living community. I'd just joined Airbnb a few weeks earlier. And I felt dizzy—but not from the altitude. I've jumped onto a few merry-go-rounds in my life, so anxiety is a familiar state. But this felt very different. Heavier. Like I was hiking the trail with 180 pounds strapped to my back. At the time, I didn't yet realize that the backpack was filled with my past identities.

I'd shared with my dad that I was feeling out of place in the land of the young. But as Sylvia Townsend Warner describes in the quote that starts this chapter, when you're too focused on your historical wardrobe—rather than the person inside those clothes—you lose track of the authentic and special gifts you have to offer.

Professor Herminia Ibarra is one of the world's leading authorities on career transitions and the sense of liminality that occurs during this passage. Many of us attach much of our sense of identity to our work, so it's natural that a certain ambiguity and disorientation can occur when we're in transition—especially when we stray off our normal hiking path. When you're "married" to your work, it's no surprise that a transition can feel like a divorce.

In tribal societies, there are community rituals to assist major life transitions—from women giving birth, to children becoming adults, to the passing into death. Yet, as I discussed briefly in the last chapter, we don't have these rituals in the modern workplace, the result being that our caterpillar-to-butterfly transformation often happens inside of us without much hint to our family, friends, or coworkers. Hence, loneliness and isolation can take root and grow. And when our past identity, or wardrobe—with all our past successes or failures—gets in the way of this inner transformation, we can feel betwixt and between. It's how I imagine the amateur circus performer must feel as he lets go of the trapeze bar before grabbing hold of the swinging bar ahead of him.

Elizabeth White felt that sense of liminality when she was fifty-five and in between jobs; and it didn't help that her phone had stopped ringing. This fierce, smart African American had graduate degrees from Harvard Business School and Johns Hopkins and had been a project officer for the World Bank and was eminently qualified to make a difference in so many ways and yet she was barely eking out a living through occasional on-and-off consulting gigs. She felt invisible and in free fall. It was as though, as she puts it in her TEDx talk, she had "entered the uncertain world of formerly and used to be."

But pretty soon, she realized that she wasn't alone, and she started noticing that other midlifers who'd been doing pretty well were also suddenly having trouble making ends meet.

Elizabeth quickly learned that while we may not always be able to reset our careers in midlife, we *can* reset our mindset and expectations. In other words, evolve. Elizabeth is now sharing this hard-won wisdom with others in speeches and a book as well as through creating midlife "Resilience Circles." She says, "When everything you know has been your identity at work, and that rug gets pulled, you don't know who you are. But a Resilience Circle pays witness to the fact you still exist, are evolving, and you're lifting the veil so people can see the authentic cracks in your veneer."

For me, the cracks in the veneer took the form of a tape playing in my head on an infinite loop: *Will I be as good in this new role as I was as CEO of my own company?* Fear seemed to be in the air during this time. Between 2006 and 2011, I had four friends commit suicide, in part because they couldn't face the fear of their career or business taking a nosedive. In their midforties, they didn't realize they were at the lowest point of the U-curve of happiness that was about to start ticking upward again. It was a grueling period for me as well. I woke up every morning, meditated, and then listened to k.d. lang croon "Hallelujah" as my way of emboldening myself for another day.

In the absence of a ritual to help me make my passage into my new identity, I turned to books, including Professor Carol Dweck's work in *Mindset.* She's shown that those with a "fixed mindset"— that is, those who see their skills, attributes, and identity as static and impervious to change—are always trying to prove themselves: often overly concerned with how others see them and focused on avoiding repeating the mistakes of the past. On the other hand, people with a "growth mindset" believe in their ability to evolve and change and are willing to accept the risk of making mistakes for the sake of self-improvement. My father's question helped me to turn toward my curious future, rather than fixate on my comfortable past, and to adopt a growth mindset in my early days at Airbnb.

And, not coincidentally, the idea of "mindset" became a source of conversation for Brian Chesky and me with respect to how we could create a company culture dedicated to developing a growth mindset. You evolve—as an individual or as a company—when you take the risk to seek constant improvement.

DONNING A NEW COSTUME

One myth about elders is that we're not motivated to change as we age. That we get set in our ways. That our body, mind, and spirit atrophy based upon our narrowing collection of habits. This can also be interpreted to mean we don't want to introduce ourselves to new environments because they will inflict change upon us. I'm learning Spanish in my late fifties and discovered that a habit or custom translates as *costumbre*. How many of us are open to donning a new costum(br)e in the second half of life?

I came across all kinds of fascinating studies in researching this book, but one of my favorites comes from Jack Zenger and Joseph Folkman, called "How Age and Gender Affect Self-Improvement" (Harvard Business Review, 2016). Drawing on Carol Dweck's work on fixed versus growth mindsets, they studied seven thousand businesspeople through self-assessments and 360-degree reviews from coworkers. They found that older people were more open to self-improvement and less defensive to criticism because they had evolved over time to focus on *im*proving instead of just proving themselves. And the researchers found that the more self-confidence individuals have, the more willing they are to change.

Moreover, Zenger and Folkman found a direct correlation between age and self-confidence. This was particularly marked for women who continue to grow in their willingness to change well into their sixties—at the age when men start to decline. In sum, our evolution doesn't end at midlife. It may accelerate.

Our career can be an existential anchor, tethering us to our identities. That's why some of us can feel so unmoored when we lose a job or feel disoriented in a new one. It's also why we may feel angry that ageism or youthful cronyism (the young hiring the young) derails our career just when we feel at the top of our game. Yes, obstacles can grow as we age, but so can our ability to weather the storm.

Maybe our growing self-awareness, and our willingness to change our costume, can allow us to start lifting the burden of too many shed identities. When you've worn out all your roles, cast aside all your costumes, and relinquished your customs, you're left with yourself, in its purest form. That's when it starts getting interesting. As I mentioned in chapter 2, an elder is an editor. As we enter midlife, we embark upon a creative evolution that amplifies our specialness while editing out the extraneous. After a lifetime of accumulation, we can concentrate on what we do best, what gives us meaning, what we want to leave behind. We become unmasked.

Your résumé is built on the verb "to resume," but your second half of life may be more about shedding a skin than resuming wearing the same coat. Author Kathleen Fischer suggests that people later in life "must undergo a conversion, an experience of losing our song in order to be able to sing it in a new key."

One of my role models, Randy Komisar, sixty-three, taught me a few things about singing out of key, changing identities in midlife, and being all the better for it. Today, Randy is a partner at the prestigious venture capital firm Kleiner Perkins Caufield Byers. But he has shed many a costume to find the one that finally fit. As he told the *Harvard Business Review* in 2000, "By conventional standards, my résumé was a disaster. Eleven companies in 25 years, not to mention a crazy quilt of jobs: community development manager, music promoter, corporate lawyer, CFO at a technology start-up, and chief executive at a video game company, just to name a few. I zigged, then I zagged, then I zigged some more. By my résumé alone, no one should hire me. Except that these days, plenty of companies would. And they do. At last, my 'non-career' career makes perfect sense—to them and to me."

Randy worked closely with Bill Campbell ("the Coach" mentioned in chapter 2) in three different companies: Apple, Claris, and GO. At age forty, Randy realized he was losing a half step relative to his adrenalized younger self, as he explained, "I saw I needed to move from stamina and speed to judgment and equanimity. At that time, I started a meditation practice that still serves me today. By becoming more self-aware and conscious, I wisened up. I could observe all these identities I was carrying around. I realized I had to free myself not from just my past failures, but also my successes. If you're carrying the full weight of your past, you can't learn today, nor can you make room for others. I also learned in my forties I had to right-size my ego."

The challenge with having worn too many costumes isn't just the fact that they weigh you down, but that these past wardrobes also distract you from ones you might don in the future. Pir Vilayat Inayat Khan, the former head of the Sufi Order in the West, offers this suggestion for evolving your identity, "To transmit our know-how to the next generation, we need to change faster than ever before—in fact, even faster than the young themselves. . . . If you don't know that you can be a new person, you will continue dragging your old self-image into the brave new world. You will be outrun and pronounced redundant, unable to make a contribution to the inexorable advance of evolution on our planet." Sufis, like the poet Rumi, were the first to become "whirling dervishes" as a means of shedding the earthly identities to achieve a transcendental state.

REFRAMING VS. REINVENTING

The world is constantly changing—as are we. Which makes it that much more important, in periods of transition, to evolve out of outdated perceptions of who we are, or our ill-fitting costume, and reframe them with ruthlessly edited beliefs that connect with our soul. Melina Lillios, fifty-four, was a high school English and drama teacher for fifteen years in Honolulu as well as a teacher of creative writing and drama to fifth and sixth graders. She also taught communications to college students for a dozen years, but the passing of her mother was a poignant rite of passage for her in 2004. She realized that while she loved her students and creating a learning environment, she was tired of being part of the "system" and answerable to rigid educational authorities. So she took some time off from teaching after her mother's passing and reconnected with her love of travel. She'd been a certified travel agent since high school, and the idea of creating a travel business based upon her personal mantra came to her like an epiphany.

Melina asked herself, *Why can't I take my love of teaching and combine it with my love of travel?* And, as a "strong-willed woman of Greek and Brazilian heritage," she recalls, "my mother's death gave me a sense of urgency to become an entrepreneur and control my destiny." Thus, Live Laugh Love Tours was born.

But, as exciting as this new venture was for her, she had to push through her own mindset demons. "I had this notion I 'wasn't good with money' that had haunted me in my twenties and thirties. I knew I was very creative, but I had to remind myself how linear and detail-oriented I had been throughout my life. I had to become confident in my logistics capabilities because running a two-week overseas time-of-your-life trip is all about the details." So Melina took baby steps in getting Live Laugh Love off the ground. As is true of many later-life entrepreneurs, she started the business part-time.

The more Melina focused on the essence of her mission—changing her clients' lives through travel—the more committed she was to owning her newfound identity as an entrepreneur. And the business blossomed. Even her first tour sold out within three weeks. Today, Melina—like Karen Wickre, mentioned in the last chapter—says what helped her to make this midlife shift was seeing her talents as more than just a series of job descriptions or the ability to complete a set of tasks. She was able to reframe her "teacher" identity only by recognizing that while she loves educating people of all ages, she no longer wanted to do it solely in a classroom.

I, too, had to reframe my identity when I was going to sell my baby, Joie de Vivre. After more than two decades as CEO, I knew I wasn't happy anymore, which is a liability for a company whose name literally means enjoyment of life. But other than the fact we were struggling through a bad economic time, I wasn't sure what was at the heart of my discontent. I asked myself the question, *What was it that compelled me to start this company in the first place?* As confused as I was in 2008–2009, I knew the answer. I started my company as an entrepreneur to seek "creativity and freedom." Those were the two qualities that defined success for me. But, now, I didn't feel either of these and, with thirty-five hundred employees, and so many different hotel owner groups we were responsible to, I didn't see this changing anytime soon. So my very private decision to sell a company I never imagined selling had so much to do with realizing that creativity and freedom were my north star and it was time to wander in the wilderness again seeking a way to express these two qualities. Sometimes, then, the reframe of your identity is not an internal shift in your values, but an external rearranging of your life to once again give priority to that which is most life-affirming for you.

A couple of years into my time at Airbnb, when the company and the home-sharing industry were becoming a mainstream phenomenon, and my role as Brian's mentor was getting some attention in the media, many longtime colleagues from the hotel industry would say to me, "Congrats on 'reinventing yourself.'" But, to me, it didn't feel so much like a re*invention* as a re*intention* of how I wanted to show up in the world. It meant I could evolve to make my new costume, as Sylvia Townsend Warner put it, "not just a thing one wears," but rather "a thing one does and is."

MY MASQUERADE HISTORY

We're all born in our "birthday suit." But being a Halloween baby, born on the thirty-first of October, I got used to life as a constant costume party. A creative introvert as a child, the way I blossomed as a teenager was by collecting accomplishments. My sense of identity was defined by my achievements. I was the youngest in my graduate business school class at Stanford and then started my hotel company just a couple of years later. My first hotel, the funky Phoenix in San Francisco's Tenderloin, became a world-famous rock 'n' roll motel where I babysat Sinead O'Connor's young child, served Linda Ronstadt breakfast in bed, and lent cuff links to JFK Jr. for a wedding in our courtyard. By the time "boy wonder" (me) was profiled in *People* magazine soon after turning thirty, I was already well on my way to becoming an admiration addict.

I spent nearly two dozen years as a hospitality disruptor, expanding my little empire (or so I saw it) to more than fifty boutique hotels all over California before selling Joie de Vivre Hospitality at the bottom of the Great Recession. I thought I'd be CEO of Joie de Vivre until I was eighty years old. But, virtually overnight, my calling became a job and the high wore off. For many of us, there's a gradual "molting" that occurs before the world sees our new identity. During my molting period, I felt lonely and occasionally confused because it was hard to share my intention of a radical identity change. But, given that I had nearly two years to consider this evolution, it was harder for others to accept me so suddenly stripping away my identity as the leader of my company than it was for me to do it. It's no coincidence that "costume" and "custom" sound alike, as our costume—in my case, a rebel hotelier—can fit like a snug habit, and peeling it off can be as painful as ripping off a bandage. I'd gone through this feeling of being raw and naked once before, but this time with Airbnb was different.

One of my first lessons as a Modern Elder was that I'd need to "strategically forget" part of my historical professional identity. Airbnb didn't need two CEOs, as Brian had substantial potential to be one of the best of his generation. Nor did they need me, the curious interloper who had only just recently learned the term "sharing economy," pontificating wisdom from the elder's pulpit. I was no longer the "sage on the stage" but was instead transitioning into the "guide on the side." More than anything, in those first few months, I just listened and watched intently with as little judgment or ego as possible. I imagined myself as a cultural anthropologist, intrigued and fascinated by this new habitat: a modern, male Margaret Mead amid the millennials.

Crossing professional boundaries truly is akin to an anthropological expedition. For one, you learn new languages. In my case I discovered that young women call each other "dude" and that when someone is "down" for something that really means they're "up" for it. And while there weren't formal tribal rituals per se, there were cultural norms that took some acclimation. Fortunately, unlike many of my fellow boomers undergoing a professional transition, I wasn't invisible. I was an aging hospitality rock star, who happened to be on the hip Burning Man board of directors, and everyone knew I had

Brian's ear. So, for sure, my acclimation was easier than it might be for others.

It looked pretty good from the outside, but, internally, it wasn't pretty. Admittedly, much of my past identity was wrapped up in all the admiration associated with being on center stage publicly. Now I was behind the curtain, giving stage directions to the lead actors. I'd gone from headliner to acting coach. Fortunately, the three founders had a growth mindset, were very smart, and had no qualms about taking advice from a generational outsider old enough to be their dad. Fortunately, as you read in chapter 2, I learned as much from them as they did from me by mentoring privately and interning publicly.

I also experienced a sense of liberation that surprised me. Back at Joie de Vivre, I was weighed down with "boss baggage": the worry of whether I was venerated or loathed in my role as the holder of power and the public face of the company. As I evolved in my early days at Airbnb, I realized I could choose my own role, write my own script. Or maybe there was no script at all? Plus, as is true of many people over fifty, I was more and more drawn to mission-driven, rather than ego-driven, pursuits. And helping lead the charge with my younger comrades in the burgeoning movement to democratize hospitality— as the liaison and leader to millions of hosts and tens of millions of guests—gave me a profound sense of mission.

As I edited down my identity to what felt essential as a leader in the company, it became apparent that my influence was going to be less about pronouncements from a pulpit and more about how I showed up as a role model. This led me to an exercise in personal reputation building that I haven't before shared publicly. But it's key to what helped me to be effective as a Luddite, twice the age of most tech-minded employees at Airbnb.

INTENTIONALLY BUILDING YOUR REPUTATION

No matter what your new role is, and no matter where you sit on the organizational hierarchy, it's important to remember that your larger role is that of a role model. The more millennials seek your counsel as a Modern Elder, the more help you will have in deciding what kind of essential questions to ask and what kind of person you want to become. Once you realize this, you begin to take more seriously how you show up and how your reputation or personal brand translates to others. In an era of YouTube and Instagram, the younger generations are becoming increasingly adept at developing their personal brands, so you should make it part of your evolution as well.

As I approached my three-month anniversary at Airbnb, I began seeing the influence of my words and actions, which prompted me to create my personal, private code of behavior. As I wrote in my book *Emotional Equations*, leaders are the emotional thermostats of those they lead, and our habits as leaders can spread like a contagion. The foundation of my code was respect: how to show it and how to earn it. Brian asked me to help evolve Airbnb into a hospitality company—from the inside out—and I knew that at the heart of hospitality is respect. I made a list of habits that I hoped would be emulated among not just my fellow employees, but also the broader Airbnb community of hosts and guests. Taking this very deliberate approach to defining my reputation, as well as the behaviors that would back it up, is something I never tried as CEO of my own company. But, in a completely new habitat, it felt like a way to emphasize the core of who I was and what I stood for. It didn't just help me lead with intention, it helped me evolve into a more intentional identity. One collateral benefit of this approach is it meant, as a senior leader in the company, I was influencing the group norms of the teams I was a part of as well as the meetings I would attend. Modeling respect could have a domino effect on others around me. In sum, one of the most effective ways to change others harkens back to the famous Gandhian tenet: exhibit the change you want to see.

Here are some other ways I intentionally evolved my identity so that I could make a difference at Airbnb:

- (Almost) always arriving on time for meetings, which suggested I respected people's time and helped to create a culture based on not wasting others' time.

- Responding expeditiously, especially to emails from hosts and guests; my rule was that I needed to respond to every incoming email, which could number more than four hundred on a busy day, within twenty-four hours, even if my response was just to acknowledge receipt and clarify when I'd get back to them. When I saw an upset email from an employee, guest, or host, I would do my best to drop everything and respond within ten minutes of seeing the correspondence (obviously I had to build some space into my schedule for this kind of responsiveness).

- Giving feedback to others in a timely manner, especially with employee reviews but also real-time private feedback, doing my best to listen first before giving feedback.

- Showing gratitude to those at all service levels of the Airbnb hierarchy—dishwashers in our company cafeteria, the security staff, those at the reception desk—to remind myself and others that looking after our customers isn't the only way to demonstrate hospitality. Everyone deserves the same respect.

My goal was to show my young techie comrades that responsiveness builds trust and respect, and if you embody that way of being, it's so much easier to find solutions and resolve conflicts. So I was very observant about who took responsiveness seriously and who didn't seem to have the empathy and agility to exhibit this quality. And, then, I would do my best to give them some private tips (mentor privately) on how they could improve. One of my direct reports called these conversations "Chip's Stealth Boot Camp." Pretty soon small (one could even say "stealth") actions and one-on-one communications, rather than big companywide speeches like the ones I'd given in my CEO days, were part of my evolving identity.

When I explored this reputation I was building one-on-one with the younger folks with whom I worked most, they arrived at ways of describing me that were as precise as my DNA: "emotionally reliable," "optimystical" (optimistic and spiritually inclined), "decisive and driven," and "a story untangler," as one person told me: "You listen *for* my story, not just *to* my story, and you propose solutions." Our reputation is one of the few portable assets we can count on our entire lives. In fact, the cosmic bellhop delivers it to our new workplace even before we've arrived physically. So take your reputation seriously.

You can accentuate the positive in your evolving identity in all kinds of ways.

Build a collaborative bridge: You may have industry connections that your colleagues don't have due to the fact you've been on the planet a few more years. As the only senior executive at Airbnb with a decades-long travel industry background, it was essential that I take on the role of an elder statesman, or in modern parlance, a secretary of state. That meant inviting the CEOs and senior leaders of some of the largest hotel companies in the world to our headquarters for a deep immersion on Airbnb and why it appealed to millennial travelers. Why? It was harder for those who feared being disrupted by our entrance into the lodging marketplace to view us as villains if we were genuinely reaching out to them. And I always did my best to be deferential to Brian, the CEO, and not slip on my old costume and steal the stage, even when surrounded by those from my former industry.

Be humane and humorous: Writer Henry Miller suggested the most comforting thing about growing old gracefully is the ability not to take things too seriously, and the big difference between a sage and a preacher is the ability to occasionally laugh at life. In a company that was doubling in size every year, and under a microscope for all kinds of reasons, it was easy to lose our sense of humanity as well as our sense of humor. So being accessible, real, and, occasionally, real funny was part of my evolving identity.

Be calm and curious: I'll talk more about this in the next chapter, but if I was the smartest person in the room, I was in the wrong room. One young colleague, Clément Marcelet, told me that former French president François Mitterrand used to tell his driver, "Slow down, we're late," when they were stuck in rush-hour traffic. The point is that sometimes you just have to accept that it's going to take longer to get where you're going; doing things faster isn't always the answer and can become a problem in and of itself. For me that was certainly true when it came to learning the ropes at Airbnb. Being a calm and curious presence in the room and asking open-ended questions that helped us to see our blind spots became part of my growing reputation in the company.

Be present: Presence is far more intricate and rewarding an art than productivity and can be the hallmark of an elder. In a culture that often measures our worth as human beings by our efficiency, fast iteration, and answers, I was a bit of a rebel. The cult of productivity has its place, but worshipping at its altar can rob us of our sense of curiosity, joy, and wonder and rob a company of its ability to self-reflect.

FEELING TOO OLD TO EVOLVE,
TRY BECOMING AN INTERN

Sometimes we get a shock to the system that wakes us up and tells us it's time to evolve. For some that can be a health scare that reminds us our time is precious. For others it can be the end of a marriage, losing our job, or the approach of a milestone birthday. Yet in the absence of alarm clock events like these, it can be hard to muster the courage and motivation to shed a costume that has historically fit us so perfectly. If you're feeling like you're easing into the winter of your life, but want to remember what it's like to be in midsummer, you might consider seeking out an internship as a low-risk way to try on a new costume or identity.

Paul Critchlow had a storied career, spending thirty years with Merrill Lynch where he ultimately became head of communications. But, he told me, "The summer of 2016 loomed, for me, as uneventful. I'd retired a year earlier and I was feeling a little bored, restless, left out. My plans to do some personal writing of a memoir, some consulting, charitable work, and travel weren't quite cutting it. Then my neighbor Sally Susman, head of corporate affairs for Pfizer Inc., the pharmaceutical company, took me to lunch. On a transatlantic flight, she'd watched this film, *The Intern*, and she loved how all the characters—younger and older—affected, changed, and enriched one another. She was wondering whether I'd be open to being an intern for the summer. Why not?! Later, Sally confided her worries that I'd be insulted or our friendship somehow damaged. I confessed my fears that the young people would reject me; the staff, resent me; or I might come across as an old out-of-touch know-it-all. We both turned out to be wrong." At seventy, Paul was the oldest of some two hundred interns who were mostly around age twenty.

On his first day, Shalini Sinha, a bright grad student from Georgetown University, approached Paul. She asked if Paul would be her mentor. Shalini's main worry was how to tell her father, a traditional Indian patriarch, that she wanted to remain in the US to pursue her career. Paul told her she was an adult woman and she could reassure him that wherever she lives, she will always be his daughter. Paul was deeply touched later to receive an email from her. "I feel like I've been given permission to pursue my own dreams," she wrote. Shalini became a star of the class and a reliable source of coaching and wisdom for Paul. And Paul immediately saw his value to these young people and realized he could reframe his skills and be both a mentor and an intern.

Paul was teamed with three other young interns and this "fantastic four" bonded quickly by being transparent. Paul says, "They encouraged me to be briefer in my communications. I urged them to dig a little deeper. I taught them about classic media relations techniques. They taught me about social media. With their help, I opened my first Facebook account and toned down ('You're not looking for a job, Paul') my LinkedIn profile." He taught them office etiquette; they taught him how to communicate with a millennial. Reciprocity and mutual respect allowed Paul to give some feedback to his teammates about the lack of eye contact they offered due to being distracted by their gadgets. He says, "I noticed that they barely looked up from their laptops or devices when others approached." One of his teammates took him aside and said, "Paul, I've noticed that when someone comes into the room, you stand up, introduce yourself, and shake their hand. Should we be doing that—and why?" I told him, "Yes. It's courteous, shows respect for the other person, and establishes you as a presence to be dealt with." All three of his teammates began to follow suit.

As outlined in the *Fast Company* article in the appendix's "My 10 Favorites" (see the "Articles" category), Paul's experience was life-affirming both for him and all those around him. Yes, he was an intern, but he was so much more than that. The intergenerational transfer of trust, respect, and learning he experienced that summer was invigorating and inspired him to start attending writers' conferences by helping him see he had even more of a story to tell in that memoir he'd been trying to write. He says, "This experience allowed me to distill a lifetime of experience into a cohesive narrative. Of all the titles I've held through the years, Senior Intern at Pfizer will be among the most treasured. My wife, Patty, calls it 'the gift of a victory lap.'"

He recommends an internship for anyone who needs to open up their life. And while some might consider an internship "beneath them" and bemoan the loss of status or stature they had in prior roles, Paul felt very differently. "As an intern, when I stopped having management responsibility, I suddenly found I could stop and ponder and wonder at things I'd walked past without noticing for years. This process frees your mind from your conditioned instincts and suddenly you're thinking outside the box again, like when you were a child and could imagine doing anything. And, while I occasionally miss the power, perks, and prestige of my former corporate life, I appreciate my freedom and lack of stress."

For Paul, the experience made him realize he had more to contribute—and more to learn. He decided to open a communications consulting practice and named it Black Cat Communications LLC, after his little pet cat. Sally came up with his company's slogan—"Nine lives"—and after he formally pitched her, Pfizer became his first client. Bank of America soon followed. Today, his business is thriving, with other client prospects stepping forward, and he faces the "nice problem" of whether or not to expand. He models his consulting on his experience as a senior intern and is excited, for the first time in his long professional career, to be an entrepreneur. "Older people have a lot to contribute," he's concluded. "They just have to be asked."

Seventy-one-year-old Doug McKinlay, an advertising professor at Brigham Young University, didn't wait to be asked when he approached a friend at a Dallas-based ad agency, the Richards Group, about becoming a summer intern as a way of staying relevant in an increasingly young and digital-savvy industry. The company paired Doug with a twenty-five-year-old creative exec, with whom he quickly formed a symbiotic relationship, benefiting both men, as well as the agency. Doug now suggests that all advertising professors work inside an agency every five to seven years to ensure they're up to speed on what's new in the industry.

Finally, I was fortunate enough to be able to help secure senior internships at Airbnb for Debbie and Michael Campbell. Before their sixtieth and seventieth birthdays, respectively, the Campbells chose to start traveling the world, staying exclusively at home shares booked through Airbnb. They sold their Seattle home and their boat, said good-bye to friends and family, and started their sojourn. They got a little famous along the way being profiled as the "Senior Nomads" in a cover story in the *New York Times*. And, just after their thousandth day, having stayed in more than 160 homes in nearly seventy countries, they had become our most prolific guests and they wanted to share some of their learning with Airbnb employees. So they joined us in the fall of 2017 for their ten-week internship at our San Francisco headquarters so that Airbnb employees could hear how our platform could better serve the needs of our most active guests. Given that Airbnb's average guest is ten years older and our average host is nearly fifteen years older than the average age of our employees, Debbie and Michael appreciated translating the needs of our large guest and host community to those creating the software and rules that define our growing home-sharing marketplace.

At the end of a masquerade ball the masks are taken off and people show their true character and essence. In the latter part of life, much the same thing happens. As cultural anthropologist Angeles Arrien wrote in *The Second Half of Life*, "When we move beyond our ego and worldly identity, we can take eighth-century Buddhist sage Hui-Neng's advice: 'Show me the face you had before even your parents were born.'"

Now let's explore a few practical ways you can evolve your identity and don a new costume in your professional life.

ModEl Practices to Evolve Your Identity

1. TRY AN "IDENTITY CLEANSE."

Around the age of forty, I started a practice of doing a quarterly three-day juice cleanse to reset my metabolism, remove toxins from my system, and become more conscious of my senses and my connection to others. We can apply a similar cleansing practice to our identity as well.

Swedish gerontologist Lars Tornstam believes that one of the key development tasks of the elder is the construction of a life story that feels right and true. Maybe this is part of the reason elders can tell and retell stories from the past. And Erik Erikson suggested that each of us has an "invariable core" or an "existential identity" that is an integration of the past, present, and future. An "identity cleanse" allows you to purge some of the baggage of your LinkedIn profile and become more conscious of what's essential in your experience and history.

Reserve at least a couple of hours for this exercise as well as find a place to do this where you won't be disturbed or distracted. I recommend doing this by yourself, but there is some preparatory homework you could ask a minimum of a half-dozen coworkers, friends, or family to complete. Ask them to answer the following: "When you think of me in good times and bad, what are the core qualities that I exhibit? What are the positive ones? And what are the more challenging ones?" Before you read people's answers, answer these questions yourself, being as candid as you can, knowing you don't need to share this with anyone else. When in doubt, consider feedback you've gotten from past employee reviews. Make your list and then compare it with the answers you received from others.

Can you identify your identity? What are the durable traits or qualities you want your reputation built upon? If you're having a hard time determining them, think about when you feel most "in the flow" at work or what you're doing when you easily lose track of time. You're probably experiencing some natural talent or aptitude. What habits or customs can you incorporate into your daily life that back up this trait or quality? For example, if you like that your invariable core is recognizing and appreciating people, does it make sense to create a habit that you will privately recognize two people with specific feedback in person at least, on average, twice per day?

And, then, what qualities are you ready to part ways with? In other words, which qualities are like toxins best removed from your system? The capacity for change with a ballast of continuity defines the Modern Elder.

2. REDEFINE YOUR REPUTATION.

So, whether you're in a new workplace trying to find the right costume, or wanting to trade your old costume in for a new one in your current workplace, or even still hanging in the liminal space between, imagine if your personal reputation or brand was a consumer product. What would be your value proposition? What are the three to five qualities or adjectives that people would use most commonly to define you, and what habits or customs are foundational to that reputation you wish to build?

But your reputation or brand won't feel authentic if it doesn't align with who you are. Melina Lillios felt so strongly about her personal mantra to "live, laugh, and love" life that it became the name of her tour company. Gandhi clarified the connection of beliefs to destiny in the following linear, poignant way: "Your beliefs become your thoughts. Your thoughts become your words. Your words become your actions. Your actions become your habits. Your habits become your values. Your values become your destiny." So, at your core, what beliefs define your reputation?

3. TURN WISDOM UPSIDE DOWN: BECOME AN INTERN.

If you're stuck in a rut and find yourself just cursing millennials, you may be longing for a time long past: the time when elders were venerated and powerful. That era ain't coming back, so it's time for you to start slipping into the costume of the Modern Elder who is both a mentor and an intern. For many of us, that latter role, the one Robert De Niro so perfectly embodied in the movie *The Intern*, is ill-fitting, in that it doesn't feel just or appropriate for someone our age.

Don't let that discourage you from reaching out to a company you're intrigued with. The film *The Intern* has paved the way for a cultural phenomenon, so you might be surprised by the positive response you get (it grossed more than $200 million in revenues— which means *a lot* of people went to see it). Or, if this seems like too challenging a proposition, consider another way to try on a new identity. Volunteer at a local homeless center. Live in a foreign land and learn a new language. Do something that helps you lose your balance. Become liminal. A freshly evolved identity prepares you for Lesson 2, growing your ability to learn.

[5]

Lesson 2: LEARN

There is something I don't know
that I am supposed to know.
I don't know what it is I don't know
and yet am supposed to know,
and I feel I look stupid
if I seem both not to know it
and not know what it is I don't know.
Therefore, I pretend I know it.

This is nerve-racking
since I don't know what I must pretend to know.
Therefore I pretend to know everything.

I feel you know what I'm supposed to know
but you can't tell me what it is
because you don't know
that I don't know what it is.

You may know what I don't know,
but not that I don't know it,
and I can't tell you.
So you will
have to
tell me
Everything.

—R. D. LAING

"Is your head swimming?"

"No. It's drowning," was my response to a fellow boomer who asked me this question as we shuffled out of a presentation with Airbnb's genius data science team. It's probably the question I should ask you after just reading psychotherapist R. D. Laing's mind-twisting quote above. As we discussed in the last chapter, being in the midst of a career transition can create a confused, liminal state. The natural reaction to this fear of survival could be fight, flight, or freeze. But evolving into a learner who adapts is your best means of swimming and not drowning.

If you're feeling a bit of trepidation about reading this chapter because you feel you have no learning left inside of you, I offer a simple quote from ancient Chinese philosopher Lao-Tzu who said, "To attain knowledge, add things every day. To attain wisdom, remove things every day." Once again, being a prudent editor is a critical part of learning how to live and learn later in life.

Our world is awash in knowledge, but often wanting in wisdom. Based upon our childhood approach to learning, we believe that information produces knowledge, which leads to wisdom, but the correlation isn't perfectly direct. Too much information without context can create fog. A lighthouse of knowledge may provide some sense of safety, but often what's required when grappling with a vexing issue is the very uncertainty of sailing into a dark storm. And, yet, our gut reaction—especially in today's data-driven world—is to try to digest all available information quickly and spit out a brilliant answer. Or, as R. D. Laing suggests, don't let on to what you don't know.

Picasso said, "Computers are useless. They only give you answers." Just think about how learning has evolved in the past thirty years.

Management scholar (Carnegie Mellon University) Professor Robert Kelley has shown that the percentage of knowledge necessary to retain in your mind to perform well on the job was about 75 percent when the youngest baby boomers entered the workplace. For the other 25 percent, we accessed all kinds of manuals, books, and other sources. But today that 75/25 mix has moved to 10/90 as it's less essential for us to remember everything in the era of search engines and social media; after all, why cram our brains with facts and figures when we can query friends, or simply "Google it"? This is actually reassuring since the flip side of this story is that the relevance of so much knowledge is decaying at a faster and faster rate, particularly in the tech world where it's estimated that about 30 percent of technical knowledge becomes obsolete each year. To stay relevant, it's not just about learning something new, it's also about learning new ways to access the information at our fingertips.

Many of us fear that our mental functioning naturally cripples with time because brain cells die. Yet growing research shows that neuroplasticity, or the brain functioning like a muscle such that when it's well used it stays fit, allows many adults to retain their full cognitive abilities late into life. Neurologist Marsel Mesulam has shown that "Superagers," those who see almost no cognitive decline with age, tend to have something in common: they consistently work on difficult tasks that require ambidextrous use of their mind.

Throughout a person's lifetime, the brain is continually reshaping itself in response to what it learns. Swiss neuroscientist Lutz Jäncke studied people who were learning to play a musical instrument. After they had been practicing for five months, Jäncke noted significant changes in the regions of the brain that control hearing, memory, and hand movements, even in participants who were sixty-five or older. This joins a growing number of studies demonstrating that brain plasticity continues late into our lives.

Peter Drucker, maybe the greatest management theorist of all time, recognized that it was never too late in life to learn a new skill. After all, he wrote two-thirds of his forty books after the age of sixty-five. His seventy-year career and his way of "living in more than one world" is a role model for all of us. "What matters," he wrote, "is that the knowledge worker (a phrase he coined in 1959), by the time he or she reaches middle age, has developed and nourished a human being rather than a tax accountant or a hydraulic engineer." Organizational Behavior expert (Rice University) Professor Erik Dane similarly warns older workers to beware of behavioral rigidities and "cognitive entrenchments" that can start to rule your life. He and other researchers have found that many successful scientists tend to be polymaths—that is, in addition to their scientific expertise, they have artistic, literary, or musical avocations. Older brains often flourish with a diverse set of sensory and intellectual inputs.

Drucker lived to age ninety-five, and one of the ways he thrived later in life was by translating his curiosity into diving deeply into a new subject that intrigued him. He'd do this every couple of years on a diverse collection of subjects that had nothing to do with his business career, from Japanese flower arranging to medieval war strategies. He imagined that, on occasion, a "parallel career" might sprout out of this curiosity. I've been following Drucker's lead for a dozen years now, having deeply studied all kinds of subjects that had nothing to do with being a hospitality leader: the nature of our emotions, the history of festivals and why they are making a comeback in the twenty-first century, the geological origins of why hot springs exist, and the importance of meaning in one's life. This led me to turning the first topic (emotions) into a bestselling book and the second topic (festivals) into an online start-up that also inspired me to create the "Airbnb Open," a festival that has attracted attendees from more countries in the world than virtually any other festival or conference.

This kind of "serial mastery"—or creating unique competencies in various areas—helps people to remain flexible and open to new, unexpected change. Drucker believed this appreciation for learning makes for a better leader—and I believe that it makes for a happier and more fulfilled life, as well.

ADOPTING A BEGINNER'S MIND

"The mind of the beginner is empty, free of the habits of the expert. Such a mind is open to all possibilities and can see things as they are." So said Shunryū Suzuki, who helped popularize Zen Buddhism in the United States. Part of the practice of Zen Buddhism is creating a safe space for the "don't know" mind, a place beyond knowing and not knowing. A place where you can contemplate and discern. This space is what allows your thinking to steep like a good cup of tea. Unfortunately, most of modern adulthood doesn't offer a whole lot of space to steep.

Many a company's founding story came out of the asking of an innocent question. Reed Hastings got the idea for Netflix after a $40 late fee on a DVD rental prompted him to ask himself "What if DVDs could be rented through a subscription service, so no one would ever be hit with late fees?" Steve Wozniak and Steve Jobs's idea for Apple came out of the question "Why aren't computers small enough for people to have them in their homes and offices?" With Airbnb, Joe and Brian's idea to set up three air mattresses on their living room floor and open their apartment to strangers was predicated on the question "Why can't we be in the B&B business?" This inquiry was based upon two simple premises: like many relatively recent college grads, they were broke and needed to pay their rent, and, there was a design conference in San Francisco and all the hotels were full. They didn't spend months or years writing a business plan. They didn't research the regulatory environment for such a business. They didn't raise money. They just asked a question and started blowing up air mattresses and advertising this crazy idea online.

Innocent questions have been the fuel for innovation since the beginning of time. Back in 1752, Ben Franklin wondered if lightning could be electricity in the sky, but he wanted to test it, so with a kite and a key (and a whole lot of courage) he was able to prove his premise. In the 1940s, the invention of the Polaroid instant camera was seeded by a three-year-old's question. Edwin H. Land's daughter grew impatient after her father snapped a photo and wondered, "Why do we have to wait for the picture, Daddy?"

Maybe we all should think a little more like a child, as question-asking peaks at age four or five and steadily drops off from there. Harvard child psychologist Paul Harris says a child asks about forty thousand questions between the age of two and five. Yet our educational system encourages us to seek answers, not questions, so by the time we graduate into the workforce, we feel like the simple questions have been educated right out of us.

William Yeats wrote, "Education is not filling a pail. It's lighting a fire." In my early days at Airbnb, I was able to stoke a fire in the company by being catalytically curious. I didn't know any better. Being in a tech company was new for me. And so my beginner's mind helped us to see a few of our blind spots a little better, as my mind was free of the habits of being the expert, partly due to some of the work I described in the last chapter. I could channel my little kid energy, asking a lot of "Why" and "What if" questions, whereas most senior leaders are stuck in the "What" and "How" of business.

One of the first questions I asked was, "Why do Airbnb hosts— who are not our employees—care about the quality of hospitality they offer?" This was a fundamental question since part of my role was to help create a world-class hospitality company when it's not employees delivering the service, as it had been in my experience as a hotelier. I asked this question of those within the company, and in focus groups and social events with hosts. While there were many answers, the two primary ones I heard were: (1) many hosts rely on their financial security by home sharing and, thus, anything that makes their listing look better—guest reviews, search rankings, or special designation—helps them meet their financial goals; and (2) the act of opening your home or apartment to a stranger creates a kind of immediate intimacy, so many hosts take their hospitality skills very seriously because it's such a powerful way to foster human connection. For many of our hosts, the better they feel about their hosting, the better they feel about themselves as a human.

The more I learned, the more I realized psychology was at the very heart of this new grassroots form of hospitality. So that first "Why" led to many more beginner's mind questions:

- Why is our review system the way it is?

- Why do we have hosts review guests? (My "hotel brain" had a hard time understanding this in my early days, as a hotel would never review a guest in any online public way.)

- What if we more directly linked the quality of host performance with their search rankings?

- Why has our Superhost program, celebrating our best hosts in the world, not grown since 2012?

- Why don't we create a private dashboard for our hosts that shows their effectiveness in meeting hospitality standards as well as champions their progress?

Over my first year at the company, using both motivation techniques—extrinsic (1) and intrinsic (2)—with our hosts, we improved the feedback loop system that helped our hosts understand how they were doing and incentivized them to constantly improve.

Early in my tenure, I sat with Laura Hughes, our director of hospitality, and hypothesized, "What if improving our review system could create a more effective feedback loop so guest satisfaction might surpass the hotel industry, even though those delivering the service aren't our employees?"

It seemed like a blasphemous thought, especially given my professional history. But with a variety of changes we made in the system in 2014—including creating more confidentiality for private feedback and modifying the timing of revealing guest and host reviews so it was simultaneous, which meant less fear of retribution (i.e., a host leaving a guest a bad review because the guest posted a bad review of them)—Airbnb guest satisfaction with their hosts, based upon the hotel industry standard of Net Promoter Score (NPS), grew to 50 percent higher than the average for the hotel industry over the next couple of years. Yes, you read that correctly! Independent hosts, who are not our employees and have not received in-person formal training, were able to deliver hospitality experiences that guests far preferred over the hotel industry. Hence, Airbnb's rapid growth, which began with an innocent and childlike question, has been fueled by ecstatic guests who appreciate the personalized hospitality our hosts offer.

INDUSTRIES AND EXECS THAT DON'T LEARN WILL BE DISRUPTED

After the fact, this may seem obvious since hosts are microentrepreneurs and may have more incentive than a hotel employee to deliver great hospitality. The irony is I chose to sell my hotel management company and brand in 2010 because what had been the "Hospitality business" (big "H," small "b") had become the "hospitality Business" (small "h," big "B"). When I started in the hotel business in the mid-1980s, many grand hotels were like family heirlooms, and owners like the Swig family operated their Fairmont Hotels as bastions of good taste and service, treating their employees almost like extensions of their family.

But private equity firms and public market real estate investors discovered that hotel real estate often offers higher returns than other forms of property ownership, so many of those grand hotels got swallowed up by investors focused primarily on bottom-line returns, often fixated on quarterly results. In the process, "Business" took precedence over "hospitality" and those of us managing hotels for these new owners lost some of our hospitality spirit in the pursuit of maximizing financial gains.

While I sold my management company and have sold a few of my hotels, I still own (with partners) the real estate of nine hotels, many of which are managed by Joie de Vivre. So I offer the following set of "Why" and "What if" questions to my fellow hoteliers. Even if you aren't in the hotel business, these questions can get you thinking about how to apply a childlike curiosity to the challenges in your own field:

- Why has growth in hotel guest satisfaction been stagnant for so long?

- Why do more than 70 percent of Airbnb hosts and guests review each other in their peer-to-peer review platform, yet only 5–10 percent of hotel guests fill out their online guest satisfaction survey after a hotel stay?

- Why don't we have a feedback loop that helps an individual hotel employee—whether a bartender, a bellman, or a front desk agent—know in real time how they're doing? (Most hotel employees only get reviewed once a year by their boss and, unfortunately, the average employee in a hotel often stays less than a year, so there's no formal feedback from their boss and no effective means of capturing guests' recognition of above-the-call-of-duty service.)

- What if the hotel industry embarked upon a whole new service approach using mobile technology, allowing employees to receive real-time feedback from guests, and the hotel to determine in real time what parts of the business are struggling to keep up with guest expectations (almost like a "heat map" that would allow a general manager to immediately shift resources to solve momentary service need gaps)?

"Disruption" seems to be the buzzword of the era when it comes to business. But disruption has been around since the dawn of free-market competition. It's just become more abrupt in the age of technology when an innovative new business idea, like home sharing or file sharing, can take off and go global so quickly. Virtually all industries and companies are vulnerable, but the ones that are most ripe for disruption have a few things in common. They are those that don't ask lots of "Why" and "What if" questions, have stopped learning, and have these qualities:

- Grown complacent by past successes and haven't evolved their product offering much;

- Lost touch with their core customers' evolving needs and have no way to track this well;

- Didn't imagine a whole new set of customers, with different needs, entering the market;

- Don't take new competitors seriously, potentially because they feel competitively safe due to their historical regulatory environment; and

- Have no clue what the true essence of their product offering is.

That last bullet point may seem a little ethereal, so let me explain and offer a shortcut. Most businesses get commoditized over time such that they become just transaction machines. The lack of new oxygen (innovators and rebel thinkers) in the system means they define their business and its appeal in a very bottom-line way. Professor Theodore Levitt asked a simple question long ago that Peter Drucker popularized: "What business are we in?" Simple, yes. But you may be surprised at how subtle, sublime, and valuable this question can be as a learning exercise for your organization.

This simple question helped Joie de Vivre to discover we were in the "identity refreshment" business, as our most loyal guests (to a particular boutique hotel) almost felt like the personality of the hotel rubbed off on them. A hotel guest at the Hotel Vitale, for example, who sees that property as "modern, urbane, fresh, natural, and nurturing" might experience staying in that hotel as an amplified mirror for their ideal self. Discovering our company's unique value proposition in the marketplace, designing hotels that captured this "*you are where you sleep*" experience, and then marketing them in a way that subtly speaks to "identity refreshment" is a core reason Joie de Vivre grew so successfully.

So, before you and your company get disrupted, try the exercise at the end of the chapter and disrupt yourself by getting curious about the essential differentiator of your product or service. This can be just as valuable for a large company as a small one, and, frankly, larger companies are more vulnerable to disruption.

CREATING CATALYTIC CURIOSITY

Curiosity is the foreplay of discovery. While creativity and innovation get the headlines, curiosity is the elixir that gives them stamina. So why aren't more of us curious in the workplace? Why do we feel the need to put on the façade of a know-it-all when obviously no one knows it all?

Being curious as a way to catalyze courage, learning, and creative thinking is something that requires confidence. Modern Elders can use the confidence capital they may have accrued over the years and spend it on behalf of themselves and their teams. In some cases, your seniority may have earned you the right to ask, "Why?"

Alan Eustace was a fifty-seven-year-old Silicon Valley engineer in free fall. No, I'm not referring to the sad truth that many older engineers are discarded by their employers. I'm referring to the fact that Alan holds the world's record for the highest altitude free-fall jump. In 2014, after years of preparing, he fell from 135,889 feet in the stratosphere, becoming a human projectile falling at a rate of 821 miles per hour. I get a nosebleed over ten thousand feet, so I was particularly impressed when I had the honor of spending a few minutes talking with him about the near decade he spent as the head of engineering globally at Google during their most significant early growth years.

Alan was a rock star technologist in 2002 when he joined Google, which was then just four years old and bringing in very little revenue. And he was about fifteen years senior to its founders, Larry Page and Sergey Brin, who had set out to hire very senior technical leaders who'd become available in the wake of the disintegration of some of the great research institutions like Xerox PARC and Bell Labs. Yet "Larry and Sergey weren't interested in how you did things before," Alan says. "They just wanted it done the smartest way and they wanted to have confidence that you weren't taking the easy path by just repeating what you've done before." He acknowledges that his role was to translate the young founders' vision into operational reality based upon his depth of experience. But, more than experience, curiosity was a core quality that the founders sought in their engineering leaders. And many older technologists at Google felt confident enough in who they were that they didn't mind asking the occasional naive question as long as it showed some ingenuity in their thinking.

Psychologist Karl Weick suggests that the right attitude for learning and creativity is to "argue as if you are right and listen as if you are wrong." Futurist Paul Saffo coined this approach as "strong opinions, weakly held." It is this balancing act between confidence and doubt that defines great leadership in a learning organization.

I was known around Airbnb as being one who asked the occasional "airball" question. I'm a big basketball fan, so I know what a faux pas it is to shoot and not only not score a basket, but not even hit the backboard or rim. Of course, I was a bit of an idiot when it came to technology, so many of my questions were elementary. But I came to realize that my courage to make humble inquiries was akin to how I viewed my shooting percentage. Occasionally, I would ask a simple question that uncovered a company blind spot. That would be like making a three-point shot far away from the basket, but I still found that maybe only one-third of my questions "made a basket." A 33 percent shooting average on the basketball court from any distance isn't enviable and means you might not be suiting up that much longer. So over time, I realized that some of these questions were better left for a one-on-one with a colleague than for a whole room of people.

One day, after throwing a few airballs in a meeting, I commented about my private shooting percentage calculations to a younger colleague. He had the perfect response: "Maybe we're playing baseball at Airbnb, not basketball." I gave him a curious look, so he continued, "A .333 batting average in baseball means you're one of the best hitters on the team. You're also proficient at hitting home runs in the conference room (big ideas that expose new opportunities), so you earn a high slugging percentage (baseball players who hit a larger percentage of homers than the average player) like Hank Aaron or Babe Ruth."

This kind of shift in my thinking gave me confidence to take a few more swings at the plate, as Ruth is famous for being both the home run *and* strikeout king. So ask yourself, is your company playing basketball or baseball when it comes to being open to curious questions? As the greatest basketball coach of all time, John Wooden, put it, "It's what you learn after you know it all that counts."

A GREAT QUESTION LEADS TO A QUEST

There was a time when answers ruled the world. But, thanks to search engines, answers are plentiful, and an insightful question may be worth a thousand Google searches. "You can tell whether a man is clever by his answers. However, you can tell whether a man is wise by his questions," says Egyptian writer and Nobel laureate Naguib Mahfouz. The root of the word "question" is "quest." And through the process of reflection, every question can become a quest, a journey of self-discovery, the facilitator of a sojourn into uncharted territory.

Just as great questions fertilize the minds of individuals, so do they nourish the corporate soul of a young start-up. And in older and more established companies, they wake people up, create the kind of environment that breaks bad habits. Author David Cooperrider suggests in his book *Appreciative Inquiry*, "Human systems grow in the direction of what they persistently ask questions about, and this propensity is strongest and most sustainable when the means and ends of inquiry are positively correlated." In other words, if the question has blame attached, like "Why is our market share dropping and who is to blame?," that creates a finger-pointing organization. But if instead the question is, "We're not performing as well as we used to; do we have a blind spot or a systemic problem, and what can we learn from our competitors?," that's a very different framing that influences the psyche of the organization. Show me the typical question that emerges from a meeting of any company's leaders, and I'll show you the culture of that organization.

Socrates, famous for turning the act of inquiry into an art form, played the role of the perpetual student and modeled it for his young mentees. He blurred the distinction between who was learning and who was teaching and, as such, he appeared less like the wise old man, but more like a mature, fully baked version of what his young students aspired to be. Socrates's method of questioning can create a systemic way of thinking about any topic. A curious mind begins with the premise that things may not be what they seem on the surface, and that exploring the scaffolding of one's point of view may help you uncover faulty or beautiful assumptions that aren't necessarily obvious at first glance. A Modern Elder can be the Socrates in an organization filled with young, fertile minds. When Eric Schmidt was CEO of Google, he said, "We run the company by questions, not by answers." Their Friday afternoon companywide meetings were famous for the wise questions that were posed from line-level employees to leadership.

Socrates believed the unexamined life wasn't worth living. Similarly, an unexamined company isn't likely thriving. Catalyzing curiosity as an individual or an organization requires a well-crafted alchemy of humility and confidence and, absolutely, a profound sense of respect for the one being questioned. The questioning style should also be relatively spontaneous and involve just as much listening as talking: don't act like an attorney badgering the witness with a set of prepared questions that don't reflect the direction the conversation is taking. Most important, you need to craft rules of engagement that are appropriate for your organizational culture. I'll give you some more suggestions in the ModEl Practices section at the end of the chapter.

Peter Drucker wrote a quarter century ago, "The leaders of the past knew how to tell; the leaders of the future will know how to ask."

In a constantly changing world, great questions may be more important than answers. Traditional elders had the clever answers. Modern Elders have the catalytic questions.

STAY ENROLLED AS A STUDENT

Teaching and learning are symbiotic. You can't be a teaching legend without living on the learning edge. This is why the best companies to work for are those that develop a dynamic learning environment in which everyone is invited to teach a subject even if it has nothing to do with the company's core business.

At our first "One Airbnb" global gathering of all our employees, we were encouraged to give a short "skill-share" talk to a subgroup of employees who were interested in the subject matter. I spoke about my love of festivals and created a tool that matched each person with a set of global festivals that fit their celebration archetype, as some of us want wild and crazy and love music while others prefer a more intimate art and culture experience in nature. Everyone in my group tested the tool, which led to a rich discussion on how we could use all the data points we receive from our customers to help match them not just with homes that fit their interests and design tastes, but also with things to do when they travel to this particular place.

Author Liz Wiseman spent seventeen years at Oracle Corporation and led the creation of Oracle University. In her book *Rookie Smarts: Why Learning Beats Knowing in the New Game of Work*, she speaks to the value of creating an organization in which everyone is occasionally a rookie at something. Liz believes that creating an informal peer-to-peer learning environment is good for everyone as it takes us out of our habitual roles. This can lead to an environment of what Liz calls "fluid leadership"—the notion that modern organizations need leaders who are willing to take charge but who are also willing to follow someone else's lead. She says, "We need to stop looking at leadership as a managerial position that we undertake or are appointed to, and see it as a role that we step into and out of. The best leaders need to remain great followers, knowing when to be big and take charge and when to be smaller and follow someone else's lead."

One of the challenges for older workers is they go on cruise control and sometimes need a speed bump to open them up to learning again. Liz writes, "I have found that people are most open to learning when they are: brand new to their role, facing a daunting challenge, coming out of a painful failure or loss, returning from an epiphany outside their normal terrain, and at a loss of how to get to the next level of their career. . . . In each scenario, individuals are working without a script: they've encountered an unprecedented situation."

Liz described such a spike in her own development as a leader. In her midthirties, she faced the trifecta of leadership challenges: her already demanding job as a vice president at Oracle was getting bigger, she had three young children, and she was also caring for her ill father. As her responsibilities expanded, she found that the old-school approaches to leading (like telling, selling, and compelling) simply weren't working. And, while she was technically "the boss," she felt more like the student than the teacher.

When a colleague suggested she deal with unruly children by only asking questions rather than giving directions, she was just desperate enough to try it. It not only transformed bedtime at home, it changed the way she led at work. She learned to spend less time telling people what to do and more time asking good questions—the type that give other people an opportunity to figure things out for themselves. It was a personal breakthrough and an important lesson that she's been able to share with countless other leaders.

She recalls, "I was so busy, I simply couldn't do anything more. But, because I was at a loss, I was willing to do things differently. It was the very fact that I was juggling too many balls (and a few knives) that I was forced to learn new tricks." The best teachers are those who stay enrolled as students.

THE RISKS OF BEING IN A PLACE WHERE YOUR ANSWERS GET QUESTIONED

Stanford professor Robert Sutton says, "At places where intense innovation happens, they often combine people who know too little and people who know too much. The tension between massive knowledge and fresh thinking can spark a fundamental breakthrough." So Modern Elders and young entrepreneurs can symbiotically create catalytically curious organizations. But why don't we see this type of culture as a fundamental part of every successful organization?

Here's how to avoid the traps that inhibit a questioning culture in many organizations:

1. **Avoid Using Questions Like a Hammer.** In companies that swing the questioning pendulum too far in the direction of intense inquiry, you often find know-it-alls using questions as a way to stroke their ego and show off. When questions are used as a hammer to drive an existing viewpoint rather than as a flashlight to shine light on new ones, you don't elicit productive reflection. To remedy this, focus on empowering rather than disempowering questions, which we'll outline in the ModEl Practices section of this chapter. When in doubt, offer a healthy mix of authentic empathy and sharp curiosity in your questions. I once offered the following private feedback to a constant questioner who was grandstanding a bit and creating unneeded tension in the room: "Wisdom is whatever is left after you've run out of your opinions. Be careful not to use questions as a means of just expressing a strongly held belief."

2. **Know When It's Time for Questioning and When It's Time for Efficiency in Decision-making and Execution.** A questioning culture can slow things down and, if it's a hierarchical organization like the military, it can lead to confusion in strategy or lack of leadership direction. So it's important to recognize if your organization isn't built for questioning at times when the pressure is on, deadlines are looming, and stakes are high.

3. **Foster Candor and Psychological Safety.** Part of the reason many employees don't feel comfortable asking tough questions is a fear of reprisal for being a "troublemaker"—or even losing their job. Author Edgar Schein poses a very important question that leaders can be asked as a measure to determine the level of psychological safety in an organization: "If I am about to make a mistake, will you tell me?" If there is not enough candor and safety built into an organization's culture to honestly answer yes, then the next question becomes, "What do we need to do differently to develop and create that kind of culture?" Without it, people may take a less candid CYA (Cover Your Ass) approach to communication.

4. **Be Clear That Alignment Is the Ultimate Goal of Questioning.** A questioning culture is not synonymous with democratic decision-making, although they're often confused to be the same. Companies that do this well make very clear when it's the right time for questions and potential disagreements and when it's time to align. It's critical to be explicit about this. Pat Lencioni's book *Five Dysfunctions of a Team* (which we used as an Airbnb leadership team) gives good direction on how to clarify the difference between debate and alignment.

5. **Make Sure Senior Leaders Are Actively Engaged in the Questioning Process.** If senior leaders don't actively take part in

the questions and debate, whether it's because they're not in the room or because they are preoccupied on their phones or laptops, it sends a deadening signal to everyone else. Additionally, when a truth has been uncovered through the questioning process, but senior leadership doesn't see it or take action, this can dissuade energy expended by the group in a future debate.

Modern Elders often have deep domain expertise that can be helpful to an organization, but only if you serve up that expertise with a humble mixture of teaching and learning. I discovered quite quickly that the traditional hospitality model of hotel operations wasn't all that relevant to many of the needs Airbnb had in providing customer service, nor was it relevant to our hosts. So it was essential for me to discern what portion of my expertise was worth sharing and what I needed to question.

Professor Erik Dane, who studies cognition in the workplace, has shown that "cognitive entrenchment tends to increase with expertise," but that you can create a dynamic culture that encourages after-action reviews to help accelerate learning for everyone, especially those who are most experienced. An elder who doesn't doubt, and is assured in their historical knowledge, is that carton of milk at risk of curdling. Additionally, Dane posits that those with great expertise in one area should focus attention on discussions outside their domain to fertilize the mind with other perspectives and potentially break some habitual thinking.

Often, an elder expert is brought into an organization to solve a problem in their area of domain expertise. But just having them focus their mind on this area to the exclusion of anything else can be counterproductive to both the elder and the company. For me, I found that bringing a beginner's mind to areas of the company where I was relatively clueless helped create a more catalytically curious company, and I was the occasional midwife to epiphanies in a few meetings.

Albert Einstein had a certain reverence for this way of thinking when he wrote, "The important thing is not to stop questioning. Curiosity has its own reason for existing. One cannot help but be in awe when he contemplates the mysteries of eternity, of life, of the marvelous structure of reality. It is enough if one tries merely to comprehend a little of this mystery every day. Never lose a holy curiosity."

If you knew you were going to live to one hundred, you might take up the violin at fifty. Learn a new language, become a tournament-level chess or bridge aficionado, take some dance classes, or, in my case, jump on a rocket ship tech company. Your curiosity doesn't have to be confined to the workplace.

Now that we've been open to evolving our identity and elevating our ability to learn, let's explore in the next chapter how we apply our decades of understanding other humans to becoming a master collaborator.

ModEl Practices to Grow Your Capacity to Learn

1. STOKE YOUR CURIOSITY.

While it contradicts the stereotype that older people become more narrow-minded and set in their ways, there's glorious evidence that postfifty, many elders return to a childlike sense of wonder. Beyond wonder, there's also a sense of mature, jaw-dropping awe that helps many of us appreciate just how small we are in the greater cosmos. This sort of right-sizing helps us get curious again, but with the benefit of the pattern identification of a wise elder.

So I invite you to consider these questions: "How can you become more curious? What's a subject—unrelated to your work—in which you could become one of the world's leading experts?" Your biggest challenge is just making time in your schedule for wondering about the world. You can only say a full-fledged yes to new activities when you've properly edited your life and deleted some of what feels extraneous.

And how about exploring a learning or leadership development program like StartingBloc, Camp Grounded, Summit Series, TEDx, Hive, Aspen Ideas Festival, Renaissance Weekends, or Road Scholars (note that some of these require an application or are invitation-only)? I've listed these roughly from youngest to oldest with respect to the age demographic of attendees. Choose one that will give you the most interdisciplinary and intergenerational diversity. You're likely to learn more from people who don't look and act like you.

Aging with vitality exists when you create the perfect alchemy of wisdom and curiosity. Author Martin Buber suggests in his book *I and Thou*, "To be old is a glorious thing when one has not unlearned what it means to begin." Essential for a Modern Elder is the desire to experience something new and unexplored rather than regress into what is comfortable and familiar.

2. QUESTION ASSUMPTIONS ABOUT THE ESSENCE OF YOUR BUSINESS.

You ought to constantly be asking the question, "What business are we in?" At a meeting or off-site retreat of your executives, set the room up so that everyone pairs off and sits facing each other. One person goes first at answering this question, then the questioner poses the exact question again, but the answerer can never repeat their answer. For example, at Joie de Vivre, the typical first answer to the question was "We're in the hotel business." The questioner asks again, "What business are we in?" This time the answerer might get more specific and say, "We're in the boutique hotel business." You keep this going until you've asked the question five times and received five different answers, and then you flip it so that the questioner now becomes the answerer. Then everyone shares with the whole group. You may be surprised by how this exercise unveils your company's true differentiating essence. Or, if you want to focus on yourself rather than the company, ask the repeating question, "What mastery do I offer?"

3. LEARN TO CRAFT CATALYTIC QUESTIONS.

In his book *Humble Inquiry*, author Edgar Schein writes, "It is the highest-ranking leaders who must learn the art of humble inquiry as a first step in creating a climate of openness . . . the art of questioning becomes more difficult as status increases. Our culture emphasizes that leaders must be wiser, set direction, and articulate values, all of which predisposes them to tell rather than ask. Yet it is leaders who will need humble inquiry most because complex interdependent tasks will require building positive, trusting relationships with subordinates to facilitate good upward communication."

And, yet, if this is true, then why the heck don't we teach the fine art of inquiry in more graduate business schools or corporate universities? We need to adapt our thinking about the value of questions, moving from thinking of them as blundering ignorance to appreciating them for their blessed innocence.

A question, thoughtfully conceived, can illuminate a room, a company, a life. Yet conceiving the proper question and then crafting the way of expressing it is an art. Here are some helpful guidelines that can make anyone an inquiry artist:

- **Empower:** Ask questions that give the receiver of the question the feeling of being valued and that her opinion is worthwhile and respected such as, "How do you feel about . . . ?" or "Help me understand why you proposed that option?" or "Could you explain a little further?" Or use a beginner's mind and start your inquiry with, "Pardon me for bringing up something that might be obvious for everyone here . . ." or "Help me understand . . ." Subordinates can tell when the leader is asking questions to genuinely learn. The kind of inquiry I'm talking about derives from an attitude of interest and curiosity. It implies a desire to build a relationship that will lead to more open communication. It also implies that one makes oneself vulnerable and, thereby, arouses positive helping behavior in the other person.

- **Listen:** Schein writes, "Try to minimize your own preconceptions, clear your mind at the beginning of the conversation, and maximize your listening as the conversation proceeds. In fact, the most important diagnostic that the other person will use to decide whether or not you are interested is not only what you ask but also how well you hear the response. Humble inquiry can reduce the status or deference gap and lead to a more informal open exchange."

- **Put Your Heads Together:** "Question-storming" exercises can be used as a substitute for conventional brainstorming sessions. The idea is to put a problem or challenge in front of a group of people and instead of asking for ideas, instruct participants to generate as many relevant questions as they can. One helpful rule is to ask that each inquirer start their brainstorming inquiry with a "What if" or "How might we" question. "What if" questions tend to have an expansive effect allowing us to think without limits.

- **Be Goal-Oriented:** Is there any collateral benefit you want to result from your inquiry? Ask yourself, "What do I want my question to accomplish?" Find an answer, reveal a blind spot, help someone establish their authority or regain their confidence, test underlying assumptions that haven't been voiced, dive deeper into a subject that has previously only been superficially explored?

- **Go Off-Script:** One of the ultimate opportunities to use questions in a catalytic fashion is in a job interview. As an interviewer, if you ask scripted questions, you will get scripted answers. So this is your opportunity to get underneath the surface with a candidate in a way that helps you explore their leadership and emotional DNA. After interviewing thousands of candidates, I've found these three questions to be the most catalytic in terms of learning more about a candidate:

  (a) In some ways, we're probably all occasionally misperceived at work. People see us one way, but—in truth—we're different than that. What's the most common way you're misperceived?

  (b) What's the biggest mistake you've made in your career? And why did you answer the question with this particular mistake?

  (c) At what skill are you world-class? And I'd be honored if you gave me some evidence of that talent?

[6]

Lesson 3: COLLABORATE

"When your capacity for sharing wisdom is stunted, so will be your fortune in receiving."
—CHUNGLIANG AL HUANG AND JERRY LYNCH

"Can we find a more private place to talk?"

A fifty-three-year-old engineering manager at Airbnb had reached out to me after reading my *Harvard Business Review* article in April 2017, entitled "I Joined Airbnb at 52, and Here's What I Learned About Age, Wisdom, and the Tech Industry," and asked if we could speak. He suggested we meet in the Santorini Café, one of the impressive grazing spots inside Airbnb's headquarters. When we arrived there it was busy, which seemed to make him a little anxious, so he suggested we move outside the café, where there were fewer people.

As I listened to his story, I understood why he felt awkward having a conversation about our age in such a public place, teeming with his colleagues. It reminded me of the encounter with Bert Jacobs that I wrote about at the start of this book, which for a moment made me wonder if I was an idiot for being so public about my age. But in reality, I wasn't stupid. I was privileged. My long history in the bricks-and-mortar hotel world was precisely why I'd been brought into the company. But this fellow employee—let's call him "Q" since it felt like we were creating a secret society—had joined the company as part of an Airbnb acqui-hire, that is, when a larger tech company purchases a smaller start-up, typically for its engineering talent. Across Silicon Valley, and especially in engineering, tech companies tend to skew toward a younger workforce—but since Q joined Airbnb as part of a group hire, he felt this provided a different context in which to be seen and he was appreciative of the opportunity.

It was clear Q loved Airbnb and he was diligent about updating his coding skills every two to three years to stay current. For all his engineering experience, he still had that beginner's mindset I outlined in the last chapter. Due to his strong interpersonal skills, Q acted as a trusted adviser to younger engineers and in return felt refueled by the energy and idealism of those who were nearly half his age. Q was the kind of employee any CEO would appreciate, but the greatest contribution he felt he could make at this young company was to help create stronger internal teams by modeling great collaborative habits he'd learned over his years in Silicon Valley.

I asked him if he might join an internal Wisdom@Airbnb affinity group of employees primarily over the age of forty, one of the first of its kind in Silicon Valley. The intent of this group was to explicitly foster more sharing of wisdom across generations, as well as to create a support network for age-comparable peers. He looked at me like I'd suggested we jump off the Golden Gate Bridge. He responded by describing the challenges he'd faced when he'd first signed on as an engineer over fifty at one of the world's most-prized tech companies: "When I joined, I didn't have to prove myself as a manager but I did need to earn trust in a younger workforce so that when I did eventually have a team, people would be fine working on my team. But I definitely had to prove myself in my engineering skills. It's literally starting on the front lines of engineering and working up."

As a result, he told me, "My first six months at Airbnb were no sure thing because I wasn't being judged based on my skill as a manager despite being hired as one. I was being judged on being able to add impact as an engineer to see if I would then be moved to an actual management position." He then went on to tell me how, ironically, the key to proving his value as an engineer at Airbnb had been to draw on his managerial, emotional, and observational skills to model collaboration and build trust, before transitioning to an actual management position. "And now I feel I'm thriving."

Q also reminded me, with a smile, that the first time I ever met him, I remarked, "Aren't you a little old for an engineer?" (and that was before I realized he was in his fifties as I thought he was ten years younger) and complimented him on his "good skin." So the irony of my suggesting he join us on this age-focused internal affinity group was not lost on me. As he reminded me of our first encounter, my own ambivalence about age stared me square in the face. The wise Q was mentoring me.

With five generations in today's workplace, we can either operate as separate isolationist countries with generation-specific dialects and talents coexisting on one continent, or we can find ways to bridge these generational borders and delight in learning from people both older and younger than us. Silicon Valley is famous for spawning young disruptors, but my goal for Airbnb was to demonstrate that intergenerational collaboration, virgin territory in many companies, could become our ultimate disruptor. Whether it was in novel new programs like Wisdom@Airbnb or in more subtle, quiet ways, like having employees like Q demonstrate a collaborative leadership presence on their teams, I became increasingly emboldened to prove that Airbnb could become a role model for the intergenerational transfer of wisdom—one that could be replicated across other industries and companies.

THE ULTIMATE DISRUPTOR

One of my favorite roles at Airbnb was to advise Brian and other internal HR execs on how to create more effective and collaborative teams. Through my experience leading multigenerational teams at Joie de Vivre, I had learned that an aligned and empowered team is like a crew rowing in unison. When you tap into the diversity of personality types and perspective across generations, it's similar to what happens when the crew is stroking as a unified body—rather than a group of individual rowers—at just the right pace. Rowers call this miracle of physics "swing," and it allows the elevated boat to move more quickly since there is less friction in the water holding it back.

In the workplace, generational differences can cause the kind of friction that holds back teams, or they can provide the swing to propel the team forward. As I'd learned from a good deal of trial and error over the years, a healthy team can rise above its common, petty differences and become that much more efficient and effective, the more age diverse it is. And now I was able to apply these learnings on a bigger stage.

As our Airbnb leadership team (known as E-staff) was starting to gel in 2014, it was becoming increasingly apparent that this group of a dozen leaders (including our three millennial cofounders)—which was evenly distributed with boomers, Gen Xers, and millennials—needed to find a shorthand way to deepen our understanding of one another and operate more harmoniously as a team. We started by reading the book *The Five Dysfunctions of a Team* by Patrick Lencioni and hired a facilitator from the author's company, the Table Group, to help oversee daylong and multiday off-site retreats every few weeks. This was quite a commitment of time and required a stripping away of old costumes and the summoning of our catalytic curiosity.

But what jump-started our building of alignment was the August

2014 multiday off-site just north of San Francisco in rural Sonoma County. All members of E-staff had taken the Myers-Briggs personality test privately before this meeting, and we learned our results as we gathered together in the same room. When we looked at the composition of the team across the sixteen personality types, one of the biggest revelations was that two of the founders—Brian and Nate—couldn't have had less in common. This became an "aha" moment as it was clear that these two successful founders—one a visionary designer and blossoming CEO and the other a brilliant, practical engineer and CTO—weren't often seeing the world with the same pair of glasses. They had always been respectful, but not necessarily symbiotic—and now we knew why. But, after this retreat, they began to genuinely see how their quite different strengths could complement each other and they've developed an even more powerful working partnership since then.

Beyond this big revelation, the whole group made a few other significant discoveries that led to some modifications in how we operated as a team. For example, we learned we had a lot of extroverts in the group, especially some (including me and a few of the older team members) who enjoyed brainstorming on subjects that might be peripheral to the original agenda. This riffing without clarity of purpose, or how we were going to execute and create a process for implementation, drove other more logic-based members of E-staff crazy. We also realized that we needed to feel more comfortable with debating issues openly, as a group, if there were differences of opinion that could lead to factions outside of our meetings. We learned just how valuable it was to debate, decide, commit, and align, even and especially when our differences—whether in age, background, or personality type—might have slowed us down.

Airbnb saw great rewards from this intensive work we did as an E-staff. In the year after we started these more in-depth team facilitations, we saw the company's confidence in E-staff grow (based upon the results of anonymous employee engagement questionnaires). And, at year-end 2015, partly due to our investment in E-staff collaboration, the company's outsized commitment to its core values, and some other factors, Airbnb was awarded first place on the prestigious annual Glassdoor Best Place to Work list, based entirely upon employee feedback. The best companies in the world are able to develop diverse, collaborative teams that use their differences as a strength. To be honest, I'd much rather be on a team with a wide variety of people far different from me because I typically learn more in those situations.

INTERGEN IMPROV

Imagine if Carlos Santana felt he needed to hide his age when his music career needed a resuscitation. After thirty years of rockin' and rollin', Carlos hit a rough patch in the mid-1990s. It had been twenty years since his face graced the cover of *Rolling Stone* magazine. And, though he was only about fifty, many at his then record label thought he was over the hill. But Arista Records president Clive Davis, fifteen years older than Santana, believed in him and, with his elder intuition, knew that Santana had a collaborative spirit and was young at heart. Davis proposed that Santana work with a collection of up-and-coming musical artists twenty to thirty years younger than him—including Rob Thomas, Lauryn Hill, Wyclef Jean, and Dave Matthews—to produce an album that reconnected with Santana's creative calling. Santana and his young collaborators offered the world *Supernatural* in 1999. The album went platinum fifteen times and won eight Grammy Awards and is a testament to the power of intergenerational collaboration.

Bing Crosby and David Bowie's "Peace on Earth." Tony Bennett and Amy Winehouse's "Body and Soul." Frank Sinatra and Natalie

Cole. Burt Bacharach and Elvis Costello. Roy Orbison and k.d. lang. Johnny Cash and Trent Reznor. Robert Plant and Alison Krauss. Sir Elton John and Eminem. Loretta Lynn and Jack White. Neil Young and Pearl Jam. Willie Nelson and Norah Jones. Sergio Mendes and the Black Eyed Peas. Wayne Shorter and Esperanza Spalding. Art Blakey and Wynton Marsalis and many more old jazz masters collaborating with young geniuses. The list goes on across generations and genres. Music fosters a natural improv that, at its best, allows each person to bring his or her greatest talents. Sometimes it's the juxtaposition of these talents or perspectives that creates the beauty. And you can see the joy in a young musician's eyes when they're riffing—learning from and teaching an old master. Especially when it comes to jazz, it's almost like the elder is teaching musical wisdom—how to recognize the patterns that underlie the notes and rhythms—to the young superstar on the rise. But, as evidenced by a film on intergen jazz collaboration I've listed in the appendix, *Keep On Keepin' On*, masters almost always learn something from their superstar students as well.

In music, art, science, and just about everywhere else, diversity— diversity of age, diversity of background, diversity of thought—ignites the creative spark. Why should it be any different in the workplace? Indeed McKinsey has shown that gender-diverse companies outperform the national industry averages by 15 percent. And ethnically diverse teams notch that up to 35 percent compared to their homogenous competitors. In his book *The Difference*, Scott Page outlines why progress and innovation may depend less on lone thinkers with enormous IQs than on diverse people working together and capitalizing on their individuality and shows how groups that display a range of perspectives outperform groups of like-minded experts. As John Seely Brown, former head of Xerox PARC, puts it, "Breakthroughs often appear in the white space between crafts . . . These crafts start to collide, and in that collision radically new things start to happen."

Historically, the Europeans have studied the value of intergen teams more than anyone else and their research suggests that when older workers are part of mixed-aged teams, not only are the teams more productive, so are the younger workers on the team, pointing to possible spillover effects of mixing the old with the young. For example, a well-known BMW factory study found that teams that were predominately young moved fast but made lots of mistakes. Older teams moved more slowly but made mistakes less frequently. Mixed-aged teams were the most productive. Other studies have found that intergen teams work because the older employees know how to frame problems and create accountability for results while the younger ones are faster and willing to take more risks toward innovation.

The Economist reported that Mercer, the world's largest human resources consultant, found that older workers' contributions are more likely to show up in group performance than in traditional individual performance metrics (how many widgets someone makes per hour). "It seems the contribution of older workers materializes in the increased productivity of those around them," says Haig Nalbantian, a partner in the firm.

I'm not surprised by these studies and the fact they amplify the value of the elder. How we spend our time is how we spend our lives—and in a company it's often what determines success or failure.

NOT YOUR FIRST TIME AT THE RODEO

If a team is like an orchestra, then an elder can be a master conductor who's synthesizing the distinct melodies of many musicians at once, creating an attuned sense of harmony. He or she helps create the habitat for healthy, productive teams and meetings . . . of preventing teams from slipping into a cacophony of discord. That's why it's so remarkable that younger managers get so little leadership or team-building training.

Nearly 40 percent of the American workforce has a younger boss (a number that is growing quickly), but here's a scary set of stats. When leadership development adviser Jack Zenger reviewed the seventeen thousand worldwide leaders who had gone through his leadership training program, he found the average age was forty-two. And yet the typical individual in these companies had become a supervisor at around age thirty and remained in that role for nine years—that is, until age thirty-nine—but had never received any other training prior to Zenger's program. That's a dirty dozen years between thirty and forty-two during which young managers are running the orchestra pit without any formal guidance.

As the role of conductor is increasingly falling to younger, digitally savvy leaders, this lack of formal training is becoming a massive organizational liability. It's like giving the keys of a tour bus to someone who has never taken a driver's education course, but still might be ambitious and intelligent. As reported in the *Financial Times* and *Fast Company* magazine, Uber's three thousand managers were "promoted extremely quickly and often without instruction." Sixty-three percent of Uber's managers had never led people before and as stated by a senior Uber leader, "a lack of skilled management and teamwork were the main problems in a company plagued by scandal after scandal." As a result, two baby boomer women, Liane Hornsey, as SVP and chief human relations officer, and Frances Frei, as SVP of leadership and strategy, were brought in to try and fix the problem. But this lack of experienced leadership and processes took its toll on the company, the brand, and its former CEO.

In this lack of formal guidance in many young companies lies one of the prime responsibilities—and opportunities—for Modern Elders to step into the instructional role, whether it's through the formal leadership training we can offer or the more off-the-cuff advice we can dole out in real time. Uber is in the process of a course correction, but there are countless other tech companies that scarcely know they have a problem.

Elders are as much master conductors as emotional meteorologists, whose deft pattern recognition allows them to see storm clouds surfacing on the horizon long before their cohorts. At times, a Modern Elder's role in a young digital company is to sound the foghorn or post a "small-craft warning" to a young leader who isn't as adept at sensing the friction or fissions on his team bubbling below the surface and forecasting the eruption to follow. Sometimes this bad weather system is purely associated with cofounder misalignment (thankfully, this wasn't the case at Airbnb). Harvard Business School professor Noam Wasserman found that, "Based on research from 10,000 founders, 65 percent of start-ups fail as a result of cofounder conflict." In many cases, this might be fixable with the introduction of a Modern Elder.

The number one solution researchers have found for solving this problem of ill-prepared young leaders was learning and development training for the younger boss. This is part of the reason why Brian Chesky asked me to create a manager's leadership and development (L&D) program less than six weeks after I joined the company. While the primary focus was on how we can teach twenty-eight-year-olds to lead twenty-four-year-olds, some of these young leaders were also conducting meetings with older employees like Q, whom I mentioned at the start of this chapter. And, while Brian ran effective meetings, I sat through many meetings in my early days led by a younger leader who clearly was inexperienced in the art of running an effective work gathering. At the heart of our L&D program were themes like, "How do you design an alliance with someone who opposes you or your idea?" or "How do you read the emotions in a meeting room when you're leading a group?"

I'm sure many of you Modern Elders in a workplace full of younger managers wish you could develop a similar training program. But those who aren't able to start a formal program should take a lesson from Karen Wickre, mentioned in chapter 3, who had seven different younger managers at Google in her nine years there. Karen mastered the art of mentoring privately. Once, she sat down with one of her bosses, who'd been so oppressive it sent her to therapy, and gave him some helpful hints about how she could most effectively be managed. Once she positioned her advice as something that could be helpful for his long-term career, he was open to hearing it, as opposed to seeing the feedback as a deflection of some performance problem he was trying to pin on Karen. Similarly, I didn't give advice to young managers leading meetings on the spot. Instead I asked them if they were open to some feedback and found a quiet, private time to share some thoughts that could help them be more effective. Again, because you're older and maybe less in career competition with this younger manager, they may be more open to hearing your constructive observations.

EQ FOR DQ

In the past, "connected" at work meant you had an overstuffed Rolodex. Today, it means that you have multiple technological mediums through which to communicate. But while contacts—and ways of reaching them—have their value, the true definition of "connected," which is an empathic capacity to resonate with others, is often lost in the shuffle. And this can result in missing the human gift of an in-person conversation. This face-to-face form of connection teaches us eye contact, how to concentrate on what the other person is saying sans multitasking, and how to read body language. And because your sixth sense is typically far more attuned in person, this also improves the capacity for empathy and intimacy, and even the fine art of intuition. Our mirror neurons get to play together when we're sitting across from each other.

Many Modern Elders can read humans like a musician can read sheet music or scales. Many young people, on the other hand, can read the face of their iPhone and understand its inner workings better than they can read the face and emotions of the person sitting next to them. Studies show millennials check their smartphone 153 times a day while boomers do so only 30 times. The result is that while millennials might be highly proficient in the use of emojis to express an emotional state, they are missing out on the interpersonal, face-to-face connection that creates true emotional fluency. And beware in your hasty texts on your smartphone; the "?" is just left of the "!," which can mistakenly turn a question into an angry exclamation in terms of how it's received. Efficiency can lead to deficiency, right?!

At Airbnb, I was surrounded by digitally savvy folks who might not realize that being "emo savvy" could be just the thing to help them grow into great leaders. So a question started to form in this old technophobe's head, *Will you trade me some of your digital intelligence (DQ) for some of my emotional intelligence (EQ)?* Although I never made this ask directly, this implicit trade agreement created collateral benefits for both me, as I learned how to become more fluent in tech, and the younger folks I worked with who learned how to be more fluent in human interaction. I learned more about Snapchat and WeChat and my younger colleagues learned how to do old-school chitchat.

Early in the film *The Intern*, young CEO Anne Hathaway doesn't want Robert De Niro as her personal intern because this Modern Elder is a little "too observant." Yet being "too observant" is part of what helped me succeed at Airbnb. It allowed me to create what Stephen Covey called an "emotional bank account" with those I worked with. I don't care if you're in the B2B, B2C, C2C, or A2Z world, all business is fundamentally H2H (human to human), and EQ becomes more important the more responsibility you have in an organization. Your emotional contagion grows the higher you are on the org chart.

Interpersonal skills like collaboration and empathy have a huge impact on team and company results. Many have written about Project Aristotle, a two-year project at Google that sought to determine the ingredients of the most successful teams. Initially, many thought the answer would have something to do with the individual members of the team. Conventional wisdom said simply find the best and brightest and make sure it's a diverse group: a savvy MBA, a brilliant engineer, an aesthetically minded designer, and some other brilliant oddball just to shake things up.

But what Google found in this landmark study was that the individual's traits mattered less than the collective customs and norms—both conscious and unconscious. And in particular that a sense of "psychological safety"—or "shared belief, held by members of a team, that the group is a safe place for taking risks"—proved to have the most profound impact on a team's ability to collaborate, and thus, on their effectiveness.

As an elder, we have the capacity to be what author Warren Bennis called a "first-class noticer" (a term he borrowed from Saul Bellow's novel *The Actual*). That means we pay close attention to what is happening around us, especially in times of turmoil. Young people may metabolize food faster, but older people metabolize emotions more quickly, especially the negative ones, and this is particularly helpful in collaboration. In that sense, Modern Elders are like translators; that is, we see things that others miss and translate that into the wisdom needed to make informed decisions about what course of action to take.

Q, who I mentioned at the start of this chapter, taught me a few things about the power of quiet, empathic collaboration. And over time, as he felt more comfortable with Airbnb's unique approach to inclusivity, he felt less cautious about his age. John Q. Smith (yes, that's his real name . . . no more code names) tells me that the best kind of collaborations are those that happen naturally. In his early fifties, he's had the opportunity to be both a manager and an individual contributor and he's seen many superstar engineers struggle as they make this transition.

He says, "An individual contributor may have stellar coding skills and be able to operate pretty autonomously when making decisions as an individual contributor. They're used to having 'perfect knowledge' about a problem in order to make those decisions. But in transitioning to management, you almost always have to make decisions based on imperfect information that relies on more collaboration. If this transition in decision-making isn't called out, it can be hard for people to realize why they're struggling—it takes practice. In either case, this can have a detrimental impact on their team, so part of what I do is to help them understand how to make good decisions with at best 60 percent of the information when they're used to having 100 percent when it comes to working with code."

John found that the best way for talented younger engineers to see how collaboration works was to invite them to sit in on meetings with him where they could witness the symphony of a great team. Afterward, he would help the rising technologist understand not just what decision they arrived at, but also *how* a manager comes to a particular decision even without perfect information. Many of the principles we outlined in the ModEl Practices of the last chapter, like how to ask great questions, are fundamental to the kind of education John tries to offer his younger colleagues in these informal discussions. When was the last time you invited a promising young leader the opportunity to have a front-row seat to experience a healthy, collaborative team interaction?

YOUR IMPLICIT TRADE AGREEMENT

While EQ for DQ may be the most common trade agreement Modern Elders can offer their junior comrades, there are all kinds of skills that might be bartered in a different habitat. The most obvious asset you bring to the table is your deep knowledge of and connection to an industry that your younger cohorts are looking to disrupt.

Dr. Bridget Duffy, fifty-seven, has spent several successful decades in the health-care industry and not long ago was the nation's first chief experience officer at the Cleveland Clinic. She then cofounded and became CEO of ExperiaHealth, which was acquired by the public company Vocera before they became a public company. Along the way, she's been a board member and board chair of RockHealth, the first venture fund dedicated to digital health. Not long ago, Bridget was asking the twentysomethings who run the RockHealth nonprofit where the photocopier was and they looked at her like she was a lunatic. "Just take a photo of the doc on your phone, and use an app to store it," they told her. While they were completely respectful in their guidance, Bridget couldn't help but feel a little naive.

Yet Bridget is the one who is helping them see how they can disrupt the health-care world by understanding the vulnerabilities in the system and helping them see the nuances that they'd never find in a Google search. In all industries, technology is only as powerful as its ability to enable human-to-human connection. In health care, tech done right enables the trusted, sacred relationships that facilitate healing. The young wizards can create amazing tech products, but Bridget has been the bridge builder from the digital health epicenter translating those products into solutions that touch the lives of so many.

Welcome to the world of mutual mentoring. In chapter 9, I'll introduce the idea of how companies can foster reverse mentoring relationships in which a younger coworker helps older employees increase their DQ. But, since this chapter is about collaboration, let's recognize that we're all just mirrors and reflections of each other. The more I help you grow a skill, the more valuable you are on our team, and the more your newfound skills can be learned and copied by others, adding more value still. The transfer of wisdom is more sustaining when it's not one-sided, but rather, reciprocal, when all parties have something to offer and learn.

The beauty of the implicit trade agreement is that you can make it with anyone who has something different and complementary to offer, whether it's digital intelligence, pop culture savvy, or access to different people and networks. Maybe it's the twenty-five-year-old colleague who doesn't even work in your department. You just "vibe" well. She can help you learn the 97 percent of the functions on your iPhone that you didn't know existed, and you can teach her about the 97 percent of coworkers' emotions that bewilder her.

Sometimes these trade agreements are more explicit. For example, I was the only hotelier at Airbnb for quite some time and one of the few execs who had any experience within the travel industry. So, in exchange for various digital tutorials I received, I also became a subject matter expert on how the industry operated, which aided a wide variety of teams. Even now—after leaving my full-time operating role and being a part-time strategic adviser—I get frequent inquiries from various managers in the company who are trying to figure out this industry.

Similarly, my friend Fred Reid, sixty-seven, was happy to trade his traditional industry knowledge for a crash course in the technologies of the future—and he also has a parallel story to mine when it comes to disruption, not in lodging, but in air travel.

Fred was president of both Lufthansa and Delta and was founding CEO of Virgin America. He also knows a thing or two about collaboration, as he was the coarchitect of the Star Alliance—the first ever multiairline, independently branded alliance—that became the model for airline industry collaboration. But, like me, he was a Bay Area exec who didn't know much about the tech industry when he was summoned, in late 2014, to a secret factory in the heart of Silicon Valley. He found an astonishing team of engineers, software and battery wizards, and technicians who were developing a completely new form of human transport: a flying vehicle that takes off straight up, transitions forward, and flies almost silently on a fixed wing, powered by emission-free electric batteries, and containing unprecedented, sophisticated software and flight controls. If it sounds like something out of *The Jetsons*, that's because it is; the vehicle can take off and land from a tennis court or your driveway. It's like a taxi or Uber in the air.

The company team behind this new form of robotic air travel, Zee.Aero and its subsidiary Kitty Hawk (with Google cofounder Larry Page being its primary investor), needed a seasoned exec like Fred to be their expert when it came to the complicated governmental regulatory process for airplanes in multiple countries, as well as to develop a branding, marketing, and communications strategy for this new venture. And they needed him to do so in collaboration with a talented senior leadership team, some of whom were three decades his junior. Like me, Fred had to enlist the help of his younger and more digitally fluent new colleagues in order to adapt to this new habitat. He says, "I was quite self-conscious arriving in the midst of this secretive project, and working with young superstars from Tesla, Google, NASA, Boeing, DARPA, and other stellar companies. So there are days I feel out of my element, but then I have to remember of the team of over a hundred people, there is exactly one person who has run an operating company at the COO/president/CEO level multiple times. That would be me. It reminds me they need me as well."

Fred is learning as much as he's teaching the leadership team and he's valued for the combination of his historical knowledge as well as his openness to new ideas. Without that latter ingredient, he wouldn't have lasted longer than a week in a company creating flying cars. He says, "I'm trading my experience happily in return for what they give me: awestruck wonder and the ability to participate literally in the making of history—producing a product and service with vast utility for society around the world."

You might be a midlevel exec with deep experience in enterprise software sales who could help some young disruptors who don't have your industry knowledge or your extensive Rolodex. Or you might be a nonprofit manager who has a great history in writing grants to fund your organization and you could be a godsend to a fledgling, high-potential arts org that has a beautiful vision but no knowledge of how to tap into government and foundation grants to fund themselves. The key is to know your value and to be assured that your younger colleagues see it as well. Be wary that in many businesses and industries, younger workers are assumed to have the most up-to-date knowledge, so the burden is often on the older worker to surface knowledge that is timely (specialized industry knowledge that younger people don't know) along with wisdom that is timeless.

Still, I believe that building bridges across generations will happen naturally when both sides realize just how much they have to learn from each other. After all, when wisdom flows in both directions, there's a huge collateral benefit for the company manifesting as gains in creativity, productivity, and communication not to mention the savings that come from less reliance on formal learning and development programs. Creating connections across the decades, if not a generation, between those who share an employer and a mission can open up all kinds of possibilities.

The Roman philosopher Seneca wrote, "If wisdom were offered me on the one condition that I should keep it shut away and not divulge it to anyone, I should reject it. There is no enjoying the possession of anything valuable unless one has someone to share it with." Think of your workplace as a potluck with each person having their own special recipes and dishes to be shared. In the next chapter, we'll take that perspective and apply it to the final lesson: how you can give wise counsel to those who seek it.

ModEl Practices to Collaborate

1. CREATE PSYCHOLOGICAL SAFETY.

As Google demonstrated with Project Aristotle, even the most data-driven companies are influenced by the basics of human nature. The most neglected fact in business is that we're all human. Your capacity to collaborate will improve if you create team norms that help everyone feel that the group is there to support you and the mission, as opposed to undermining you.

Here are a few group norms that have proven to be effective:

- Try to encourage everyone to participate in group discussions, especially those representing diverse demographics and viewpoints.

- Lead by example, such that you don't interrupt teammates during conversations and you give credit to people for their earlier idea as you build on those ideas.

- Call out intergroup conflicts or people who seem to be upset so that you can resolve matters in person.

- Build a skill of reading body language to see who is engaged and who isn't, which may mean you have to have a one-on-one conversation after a meeting if someone feels actively disengaged.

- When discussing a subject, and a more junior person who is most familiar with the data is present, give them sufficient time to frame the issues. Many companies have senior execs with barely a half understanding making all the big decisions unilaterally, forgetting that the junior folks who are closest to the data can be a valuable resource.

- Use some of the skills of the last chapter by making genuine inquiries of catalytic curiosity.

2. MAKE COLLABORATION PART OF THE CULTURE.

Jonathan Rosenberg is a fifteen-year senior exec in the Google orbit who coauthored the book *How Google Works* with former CEO Eric Schmidt and is now working on another book with Eric, this one on leadership coach and mentor Bill Campbell. One collaboration trick Jonathan learned from Bill was to make sure that all action items at the end of a meeting are shared by two people rather than one. This forces team members to work together between meetings, come to mutual agreement, and present their findings or solution as a united front.

3. STUDY A PERSONALITY ASSESSMENT TOOL THAT RESONATES WITH YOU.

Even the most emotionally fluent among us can benefit from personality-typing tools to help us better read others and build stronger H2H connections. I've found them to be particularly valuable in looking at how the chemistry of a group can be affected by the alchemy of the various personality types within that group. First, if you're not aware, check in with your HR team to find out if there's a tool that they prefer or that they may be rolling out in the near future.

While there's value in learning a variety of methods, you might as well start with the one that may become predominant in your organization. If you still have an open field of choices, I've outlined in the appendix section "Personality Typing Tools" some of the best ones I've seen in various corporate environments.

4. CRAFT AN IMPLICIT (OR EXPLICIT) TRADE AGREEMENT.

There may be a specific individual—whether they are young or not—on your team or in your company who seems very knowledgeable about a subject in which you feel lost. Start building a connection with that person and, when you feel like trust has been established, ask them if they can spend some time teaching you about this subject. If this is a younger person, we might call this reverse mentoring, but no need to label it. I recommend that you make it reciprocal, which forces you to ask the question, "What do I have to offer?" A friend of mine asks an even bigger question: "If I were calling a meeting of the world, what would I like to teach them?"

Your gifts may not be too obvious to you, but, according to a *Harvard Business Review* report, here are some of the things millennials want from their boss and company: *help me navigate my career path, give me straight feedback, mentor and coach me, develop my skills for the future, develop my technical skills in my area of expertise, self-management and personal productivity, leadership or functional knowledge, and creativity and innovation strategies.* I bet you have something to offer in at least one of these skills.

Last, if you're like me, you may have industry knowledge that might be valuable to a disruptive company. It would be worth exploring in the interviewing process for a new job with a disruptor whether they truly value your knowledge or are fearful it might hold you back. Engage in a conversation with your prospective boss or a very senior leader and ask them the following: "How can my industry expertise be helpful to you and the company? And what's your biggest fear of how it might be detrimental?" Being explicit about this on the front end will tell you if you're entering a ripe habitat for you to teach, learn, and collaborate.

[7]

Lesson 4: COUNSEL

"People ask me about the common denominators of the wisest people I've encountered. . . . Here's what it feels like, what I can report: an embodied capacity to hold power and tenderness in a surprising, creative interplay. This way of being is palpable, and refreshing, and in its way jarring, hard to figure out. Among other things, it transmutes my sense of what power feels like and is there for. This is the closest I can come to describing the sense I have, at this point, of wisdom incarnate, and it is an experience of physical presence as much as consciousness and spirit."

—KRISTA TIPPETT

———

"What brings you joy at work?"

Jessica Semaan, twenty-nine, was my match. And my younger mirror. But, on this day in 2014, she was in tears . . . and they weren't joyful. She was on the precipice of leaving Airbnb, feeling washed-up before she had turned the big 3-0.

Jessica was one of the first people I met at Airbnb. She and four others were assigned to be on my Hospitality Task Force in the early days of imagining how Airbnb could become a mature hospitality company when it grew up. While Jessica and I both had a Stanford MBA in common, it was the rebellious poet inside her that felt like my mirror. She'd spent her childhood in the backdrop of civil war in

Beirut, always striving to be the "good daughter" to a young, narcissistic mother. So she jumped on the achievement treadmill at an early age and had been cranking up the speed ever since, reaching for more and more success as a means of feeling worthy. Over the course of our conversations about creating a hospitality team at Airbnb, I found us talking just as much about love, life, and fears as we did about work. Jessica reminded me of myself at that age, toggling sharply between supreme confidence and soul-crushing self-doubt. After a few effective months on the task force, she turned her full-time attention back to her Customer Experience manager job.

A year into my tenure, I was faced with creating the world's first Airbnb global host conference from scratch—with a modest budget and less than five months to plan and execute. And Brian expected me to grow the Airbnb Open into a festival of travel that would one day rival the World's Fairs of the past. But I had not one full-time person to help me get this off the ground, and all while I was running four other departments. No pressure! It had become clear that I needed a chief lieutenant, and Jessica felt like just the person. And yet, here she was, tears and all, telling me about how her toxic relationship with her boss had given her a form of amnesia—she couldn't remember why she came to Airbnb in the first place.

I asked her the question that starts the chapter because I firmly believe that one's calling in life often flows from what naturally gives you joy. When she responded, with little hesitation, that she loves to create, I shared my experience that creativity happens best in a habitat that sees and leverages your gifts. And I shared my advice that it's essential to actively seek those habitats and to think of your career as a marathon of learning as opposed to just a series of transactional sprints. I asked, "Before you leave the company, are you open to joining me on this journey to create the Airbnb Open? It will help you reconnect with your joy of being a creator and bringing joy to others. And it will help you believe in yourself again."

Fortunately, Jessica said yes and we created a stellar three-day event that sold out its fifteen hundred tickets in half a day, to hosts flying in from forty countries. Two years and two festivals—in San Francisco and Paris—later, the Los Angeles Airbnb Open attracted twenty thousand hosts and guests from more than a hundred countries and won awards for the best corporate experiential festival or conference in the world. This legacy would not have happened without Jessica.

Jessica left Airbnb soon after helping to produce the first Airbnb Open, no longer a wounded bird but rather one who was confidently ready to fly. She went on to create The Passion Company, an organization dedicated to helping people kick-start their passion project into a career. Jessica's passion was helping people find their passion. She also became a writer, whose vulnerable, powerful prose touched the hearts of many. It's not surprising that she's now studying to become a psychotherapist as well. Her life has become a journey to help people believe in themselves. And it all started with believing in herself once again.

SETTING UP AN "ADVICE" STAND

Collaboration is a team sport. But counseling is one-on-one. The word "counsel" is fraught with all kinds of messy meanings: it can refer to an attorney, a guidance counselor, a special counsel who investigates US presidents. Forget about all that. In the context of being a Modern Elder in a company, to counsel means becoming "confidant" to your younger colleagues.

My network—in people and knowledge—unwittingly turned me into the company librarian at Airbnb. I guess it helped that I've spent a lifetime being curious about people and things, which means I'm pretty well-read and well-connected. People saw me as someone who could always recommend a book or academic study to read, as someone who could connect them to an expert I'd met. Sometimes I'd simply be a friendly ear; other times, I'd offer advice on things like workplace etiquette, or on how they could improve their relationship with their boss. Often I told them things they didn't want to hear. My counsel didn't have to be particularly profound. What seems simple to many of us who have a few decades of career under our belts can be illuminating to a hungry young pup. And as my friend Rob Goldman, a vice president at Facebook, says, "Many of these young people don't know what excellence looks like yet." Without knowing it, I was setting up a sort of millennial "finishing school," while I was attending my own boomer "starting school" and taking a crash course in what it means to work as an elder in a young start-up.

I'm not sure there's anyone else at Airbnb who's been "asked to chat" by a more diverse group of employees seeking a more diverse variety of advice or contacts. These fellow employees were not my direct reports; the vast majority weren't even in departments I was overseeing. I felt a little like Lucy from the Peanuts comic strip where she sets up her version of an outdoor lemonade stand dispensing "Psychiatric Help" for 5 cents.

Since I wasn't seen as competition or a career threat to any of these colleagues, I often became a confidant to whom they could truly open up, someone who not only listened but also gave them confidence. I always did my best to say an enthusiastic yes to these invitations as it was as enriching for me as it was to them. This role did eat up a lot of extra hours, but it was worth it.

If I were to plot all those conversations across the various islands (or departments) of the organization, you'd see that I'd become a hub in the web of relationships and knowledge within the company. This served me well as an adviser to the founders, since I had a real sense of the pulse drumming beneath the surface of the company and its various teams. While the founders were steering their rocket ship—

doubling in size every year—it was valuable to have a Modern Elder on board to help them see how their company was evolving internally.

Author Neil Gaiman wrote, "Google can bring you back, you know, a hundred thousand answers. A librarian can bring you back the right one." Google may be the best search engine in the world but it doesn't yet understand nuance like a finely attuned human heart and mind. Sometimes the best option for finding the wisdom we seek isn't a search engine but instead a wise counselor or adviser. In that way, being a Modern Elder also means being the "company librarian," whose role is to help others sift through the vast resources of knowledge and wisdom around them.

So I dropped my CEO "sage on the stage" costume for two new ones: librarian and confidant. Being a "guide on the side" allowed me to help my younger colleagues better understand themselves, learn from their mistakes, and, I hoped, even find their joy at an early stage in their career.

The value of a wise adviser who can embed some of his or her hard-won wisdom into hearts and minds is so great that some industries, like management consulting, the building trades, and architecture, have adopted an apprenticeship model that helps to embed mentorship into the organizational design. Smart companies know that while their competitors may outsource "counsel" to outside coaches who may offer some general wisdom, being a wise adviser can be so much more effective when an adviser is a wise elder who is in the trenches day to day with the advisee.

THE LIBRARIAN: COMBINING "KNOW-WHO" WITH "KNOW-HOW"

I joined Airbnb partly because I was curious about what is called a "global network effect" business. Like Facebook or eBay, Airbnb becomes more relevant as it has more users; that is, when both hosts and guests are using the site with increasing regularity. In the venture world, they use the term "liquidity" (distinct from cash flow liquidity) to describe the ideal scenario when there's enough of a marketplace effect such that people choose a platform as their primary destination because they know it's full of other people.

In the role of company librarian, most Modern Elders have a "personal network effect." After all, generally speaking, the longer you've been on the planet, the more people you've met.

And generally speaking, the longer you've been on the planet, the more you've read. I've read a lot of books (and have an odd affection for academic white papers), so I have a library of information and resources in my brain to offer others and tried to put that to good use as well. My liquidity and value to the company was in sharing my "know-how" and "know-who" widely. But this didn't just benefit my younger colleagues; it's what built my professional social capital internally. And as Airbnb became more of a hot company, it's what built my reputation externally, too, as I became a first point of contact at Airbnb for all kinds of people who wanted to connect with the company.

This may all sound naively "analog" in the era of digital search engines. Isn't Google the ultimate company librarian? True, Google can find information faster and more expansively than a human can, but it may not understand the context of your search, and it's results are only as good as the words you type into the search field. In contrast, when we're in face-to-face contact with someone, our brains have so many other inputs to contextualize our "search"— who's asking the question, their emotional state (based upon body language and voice tone), what they've talked about in the prior two or three minutes, or in previous conversations—so much more than just a few words entered into a search engine. Plus, Google doesn't ask us follow-up questions like people can. Google can only see patterns programmed into its algorithm, while our maturing minds can synthesize the nuances of a question to connect dots that, at times, weren't at all expected. Having a larger data set in our minds and experience may allow us to come up with more discerning answers.

So, in my growing role as Airbnb's elder and relationship melder, I could call on the relationships I'd built to be a resource for our recruiting team as they were looking for certain kinds of customer service execs. I could be a resource for the policy team when it came to building bridges with regulators and within the travel industry. I could be a resource for the research team, drawing on connections I made through books and articles I'd written at the intersection of psychology and business, to recommend scholars who specialized in motivation theory as we explored extrinsic and intrinsic host rewards. I could be a resource for the business travel team by putting them in contact with corporate travel managers with whom I used to work. If I were half my age, like my cohorts at Airbnb, I wouldn't have had 90 percent of these contacts, or knowledge. Again, the four-wheel drive of my mind often surprised me with answers to a colleague inquiry that might surface a contact deep in the recesses of my memory. Yes, LinkedIn, Facebook, or Google helped me then create a means of introducing my colleague to my contact, but the nuanced knack of my librarian mind served me and the company over and over again.

Of course, the more you build a reputation for having a "personal network effect," the more people will seek you out. And your value to your company will only multiply to the extent that: (1) you are open to sharing your "know-who" and "know-how"; (2) you exercise confidentiality and aren't seen as competitive; (3) you are reliable and empathetic; (4) you provide true insight often through the use of questions; and (5) you have a capacity for synthetic, "gist thinking" to help the junior person understand what they really should be looking for.

If you do this, be prepared for a lot of inquiries coming your way, which may mean that you will at some point have to create some boundaries or filters for whom you can assist. Or not. I never got to that point, as I deeply appreciated how valued I felt by being an internal nexus. If you arrive at this point, I've given you advice at the end of this chapter on how you can scale and edit your counsel. Even if your sphere of influence is purely those within your department, showing this willingness to serve others will build your reputation and relevancy within the organization.

THE CONFIDANT: COMBINING CONFIDENTIALITY WITH CONFIDENCE

The formal American English definition of confidant is "a person with whom one shares a secret or private matter, trusting them not to repeat it to others." But, as I learned from one of my Airbnb colleagues, Lisa Dubost, in French this word (spelled "confident") can also mean "a person who inspires confidence in you," as both the French and English words come from the Latin "confidens." With time, I started realizing the incalculable power of simultaneously keeping confidences, while also inspiring self-confidence; of being both a trusted ear as well as a "permissionary"—in that I gave younger people at Airbnb the capacity, courage, and permission to truly "go for it." This leadership alchemy became a life-affirming elixir for me. Combining the fountain of wisdom with the fountain of youth created a level of intimacy, insight, and awareness that to me felt truly unprecedented. When I explained this to an Israeli friend, he laughed and said I was just a garden-variety "mensch."

Whatever you want to call it, this elixir was what allowed me to counsel my young colleagues, on a far deeper and more meaningful level. Venture capitalist Ben Horowitz, who had this kind of relationship with Bill Campbell, describes it aptly when, upon Bill's death, he wrote in his blog, "Whenever I struggled with life, Bill was the person that I called. I didn't call him because he would have the answer to some impossible question. I called him because he would understand what I was feeling 100 percent. He would understand me." An elder focuses as much on their protégés' essence as on their actions; as much on the "being" as the "doing." An elder focuses as much on helping people find their joy as helping them find their next job. And a true elder helps younger people think more seriously about their lifelong career journeys, not just the immediate challenges of their current day-to-day work. That's because elders know it's the complete package that matters and endures.

And yet, even in what might feel like a very sagelike role, elders still must hold on to their catalytic curiosity. Jonathan Rosenberg from Google told me about how Bill Campbell used to say that arrogance was inversely correlated with age. "He (Bill) appreciated becoming someone's mentor when they had recently failed as they were humble enough to learn." Being a confidant means finding those teachable moments when you can both radiate clarity, and keep an open beginner's mind to catalyze the questing spirit of a younger person. Think Obi-Wan Kenobi and Luke Skywalker.

Luther Kitahata, fifty-two, is one of Silicon Valley's Obi-Wan Kenobis. His career is also a good example of the fluid, multistage life you read about in chapter 3, in that his trajectory has been less a straight line and more a series of cycles: first software engineer, add entrepreneur, then executive, and now wise leadership coach. He cofounded companies in his late twenties and early thirties, then joined the founding team of TiVo, the pioneer digital video recorder (DVR) company. After eight years as a vice president of Engineering leading every aspect of engineering at TiVo, Luther went on to start and develop other companies, one of which was acquired by TiVo ten years after he left. So now he's once again part of the executive team at the company leading the next generation service, where he's being asked to reinvent the TiVo Service in response to the fast-changing, competitive environment and to better integrate its many products beyond the DVR.

I met Luther at a Wise Leader retreat I was cofacilitating in May 2017. When I heard about his resilience as an engineering leader in his fifties, I was impressed. But I was more intrigued by Luther's calm and contemplative demeanor (he reminded me of a Zen monk). I explored further and found a scientist and philosopher at heart. I discovered someone who has been asking big questions since he was young, and who started doing his own personal development work in his twenties. While continually updating his engineering skills to stay relevant in the tech world, he was also learning more than a half-dozen modalities that he would later integrate into his coaching. By his mid-forties Luther had earned his Professional Coach Certification, which gave him the unique combination of being a formally trained coach, and an experienced operations executive who's walked in the same shoes as his clients.

Luther told me, "I realized that by pursuing an executive leadership coaching career, I could bring my two worlds together—my years of experience as an executive and leader in high-tech, and my passion and years of training in personal development and mentorship. The Silicon Valley workforce seems to be getting younger as I'm getting older. And, while I've been fortunate to continue to forge a successful high-tech career, I can see that my wisdom from experience is my long-term calling card. I've found my Modern Elder niche."

So, at age fifty-two, Luther continues to reinvent himself. This enables him to better drive TiVo's new approach to product *invention*, as well as guide the cultural *reinvention* that is needed for the company to evolve. Interestingly, his approach to reinventing TiVo is as much about trust and relationships as about technologies. Luther knows that change means uncharted territory and that this can be difficult, especially for a company that is a bit old-school, at least by

Silicon Valley standards. Luther also knows that TiVo is at an inflection point and that his value to the company is far more than just helping create new engineering innovations. Thus, he approached the head of HR and offered to help facilitate change for individuals and teams through one-on-one coaching, as well as leading group training programs.

Luther is truly a Modern Elder, in every sense. He's constantly evolving as a person and leader. He is catalytically curious and focuses his beginner's mind on learning and keeping both his coaching and engineering skills fresh. He became an expert collaborator using his EQ skills and now, as TiVo launches into a new era, he's tapping into his ability to provide wise counsel to inspire others as they scale new peaks and remake themselves. He summarizes his approach to change in this simple phrase (inspired by Aristotle's "We are what we repeatedly do. Excellence, then, is not an act, but a habit."): "We are what we practice and we're always practicing something. Thus, to make changes we need to practice something new and different."

WHEN THE *TEACHER* IS READY,
THE *STUDENT* WILL APPEAR

As power cascades to young people faster and faster, we need to create armies of Luther Kitahatas who can provide wise counsel to those young leaders as they *"make fast strategic decisions in higher velocity environments."*

Those italicized words come from the title of a landmark study scholar Kathleen Eisenhardt published nearly thirty years ago in which she found that many tech industry leaders experience moments of indecision in high-stress environments. The team is looking for the leader to make the call, but often the leader feels paralyzed by ambiguous data and a lack of insight. Yet Eisenhardt also found that the companies that were able to avoid this often had one thing in common: the presence of a highly experienced confidant who acted as a sounding board for the leader; a trusted counselor who had the wisdom to help "impart confidence and a sense of stability" in uncertain times, as well as the ability to find the blind spots due to their fresh, impartial eyes. In a fast-changing competitive environment, speed of decision-making can make or break company performance, and it also can be the difference between an organization with strong leadership and one that is crippled and confused by the lack of decisiveness by a CEO or founder. It also means that young leaders who might tend to be rash and impulsive can learn to be a little more thoughtful and deliberate in their decision-making process by talking through their options with this trusted counselor.

But do younger people really want such guidance? A 2011 poll conducted by MTV found that 75 percent of millennials want a mentor, and 61 percent say they need "specific directions from their boss to do their best work"—a level twice as high as observed among boomers. Another study found that the age demographic that most want a mentor is thirty-one to forty years old, which coincides with the "dirty dozen years" we talked about last chapter where young supervisors operate without formal training. So, despite stereotypes suggesting young people want to do it their own way, they truly thirst for guidance.

And yet, many Modern Elders, like Lenny Mendonca, a longtime McKinsey consulting partner who now teaches at the Stanford Graduate School of Business, feel an obligation to "pay it back" as confidants to younger folks, but find themselves surprised by how few young people ask for informal advice. So it may fall to us elders to put out an "Advice" shingle like the one Lucy fashioned in the comics. And it may fall to us to win the trust of our younger colleagues, by asking empathetic questions, showing vulnerability, describing instead of prescribing, and proving your loyalty and commitment to confidentiality.

In the ModEl Practices section at the end of this chapter, we'll focus more on ways to build trust, as well as on how to better understand your role as a counselor, and how to keep these advice sessions from eating up all your time. As I was approached by more and more Airbnb employees, I needed to ask and answer the question, "How can I best serve this person?" as well as, "Is this an ongoing counseling role or not?" and "Will we focus more on a specific aspect of their performance, or on their overall professional development?" Since my role as a counselor was completely informal and my choice, I could optimize my counsel in a way that served the younger employee while also being conscientious of my limited calendar.

But sometimes, the role of the elder trumps everything else on your plate. And it's especially in those times that you realize your true value when you get this counselor role right. When I first met Airbnb's cofounder Joe Gebbia, for example, I could see that he was a big part of the soul of the company. In fact, it was Joe's idea to entice his fellow Rhode Island School of Design classmate Brian up to San Francisco to pursue the entrepreneurial life, and lay air mattresses out on their living room floor. Together, the two aspiring, and broke, entrepreneurs rented them out during a design conference when the city's hotels were all sold out to help make their rent check. This is how Airbnb was hatched in 2007.

In 2013, when I first started spending time with Joe, at his request, it was clear he was both a design genius always on the precipice of the next great idea—and a leader who sincerely valued candid feedback. Through dinners, hikes, and a variety of deep, random conversations, Joe and I found our rhythm. It wasn't long before I could see I would be a long-term confidant and that ours would be a lifelong friendship. After all, the origin of the word "mentor" comes from ancient Greece and means to offer something "enduring." And it felt like that would be the case for my serendipitous relationship with Joe.

As Airbnb grew in leaps and bounds, I was able to help Joe understand the relationship between the measurable side of a business, and the immeasurable. We talked at length about the importance of being a "truth-teller" with employees and how to build a culture that connected to the higher needs of employees, hosts, and guests. Joe seemed to be drawn to my book *Peak* and its message that peak-performing companies create a habitat in which employees feel inspired by a company's mission, but also understand their day-to-day impact to support that mission. Armed with these ideas, and my full support, Joe gave one of the most open and honest speeches that I've ever heard when he addressed Airbnb's employees at our first all-employee conference, One Airbnb. Joe later said he looked to me as a Modern Elder for my years of experience running larger organizations combined with heart-based leadership and a sixth sense for company culture.

Thanks to their vast networks, Modern Elders can also serve as matchmakers who facilitate those intergenerational collaborations that spawn true innovation. For example, consider how, at age eighty, well-known surgeon, inventor, and vintner Dr. Thomas Fogarty introduced CEO Anne Morrissey, forty-eight at the time and a veteran of many health industry start-ups, to ambitious young entrepreneur Jessie Becker, twenty-four, so that Anne could shepherd Jessie's promising medical device start-up, InPress Technologies, into the future.

Over the past decade, venture capitalists have expressed a growing preference for keeping founders as the leaders of their businesses as long as possible because founder-led companies tend to be more innovative, have better instincts for their competitive marketplace, and have the moral authority to make hard choices. In many cases like Facebook, Snapchat, and Uber, this means that the founders have had unparalleled voting rights relative to the leaders of traditional companies. But this kind of consolidation of power with unseasoned entrepreneurs can lead to challenging scenarios, and it certainly doesn't mean we can't pair founders with sage counsel who can help these young leaders to mature and grow.

It's hard to measure the impact of true Modern Elders. Clearly, it's not about how many widgets they produce individually in an hour. In some cases, it may be how they helped create a habitat for people to do the best work of their lives. Through being a trusted internal counselor, I assisted dozens of up-and-coming Airbnb leaders to see their unique value in the company, helping to assure we didn't lose high-potential managers in the frenzy of our growth.

These three brilliant cofounders—Joe, Brian, and Nate—were doing something historic, beyond just the phenomenal growth of the company. Rarely before has a founding trio of a company that grew to Airbnb's proportions worked so harmoniously in their operating roles for a decade. Being a disruptor can be disruptive to internal relationships given all the distractions and pressures, so this was no small feat. Airbnb is a better company for the fact that it has grown into a *wiser* company, in more ways than one. This means we don't just obsess upon our financial results; we look at our long-term impact on the communities we serve and we adapt policies and programs to be a positive force. And, given there's much less cofounders' drama than most other companies, our employees can focus on how this start-up, which became one of the world's most valuable hospitality companies nearly overnight, can live its mission helping our customers "belong anywhere."

You don't have to have a senior role or title to "hang up your shingle." As you'll recall from chapter 4, Paul Critchlow served as confidant and librarian even though he was an intern. While we may fret that our age shows as we get older, so does our wisdom, especially when we're not trying to "show it off." Chinese philosopher Lao-Tzu, author of the *Tao Te Ching*, wrote, "The Sage holds on to the One and in this way becomes the shepherd of the world. He does not show himself off; therefore he becomes prominent. He does not put himself on display; therefore he brightly shines. He does not brag about himself; therefore he receives credit. He does not praise his own deeds;

therefore he can long endure. It is only because he does not compete that, therefore, no one is able to compete with him."

Spiritually radiant, physically vital, and socially responsible Modern Elders feel generative when they create the space for those younger than them to accelerate their learning by means of providing wise counsel. Pierre Teilhard de Chardin wrote, "The future belongs to those who give the next generation reason to hope."

ModEl Practices to Counsel

1. DISCERN YOUR SPECIFIC ROLE AS A COUNSELOR.

As you're presented with an opportunity to provide counsel, ask yourself, "How can I best serve this person?" The more performance oriented the inquiry ("I'm not meeting my sales numbers, what can I do differently?"), the shorter the likely duration of your engagement. But, a development-oriented inquiry ("How can I build my emotional intelligence to create a better relationship with all of my direct reports?") will likely be ongoing, so you need to determine whether you have both the skill set and time capacity to take on that relationship.

Another way to look at it is to ask yourself, "Will I primarily be transferring knowledge (performance oriented), or facilitating awareness (development oriented)?" If you don't feel you have the skill set or time for what is needed, what other resources exist in the organization to help this younger worker? Does this person's direct supervisor have the capacity to provide this counseling? Can the HR team help? Are there internal performance management systems like 360-degree feedback formats? Are there internal or external coaches? Is there an alternative elder in the company who is better suited than you? And could you have a singular meeting with this person in which you leave them with a question that can assist them in coaching themselves?

2. LEARN THE BEST PRACTICES IN COUNSELING.

If you're serious about providing workplace counsel, there are so many different approaches to consider. I'm a particular fan of the Coaches Training Institute so I would recommend that you look at www.coactive.com. You've also seen that "presence" is a quality that I think Modern Elders embody. There are a couple of programs that specialize in presence and embodied leadership: Strozzi Institute (www.strozziinstitute.com) and Leadership Embodiment (www.leadershipembodiment.com). From my perspective, here are the proven tips in my toolbox:

- Listen both *to* the story and *for* the story and beware of prejudging. Ask empathetic questions that help you understand what's beyond the surface. At the same time, be careful with sounding like or veering into the territory of a therapist. If that's the role someone wants you in, and you're comfortable with it, so be it, but know that you can also recommend the person seek professional help or other resources. More than anything, show that you care with your engaged listening. A great counselor describes, not prescribes, and is very careful of using the words "should" or "shouldn't."

- Assuming it feels appropriate, self-reveal something about your history that helps this person understand they're not alone in what they're experiencing but don't let your story dominate their story. Show some vulnerability but also help them see how you solved this problem and offer that wisdom to them.

- While treating each mentee uniquely, consider the life cycle of an ongoing mentor-mentee relationship. In the book *From Age-ing to Sage-ing*, authors Zalman Schachter-Salomi and

Ronald Miller suggest there are five typical stages: (a) before a mentor relationship may have even come up in conversation, there is a casual, informal introduction during which time you see whether there's a comfortable rapport; (b) the "shakeout" period when you first see whether this connection has the depth and elasticity that both parties are looking for, which is also a good time to create clarity around both parties' intentions or goals; (c) the deepening of trust as the mentee reveals more; (d) the transmission of wisdom from the mentor becomes more evident as the amount of time the mentor speaks during a meeting may be twice as much as it was compared to the earlier meetings; and (e) graduation in which both parties recognize this era of the relationship is over. It's important to be clear about when this last stage has occurred as many effective mentorship relationships get spoiled when one of the two parties checks out without being explicit about the fact they're ready for it to end.

• Prove you're loyal. You do this first and foremost by explicitly committing to confidentiality. One direction a mentor relationship can go is career advice. This is tricky as the mentee feels anxious expressing that they may be or will be considering outside employment from the company. And it can be challenging for you to hold on to this information especially if this is a particularly valuable contributor or leader. But just know that the more you help this person sort out their issue in a way that makes them happy, the better it's likely to be long term for the organization. Of course, if your mentee tells you something that could prove to be an existential threat for the company or involves serious legal or ethical issues, you may need to get additional counsel.

3. SEEK WAYS TO SCALE YOUR COUNSEL.

Just like stray cats returning for the saucer of milk you put out one day, you may find many juniors magnetically drifting in your direction when you put out your shingle as librarian and confidant. You have a few options as you start finding the demand for your wisdom greater than the available space on your calendar:

- Consider formalizing your mentor role with your boss, so it becomes part of your job, not something extra you do after hours. As I'll outline in chapter 9, it's time for more companies to consider whether mirroring Google's model of engineers having 20 percent time to focus on independent company-serving innovation projects could be applied to an elder who has clearly shown his or her prowess as a multiplier of young talent. Of course, this would mean you would have to reduce your scope of other work by 20 percent unless you are fine with just adding that 20 percent to your existing 100 percent.

- Deputize some junior elders. If you've developed some effective teacher-student relationships, some of your students may have the interest and capacity to become informal mentors themselves. So, as you're approached by new potential mentees, tell them about your junior elder who has more time than you do and who has mastered many of the skills you might have offered.

- Ask your HR department if they'd sponsor a "speed-mentoring" session in which prospective mentors and mentees could meet each other based upon the variety of subjects prospective mentors feel they've mastered and can impart.

- Turn your mentorship into classes. Michael Dearing, longtime eBay exec, former Stanford School of Engineering professor, and founder of Harrison Metal, which invests in start-ups, found that each time he'd meet with a mentee, a floodgate of memories would open as many of the issues these young folks were facing mirrored his past. Seeing that he was often saying many of the same things to his mentees, Michael created a school at Harrison Metal with the primary focus being a general management class of thirty to forty people; principles, guideposts, and a leadership tool kit are offered during the twelve hours of class time. As successful as he's been in business, Michael believes this class is the biggest legacy he will leave as a Modern Elder.

Congratulations on digesting the four chapters with the four Modern Elder lessons. I trust we've accelerated your path to wisdom. Now, let's make this more personal by moving to chapter 8 in which we put all these lessons together and apply them to thriving in the second, third, or fourth act of your career.

[8]

Rewire, Don't Retire

*"From the time that I was six years old I had the mania of draw-
ing the form of objects. As I came to be fifty I had published an
infinity of designs; but all that I have produced before the age of
seventy is not worth being counted. It is at the age of seventy-
three that I have somewhat begun to understand the structure
of true nature ... consequently at eighty years of age I shall have
made still more progress; at ninety I hope to have penetrated into
the mystery of things; at one hundred years of age I should have
reached decidedly a marvelous degree, and when I shall be one
hundred and ten, all that I do, every point and every line, shall be
instinct with life—and I ask all those who shall live as long as I do
to see if I have not kept my word."*
—Nineteenth-century Japanese artist Hokusai

"Are you breathing just a little and calling it a life?"

My close friend Vanda posed this provocative query—a line from
a Mary Oliver poem—during the early days of the dot-com bust
in 2002. I was barely breathing, at least financially, as my hotel company had been hit with the first of two "once-in-a-lifetime" down-
turns in the same decade. I'd been holding my breath like a rookie
synchronized swimmer ever since. Six years later, I stopped breath-

ing. Literally. With a broken ankle, a septic leg, some bad antibiotics, and too much traveling taking its toll, I went flatline onstage after a speech. When I came to a few minutes later, I came to the realization that for me, the acronym CEO had become Can't Endure One more downturn. Major self-awareness in a few life-altering minutes.

Over the next two years, I grieved a series of suicides by middle-aged friends who didn't realize the U-turn of life can start getting better around age fifty. That's when I decided it was time to start breathing again. I changed nearly everything in my life: I sold the company I thought I'd run to my grave, ended the relationship with my life partner of eight years, and embarked on this journey of rebirth I've shared in this book.

To some, fifty may seem old, but if you're going to live to a hundred, you're not even 40 percent of the way through your adult years. So, rather than ponder retirement or reminisce about the past, take a lesson from the Japanese artist Hokusai whose one hundred woodblock prints of Mount Fuji still astound art lovers two centuries after he created them at age seventy-five. Despite his advanced age, Hokusai was confident his best art was ahead of him and this propelled him forward. Not only does this artist's masterwork feature a wide collection of dynamic viewpoints of Japan's most famous mountain, it can also serve as a metaphor for the variety of optical perspectives we can use to consider our midlife.

For some, twenty-five years of experience is one year of experience copied twenty-five times. Others believe that each day you are reborn and you begin again with a fresh perspective. Each day you take your accumulated experience and the acuity of hindsight and become more of a master. Each day you can write a new script for where you are taking "your one wild and precious life."

MASTERING THE ART OF SELF-RENEWAL

When did you "peak" in your career or is that still ahead of you? At some point in our careers—whether it's at fifty or seventy—we will face a crossroads that might look like a dead end. Maybe we got laid off, maybe we had a health crisis, maybe we just felt used up. We have a choice: rewire or retire? Not everyone realizes this is a choice; some people believe that retirement at a certain age is a foregone conclusion. But there was a time when dying at a certain age was a foregone conclusion as well and then modern medicine moved the goalposts a decade or two further down the field. Modern medicine rewired. A Modern Elder can rewire as well.

Up until this point in the book, I've primarily been talking about how you can remake yourself to stay relevant and valuable in your current job or career path. But this chapter is addressing something slightly different: what to do when we find ourselves at that crossroads where the subject of retirement becomes impossible to ignore. You will learn about how to clarify your mastery and replant it in a new garden, so that it can be harvested for many years to come.

Teenagers are given all kinds of prep to ease into the new chapter of adulthood: years of school, Scouting programs, athletic teams, charm school (whatever happened to that?!), SAT and IQ tests, career counselors, and oodles of tutelage. But we're not offered much to prepare us for the crossroads we come to when we reach the doorstep of elderhood. And that's why I want you to think of this chapter as your road map. Or maybe we should call it a blueprint, as author Mary Catherine Bateson did in her inspiring metaphor that suggests we build our years of increased longevity into our careers the way that we might build a new room addition in our home.

She writes, "Adding a room to a house is likely to change the way all the rooms are used. Midcareer renewal is potentially a more dramatic change. Rather than building something on at the back, we are moving the walls and creating an atrium in the center. The atrium is filled with fresh air and sunlight, and it presents an opportunity for reflection on all the rooms that open off of it." In other words, the increased longevity you may have compared to your parents or grandparents doesn't necessarily mean an extra ten years occurring at the end of your life. Rather, it means you have an extra decade, or atrium, in your midlife. This chapter offers you an architectural blueprint for a midlife atrium, complete with a variety of choices of how to spend those extra midlife years.

WHY REWIRE?

But first let's tackle the big, aging elephant in the room: retirement. The word "retirement" derives from the Middle French language meaning "to go off into seclusion." Finding refuge from a complicated world may be the perfect path for some people in their fifties or sixties. But, for many, the mere notion strikes fear into their very hearts. To them, and particularly if forced to stare that elephant in the face before they are ready, the idle days and opportunity for quiet reflection feel less like a peaceful sanctuary, and more like a forced extradition or violent exile. Luckily, there is another option. And as it turns out, there are many reasons to choose rewiring over retiring.

For one, it's better for your brain and body. In fact, for healthy workers, retiring even a year early may actually raise the risk of mortality. As Chris Farrell wrote in the *New York Times*, "Academics who have studied the correlation between health and working into the senior years say this: Work offers a routine and purpose, a reason for getting up in the morning. The workplace is a social environment, a community. Depending on your occupation, doing your job involves engaging with cubicle mates, bosses, subordinates, union brothers and sisters, suppliers, vendors and customers. The incentive for workers to invest in their health while employed is strong."

So it's not surprising that 70 percent of people over fifty say they'd like to still work part-time after they retire. Many people take courses at a local community center or university, or teach themselves a language, or throw themselves into a hobby (or all three). All these are ways of keeping your brain from becoming a couch potato in retirement.

There are practical and financial reasons to rewire instead of retire as well. As outlined in Gratton and Scott's *The 100-Year Life*, if you think you might live to one hundred, you should plan to save around 10 percent of your income annually if you want to retire on 50 percent of your final salary. While most of us only save about 5 percent annually, if we were able to put away 10 percent, at what age will you be able to retire? Somewhere into your eighties. Darn! So retirement at sixty, sixty-five, or even seventy may not make sense for many of us in our triple-digit age of longevity.

Plus, the longer you wait to tap into your Social Security benefits in retirement, the more you receive. For example, you will earn 76 percent more in monthly benefits if you wait to "retire" until age seventy as opposed to age sixty-two. If you expect to be on this planet a long time, if you can afford it, it behooves you to work a little longer so that you can wait to receive your Social Security benefits. You can read more about this in the appendix's "My 10 Favorites" section under "Web Wisdom."

Retirement used to be a simple and permanent transition—from full-time work to no-time work, with limited options. But today, it's become more of a process, potentially occurring in several stages over a number of years. And just as there are more options for those who choose to retire, so too are there more opportunities for those who decide to rewire. In fact, there's growing evidence that more people post-fifty wholly change industries or job classifications. Forty percent of Americans still working at age sixty-two have moved to a new occupation sometime after age fifty-five, and those who've moved to a new occupation choose to stay in the workplace longer than those who stay in the same industry or job classification during their later years.

This requires building new muscles in midlife, as well as new expectations. For example, most workers who change career paths late in the game take a step down in salary when they start over, and this is particularly true in the tech industry where salaries tend to peak at age forty-five. And for some, the psychological blow that comes with a reduction in pay and rank can be a tough pill to swallow. But, for many of these midlife workers, the reduction in pay is less important than the kind of work hour flexibility some employers or professions offer, and the fact they can work part-time or take more vacation time. Consulting, freelancing, or the gig economy are also viable options for a growing number of people in their fifties and sixties and this kind of work now represents 40 percent of the American workforce (up from 31 percent in 2005).

Entrepreneurship, teaching, coaching, working for a nonprofit: these are just a few popular examples of the many options available to those of us who choose to rewire rather than retire. So now let's look at exactly how to refresh and reinvent our skill sets to find and thrive in that fulfilling "encore career."

THE MASTER OF YOUR OWN DESTINY

Maybe, just maybe, you are starting to believe the world is your oyster, or your atrium, in midlife. You have more options than you imagined because you've learned the skill of mastery, which can be applied to learning new things.

Luis Gonzalez is an avid reader of business leadership books that helped him fight fires in the corporate world. But in his early forties, he realized that his boyhood dream of fighting real fires was burning inside of him. Luis was the chief operating officer for Inktel, a successful call center company with more than a thousand employees. He had a great career, which along with his wife, supported their four children. But, as they were getting closer to becoming "empty nesters," Luis was reminded of something he once read from a mutual role model of ours, Randy Komisar, who wrote, "And then there is the most dangerous risk of all—the risk of spending your life not doing what you want on the bet you can buy yourself the freedom to do it later." As a kid, Luis dreamed of a career in the fire service but the business world took him in a different direction. But he still craved helping others and enjoyed volunteering with the Red Cross and helping out during hurricane recoveries in south Florida.

Pursuing his dream in the fire service and leaving a successful career was a daunting decision considering the financial security he would be giving up and the inherent risks in the firefighting profession. Additionally, at forty-four, he would be joining a fire battalion with colleagues who were younger than his oldest child. So, while he was running Inktel, he went through two years of extensive training, including Emergency Medical Technician (EMT) school, fire academy, paramedic school, and then volunteering with a local fire department on weekends.

Two years into his training, and now hirable by any fire department in south Florida, he was still volunteering, Inktel was still growing, but Luis wasn't quite feeling fulfilled. One night, while out to dinner with his family, a work emergency required him to leave the restaurant and that's when he said, "This can't happen anymore." So, he decided to finally put all that rigorous training, study, and practice to good use. He applied to join the fire department with the City of

West Palm Beach and after an extensive hiring process, became the oldest person ever offered a firefighting job by this municipality.

The fire service is an environment where rookies keep opinions to themselves and follow direction. While Luis is older than the captain and chiefs, he brings a different perspective to the department. He's proven to be a mentor to many of his colleagues, as part of his mastery was leadership wisdom forged over years in the business world. As a result, his opinion and insight are sought out by his peers and officers. Luis didn't become a firefighter to hone his leadership mastery, but, just as we all carry our mastery toolbox with us everywhere, his colleagues are the beneficiaries. For Luis, peace of mind and the freedom to enjoy life far outweigh the financial impact. His adult mastery is now realizing his childhood dream.

As you'll see in so many of the case studies I'll introduce in this chapter, the seeds of someone's calling are often foreshadowed in their past. Our accumulated life experience gives us a hint of where the seeds of our mastery might lie. For me, I realize that from both childhood and my adult career as a hotel entrepreneur, I had shown signs of being adept at imagining needs of customers that weren't obvious, being able to create a cohesive team and entertain people as a social alchemist, tapping into both my internal and external antennae to hone my intuition. We often lose sight of our unique talents over the course of a long career, but the reality is you've developed some mastery along the way.

This chapter will help you learn how you, too, can repurpose your mastery to find new opportunities you hadn't imagined, and maybe in places you weren't familiar with. As your dutiful author and "librarian," I'd suggest you also look for the *New York Times* July 2017 article "Switching Careers Doesn't Have to Be Hard: Charting Jobs That Are Similar to Yours" listed in "My 10 Favorites" under "Articles" in the appendix. This insightful article, with its accompanying charts and automated career counselor, can tell you which kinds of jobs are most similar to and different from what you're doing now and help you understand what habitats might be most ripe for you.

Now that you've developed some clarity on your sense of mastery, let's apply the lessons we learned in the last four chapters with a few stories of Modern Elders who've continued to *evolve, learn, collaborate,* and *counsel*—and succeeded in rewiring themselves and their skill sets to thrive in a repurposed career.

EVOLVE YOUR SKILLS

Pam Sherman's ob-gyn father and psychoanalyst mother had big ambitions for their youngest daughter, so when Pam graduated from law school and joined a prestigious DC law firm, her parents felt like they'd won the Super Bowl. Never mind that Pam's youthful dreams were to be an actress someday. Pam slaved away in the legal trade until one day the law firm unexpectedly decided to close their doors. Pam was embarrassed and scared, and even took to wailing at the ceiling at night.

Once the initial shock blew over, Pam decided to stop looking at the shuttering of her firm as a career death sentence and instead see it as a sign that she was supposed to reconnect with that childhood dream. She took her unemployment insurance and some savings and studied acting in New York and Oxford, and pretty soon became a successful full-time working actor.

That was, until her husband moved his business to Rochester, New York, and she had to evolve once again. Repurposing her life for act three, she became a journalist for the Gannett media company, with her own column called "The Suburban Outlaw." She was also asked by a partner in the Woods Oviatt Gilman law firm if she could help lawyers to "do what you do: you know the way you talk to people, find out their stories and make them comfortable." Pam dusted off the curriculum of an Acting for Lawyers class she created for the Department of Justice and started working with law firms, marketing agencies, and then Fortune 500 companies. Her practice has grown enormously and today she is coaching leaders all over the world, helping them share their mission and their stories with passion, energy, and engagement—none of which she could have done if she hadn't been both a lawyer AND an actor. Clearly, Pam was fusing her experience in the legal industry with her ability to entertain and connect with people in this new endeavor.

Pam tells me, "I couldn't have known it then but the firm closing and that move turned out to be the best thing that could have happened to me, widening my horizons in ways I never could have imagined and forcing me to reinvent my career from lawyer to actor to writer to consultant. I just had to be flexible and fluid with respect to how my identity was going to change. It's sort of like playing dress-up as an adult as I love costume changes." And in early 2018, she returned to the stage in a one-woman show about her idol, American humorist and housewife Erma Bombeck.

QUESTIONS TO CONSIDER:

1. Is there a trend or industry on the horizon that fascinates you? How can you can start exploring it further?
2. Is there a hint from your childhood about what new career path might be meaningful for you and is there a part of your identity you have to let go of to evolve into the new you?
3. Which of your mastery skills are portable no matter what path your career takes?

REPLANT THE SEEDS OF CURIOSITY

Learning came naturally for Sherry Lansing, seventy-three, the most powerful female movie mogul of all time and the first to head a major studio. But first, she was a schoolteacher, actress, and film executive, before becoming chairman of Paramount Pictures for twelve years. While the overall movie biz may have been more gender diverse, the corridors of power were exclusively male until Sherry came along; perhaps it was a result of her unique perspective that her whole career, as she tells it, was often mentoring or being mentored without even knowing it. Like me, she loved what she was doing until her calling turned into a job and it was then she knew it was time to get curious.

At age fifty-five, she started her process of internally evolving. She knew she was going to make a transition, so she started preparing herself. Sherry was successful and philanthropically minded. She had a particular interest in cancer research having been a math teacher and having lost her mother to cancer. She says, "While I still loved the film business, sitting through another script meeting didn't feel it was going to be nearly as interesting as learning how to solve cancer."

So she started getting involved with a variety of cancer nonprofits, even as she was still working at Paramount. But even though she was used to being the most powerful person in the room at her day job, she was open to being "the dumbest person in the room" when stem cell research was being discussed. Sherry's world got much bigger as she was now sitting at tables with the smartest scientists in their fields. She was confident enough to be naive, curious enough to be occasionally valuable, and thoroughly excited to be a lifelong learner.

By the time she chose to leave Paramount at age sixty she'd planted such deep roots in her new garden—nonprofit leadership and philanthropy primarily focused on cancer—that the shift didn't feel abrupt to her. It felt like a natural transition, although many of her Hollywood friends were surprised by her decision. The internal evolution often happens without others noticing. As detailed in the biography of her life, *Leading Lady*, "After decades of accommodating moguls and movie stars, of balancing budgets and dissecting scripts, she felt liberated, as if she had shed one skin and grown another."

Sherry says, "You don't find the cause, the cause finds you." And then, you become an expert at cultivating a beginner's mind around your new passion.

QUESTIONS TO CONSIDER:

1. Think about the people in the world whose intellect and mastery you most admire. Are they scientists finding the cure for cancer? World leaders working to eradicate genocide? Pulitzer Prize–winning writers? Whatever the case may be, what is one thing you wish they could teach you, and how can you set out to learn it on your own?
2. How can you start some stealth learning even before you've made your big move to a new career?
3. Are there elder role models who have found their primary success later than expected? Can you ask them how they fed their curiosity to learn later in life?

REEMBODY YOUR COLLABORATIVE NATURE

Betty Friedan's manifesto, *The Feminine Mystique*, is widely credited as the catalytic literary force that sparked the beginning of second-wave feminism and the women's movement a half century ago. Thirty years later, at seventy-two, Friedan wrote *The Fountain of Age,* in which she tried to ignite a similar awakening for older people and, in particular, highlighted the collaborative and generative nature of what people in the second half of their life have to offer society (a link to a synopsis of her book is under "Articles" in the appendix's "My 10 Favorites" section). She writes, "In their 'late style,' artists and scientists tend to move beyond tumult and discord, distracting details and seemingly irreconcilable differences, to unifying principles that give fresh meaning to what has gone before and presage the agenda for the next generation, so it seems to me age can free us all, personally—and our aging society politically—to a new wholeness, previewing in the serious or the seemingly irrelevant efforts of our late years new dimensions of life for the next generation."

San Francisco entrepreneur Ben Davis embodies "the collaborative nature of what people in the second half of their life have to offer society." In 2010, Ben was already successful with a quarter century of experience working on civic projects under his belt, but the creative services agency he founded in 1995 was flickering out at the same time he was lit up with a new idea. In fact, he had become so consumed with one particular client, the government agency that handles California's public roads, Caltrans, and one visionary idea—creating a living environment art piece that spanned the western side of San Francisco's Bay Bridge—that his small agency was virtually on financial life support. Ben "sees God in infrastructure and loves to find ways to celebrate and glorify it," but God wasn't going to pay his employees' payroll. Ben's fascination with this new unfunded project was coming at the expense of his business and his personal finances.

He imagined engaging an artist to create a site-specific art installation of lights that would help the forgotten stepchild of Bay Area bridges (the Golden Gate Bridge is the star in this region) win new love and respect among the hundreds of thousands who see it daily. From the moment of Ben's epiphany to the grand lighting ceremony of *The Bay Lights* in March 2013, only two and a half years had passed. But by 2014, his creative agency, WPI, had a RIP stone marking its demise. Meanwhile Ben had birthed a new nonprofit organization, Illuminate.org, dedicated to rallying large groups of people together to "create impossible works of public art that, through awe, free humanity's better nature." He couldn't sell his company because he'd drained it to support the start-up of this new nonprofit. But there was no turning back for Ben now; he had found his "new wholeness," and it was full of light. He told me, "When you reach fifty, your identity can hold you back. Sometimes you have to let go of the past and court failure, flirting with what's new and passionate in your life."

The Bay Lights light sculpture required unparalleled collaboration. Luckily, Ben had also amassed an unparalleled network of talented people to call upon. And, he was blessed by partnering with a world-renowned light artist, Leo Villareal, and a stellar team of heroic dreamers and doers. Leo's visual interpretation of turning the Bay Bridge into a canvas of light became a source of great inspiration to everyone involved.

And in shared pursuit of that vision, a hearty alphabet soup of agencies came together to collectively forge a path to permission where none existed. On the technical side, more and more people kept joining the cause: engineers, electricians, LED experts, programmers, construction managers, safety managers, and so on. Along the way, writers, photographers, filmmakers, lawyers, coders, graphic designers, insurance brokers, 3-D makers, modelers, and others flocked to the challenge. Then, a vast community of Bay Area residents and art lovers came together and, within a year's time, gifted more than $8 million to make the monumental artwork a reality.

What's most impressive to Ben is the belief and generosity of an entire community—literally a cast of thousands—that selflessly invested in the vision with no guarantees. He says, "That's the real magic of the thing. My role was to help ignite a beacon of belief that served as our organizing principle to create collaboration amongst government agencies, technologists, donors, and all kinds of random other naysayers who typically conspire to say 'no' to big ideas. The integrity of the idea is what helped lead to epic collaboration."

But it wasn't the idea alone. By the time he reached his early fifties, Ben's history of seemingly disparate experiences was what helped him to build this collaborative muscle such that he could orchestrate this Herculean effort, whereas if he'd tried to do it twenty years earlier, he would likely have failed. His diverse job history had collaboration as the common link throughout, but it wasn't until those lights switched on for the first time on the Bay Bridge that it dawned on him that his résumé had prepared him perfectly for this moment. And being a little older gave him the courage, perspective, and vision to help steer people back to the mission-minded long view rather than focusing on the short-term obstacles that can sink an ambitious public project like *The Bay Lights.*

Ben believes that "when you give yourself fully to realizing a transformative vision, you cannot help but be personally transformed by the experience. Our lives, our paths, our sense of self, the world around us, was forever altered by what we had accomplished together."

QUESTIONS TO CONSIDER:

1. Is there an example of a collaboration you led and/or were the glue that held the parties together to a successful conclusion?
2. As you look at your employment history, how have your emotional intelligence skills developed so that you have an improved intuition or insight into the variety of people you work with? How can you leverage that talent in new ways in the future?
3. Do you have a vision for a passion project that is so illuminating and magnetic that it creates powerful alliances and alignment among disparate parties?

TEACH, COACH, COUNSEL

Mike Rielly thought he'd be in the golf business his whole life. It was part of his family history. Right after graduating from Stanford, he joined the sports agency IMG where, at the age of twenty-three, he started representing PGA Tour players. He spent the next twenty years moving up the ranks to senior vice president running IMG's golf course services group worldwide, spending much of his time stationed in Asia, and helping to market the careers of such notables as Arnold Palmer, Gary Player, Greg Norman, Nancy Lopez, Nick Faldo, and many others. He was almost a career guidance counselor for athletes especially as they considered their post-competitive play "retirement."

And then his world shifted. The iconic founder of IMG, Mark McCormack, died and the company fell into the hands of an investment group that had a very different perspective on the business. For two decades, Mike had been fortunate to experience Mark as a mentor, and so this shift was a shock, and it forced him to consider his career alternatives. He chose to take a lucrative severance package to give him the time to consider what was next.

But he found himself feeling somewhat vulnerable now that his professional identity had been shed, and his IMG business cards had been discarded. He made a geographic move back to his childhood home, Los Angeles, yet with each month that passed he was becoming increasingly anxious that his severance package was running out. He knew he needed to find a new career—but what? Then he remembered how in eighth grade he'd wanted to be a teacher when he grew up, so he decided to create and teach a sports business development class at the University of San Francisco. Recognizing he had a talent with young people, and that he needed an advanced degree to teach at a top business school, he enrolled in the leading graduate program in sports management, at Ohio University, where he was twice the age of most of his classmates.

After graduating, he started teaching at UC Berkeley's Haas School of Business. He loved working with students and found that his talent at helping young people consider their careers wasn't a big leap from what he had been doing for professional golfers; they were still the same seeds, only different soil. His "know-who" of sports industry contacts and "know-how" of the inner workings of everything from college and pro athletic programs to sports agency work meant Mike could give his undergrad or grad students a front-row seat to understand the sports business.

Ultimately, he moved on from being a teacher and today is the CEO of UC Berkeley Executive Education. He says, "As a sports agent, I was in the business of recruiting, selling, and servicing professional athletes. And now I'm doing the same but in a completely different industry. I recruit faculty, sell companies and individuals to be part of our programs, and service faculty and participants, all the while being an empathetic listener trying to understand and deliver on their unique needs. I realize the skills I built at IMG as a 'career counselor' for professional athletes have served me perfectly here at UC Berkeley. It's so meaningful to have this kind of impact on young adults early in their career in my role as a teacher, and similar impact on senior level executives in my role as CEO. I guess the theme of my career—my mastery—is helping others achieve their potential through career guidance."

It's no surprise that many Modern Elders choose to repurpose their experience and wisdom and share their mastery as a teacher, consultant, or coach. Lisa Pearl, for example, spent a good part of her early adulthood in school getting a law degree and a PhD. She had a clear vision—to work in the social nonprofit sector—and she pursued it. For thirteen years, she worked at the United States Holocaust Memorial Museum in Washington, DC, where she held different leadership roles. In each one she was able to create high-performing teams, build programs, implement operating systems, lead change, and experience almost every aspect of nonprofit management. She also coached and mentored dozens of staff and colleagues. She found the work extremely fulfilling and was fortunate to work with other passionate individuals.

However, she tells me, "A couple of years ago I started feeling a shift. I'm not sure if it was the 'midlife crisis' that people talk about. But I lost interest in my work and felt that I lost direction in my life. I felt that my time was running out and I wanted to have more impact."

So, Lisa decided to become a certified leadership coach and find meaning by helping others live up to their full potential. As with so many Modern Elders, tapping into your natural gift of providing wise counsel helps you feel both needed and relevant, which you in fact are. Lisa says, "If you had told me twenty years ago that I would become a leadership coach, I would have laughed. I spent so many years studying, building different skills, and trying to make a difference in this world. As it turns out, my most valuable skills were the ones that were part of my DNA—leading, coaching, and inspiring others to achieve more. That's where I was making the most impact. In a way, I came full circle and ended up exactly where I should be. Today, I feel very fortunate to be able to live my truth. It's a deeply satisfying feeling."

QUESTIONS TO CONSIDER:

1. Do people come to you for counsel? Why do people seek you out? What's your "secret sauce"? How can you build those skills in new ways?

2. Remember TiVo's Luther Kitahata from the last chapter, the engineer who was also a coach? Could you share your mastery by offering coaching and counseling more intentionally within your existing company?

3. Could you leverage your ability to teach and apply it to a whole new habitat? What industry sectors most interest you, and what knowledge or experience can you contribute to them?

RECASTING YOURSELF AS A CHANGE AGENT

You're a Modern Elder in the making. You've learned how to refine your mastery to set yourself up for a seamless and rewarding career shift in midlife. In the next few sections, I will give you a menu of options for what a new career can look like.

We'll start with how you can make change in your community and the world. Many boomers and older Gen Xers state they want work that has deeper personal meaning that connects them to something larger than themselves. A MetLife Foundation/Civic Ventures study found that as many as nine million US people between ages forty-four and seventy are already in what has been called an "encore" career that combines purpose, passion, and paycheck. And another thirty-one million say they'd like to do this in the future.

What's encouraging is that many employers are jumping on this bandwagon, helping prepare their aging workforce for ways they can serve the greater good. These employers recognize it's in their interest to be a launching pad for employees who go on to make a difference in their communities. As Julie Wirt, head of global retirement design for Intel, puts it, "We don't want to be just a great place to work. We also want to be a great place to retire from."

The aptly named Encore.org has been at the forefront of this movement, matching socially conscious Modern Elders with nonprofits across the country. Since 2009 thousands of "preretirees"—including two hundred retiring Intel employees—have joined the Encore Fellows program. And one of Encore's senior execs, Marci Alboher, has even written *The Encore Career Handbook* to help others understand how to find good work that's doing good for the world.

Peter O'Riordan is an Encore Fellow who had been responsible for a $1.4 billion business at Cisco Systems and managed teams of hundreds of engineers. He was at the company for nineteen years until he chose to participate in a companywide layoff at age fifty-four. Several other former Cisco executives introduced Peter to the Encore program where he could support a nonprofit with his leadership expertise. He chose Breakthrough Silicon Valley, an organization that helps middle-school kids who want to go to college find their way to higher education. They have a 96 percent acceptance rate, which is impressive considering these kids come from families who've never had a parent go to college.

Peter said it took some serious evolution to move from leading large teams with big budgets to being the support for the executive director (ED) of a twelve-person nonprofit with an annual budget of $1.6 million. He told me, "I recognized that it was very important not to position myself as 'the guy who knows it all,' but to come in with a humble mindset where I recognized that I had some skills, but also little awareness of how those skills might be applicable in a completely different context."

At times it was frustrating since it felt to Peter like he wasn't able to fully utilize his mastery. But his counseling role to the ED and others was a perfect fit for a Modern Elder like Peter—he could ask naive questions since he wasn't working in his traditional habitat. He says, "Counseling was easier because I didn't bring the baggage of being a subject matter expert. I had fresh eyes and it meant I could offer fresh advice. I tried very hard never to say 'Well, when I was at Cisco we . . .'"

If this sounds like an interesting path for you, some of the other resources you might consider include AARP's Experience Corps volunteering in urban public schools, and Stanford's Distinguished Careers Institute (DCI) or Harvard's Advanced Leadership Initiative (ALI), which help proven leaders find a way to make a social impact in their communities.

QUESTIONS TO CONSIDER:

1. Is there a cause that's so meaningful to you that it might almost pay you psychically if you offered your mastery to a nonprofit or social enterprise devoted to that cause?
2. Do you have enough savings to provide the freedom to pursue an "encore" career in which you potentially earn a smaller salary?
3. Are there paid positions available at companies in your community with a powerful social mission, or organizations committed to serving the common good?

REPOTTING YOURSELF AS AN ENTREPRENEUR

Learning to surf in my midfifties required an evolved, growth mindset, some courage, and, I guess, an able body. Not only do I look silly most of the time, but it can also be dangerous. Even so, I love it and have found surfing to be an apt metaphor for disruptive innovation. An entrepreneur surveys the horizon for a "swell" that looks to be more of a trend than a fad, they prepare themselves to ride this wave and—unlike tennis or skiing—there's no court time to book, no rulebook to follow, and no entry ticket to purchase. The lack of regimentation defines both surfing and entrepreneurship. In my case, I surfed two long-term trends in the hospitality industry: boutique hotels and home sharing, the latter one in my fifties. Surfing also requires adaptive attunement: an ability to make yourself at one with the wave. As we approach elderhood, we can adaptively attune ourselves to the propulsive forces in the marketplace to see how we can surf a long wave.

Many of you might be thinking, *What if I took the skills I've used in a more traditional career or company and apply them to becoming my own employer?* If you've asked yourself this question, you wouldn't be alone; the Kauffman Foundation reports that the percentage of all entrepreneurs who are fifty-five and over has grown from 15 percent in 1996 to 26 percent by 2014 and that older entrepreneurs are twice as likely to be successful in their ventures than younger entrepreneurs. This doesn't mean they're all getting rich (in fact, the National Bureau of Economic Research found that older Americans who switched from traditional jobs to self-employment saw their average annual earnings drop by over $18,000). But what they are getting is more peace of mind and a sense of autonomy to control their destiny as opposed to leaving their fate in the hands of their employer. This is why twenty-five million Americans between forty-four and seventy want to start their own venture.

The *New York Times* reports, "There's plenty of evidence to suggest that late blooming is no anomaly. A 2016 Information Technology and Innovation Foundation study found that inventors peak in their late 40s and tend to be highly productive in the last half of their careers. Similarly, professors at the Georgia Institute of Technology and Hitotsubashi University in Japan, who studied data about patent holders, found that, in the United States, the average inventor sends in his or her application to the patent office at age 47, and that the highest-value patents often come from the oldest inventors—those over the age of 55."

Gary Wozniak, sixty-two, was a successful stockbroker with a drug addiction. The addiction landed him in federal prison for three and a half years with a felony conviction and, when he came out in his later thirties, he realized he couldn't even get a job on the counter at a rental car company. Without much in the way of career prospects, Gary, newly in recovery, became an entrepreneur operating a chain of pizza parlors and a health club, becoming a commercial real estate broker, and operating a consulting business for small companies. But his entrepreneurial efforts got wiped out in the Great Recession. Gary rewired and launched RecoveryPark and RecoveryPark Farms, a nonprofit that helps train a workforce of formerly incarcerated adults and a for-profit dedicated to developing agriculture on dozens of acres of formerly vacant land in Detroit's urban core. In the last few decades, Detroit has lost two-thirds of its population, which means whole neighborhoods are vacant. In the east side neighborhood of Chene Ferry where RecoveryPark is located, 97 percent of the population had fled, so Gary and his team of ex-offenders and recovering addict employees had quite a homestead and RecoveryPark Farms now provides fresh produce to nearly one hundred of Detroit's finest restaurants.

Gary's venture is one of the 250 start-up organizations that live in a business incubator called TechTown in a Detroit industrial building where the Corvette was once designed. Gary told me he couldn't have grown his company without the support he's received with Tech-Town, where they helped refine his business model, improve his pitch to investors, and networked him with other entrepreneurs who shared best practices. The decline of Detroit's auto industry and subsequent revitalization of the area's abandoned buildings is an apt metaphor and great inspiration for those of us wanting to remake ourselves in the second half of our lives. TechTown was itself the entrepreneurial brainchild of Modern Elder Randal Charlton, who convinced Wayne State's leadership to help set up this incubator largely for entrepreneurs who are on the second, third, or fourth act of their careers. The exchange of wisdom and mentorship that comes with being surrounded by fellow entrepreneurs is part of the appeal of an incubator, so take a look in your community to see if one exists.

The partnership between AARP and the Small Business Administration can be another helpful resource. The organization and the federal agency, which both have local offices in every state, provide workshops and webinars tailored to local needs. And AARP also holds yearly pitch events and even has its own incubator, The Hatchery. Or join the many other older entrepreneurs who flock to the Silicon Valley Venture Summit and the Aging2.0 innovation accelerator conference. Finally, I highly recommend you watch Paul Tasner's TED talk about how he started a business at age sixty-six (listed in the appendix under "Videos/Speeches").

QUESTIONS TO CONSIDER:

1. What skills from your traditional career are most transferrable to a new venture you could launch?
2. How can you take small steps in the direction of starting a business to see if you feel you can balance the thrill with the anxiety?
3. What resources can you tap into to help educate you and potentially help fund your start-up?
4. Have you considered franchise opportunities, which are one of the most popular paths for entrepreneurs over the age of fifty?

RELOCATING YOURSELF AS AN EX-PAT

As the quality of Wi-Fi and health care have improved in the developing world, more Americans have considered spending their later years beyond the border. The number of retired workers receiving Social Security benefits abroad jumped 22 percent from 2009 to 2015, but it's estimated the figure is even higher since many people still get their check at a US P.O. box.

What's the appeal of moving to Costa Rica, Portugal, or Thailand? First off, it's inexpensive. Real estate may be priced at half to one-third of what it is in the US, and the cost of living is dramatically cheaper (since gross domestic product per capita may be half to one-third that of the US). In my role at Airbnb as the leader in charge of all hosts globally, I met dozens of Americans who chose to semiretire outside the US and buy a home or property with vacation rental potential, using Airbnb as the source of their retirement nest egg that will finance their extended longevity.

Then, there's the great weather, the culture, and the fact that learning a language later in life keeps your mind active. Living overseas keeps many older folks feeling young and it's easier than ever with Skype, WhatsApp, and all kinds of other means of communicating across borders and time zones. There are so many careers—from consulting to life coaching to writing or editing—that can be done from afar.

My former restaurant partner, Julie Ring, sixty-six, left San Francisco to consummate her love affair with Mexico. She bought a home in Manzanillo at age fifty-two and ten years later moved there full-time. Knowing she would become an ex-pat, she simply applied for a permanent residency visa, which wasn't difficult, and filed for working papers for Mexico. Many of her friends work for US companies part-time or consult in the US and are paid in dollars while enjoying the low cost of living in Mexico. Julie lives comfortably on $30,000 annually, whereas if she were living in the Bay Area, she'd need to earn six figures. She sells paintings, teaches the occasional cooking class, and enjoys being active in her local community starting a recycling program as well as an animal sterilization operation. And her ninety-three-year-old father and her sister and brother-in-law have all now moved down as well and live nearby. Julie says, "I am so happy I designed my life the way I have. I am rich in other ways than money. I am sure things will change when my dad transitions, but, for now, these are beautiful, precious times. I see myself in Mexico for life, maybe just not in Manzanillo. Ajijic could be my next move."

You'll see in the appendix that I've recommended International Living.com as a website that can help you imagine what it would be like living an exotic, affordable life somewhere else in the world.

QUESTIONS TO CONSIDER:

1. Did you have a childhood or young adult dream of living overseas someday?
2. Is there a foreign language you already know and are dying to use, or one you've always wanted to learn?
3. Might you consider taking a few vacations to a particular spot of interest and, while there, talk to ex-pats who've relocated to learn more about the cost of real estate and ways you could pick up some additional income if you moved there?

REBOOTING YOURSELF AFTER A PAUSE

There are all kinds of reasons you may take a pause in your career: having children, taking care of your aging parents, going back to school, making a major shift in your career, being laid off. Some of these will be planned, some not. But no matter your reason for the pause, you're likely to feel a little anxious as if you're trying to jump back onto a floating raft as it rushes down the river. This is where a growth mindset, which I talked about earlier in the book, comes in handy. While it may feel like the world is conspiring for you to *prove* yourself, focus on how you can *improve* yourself even if you've been out of the sandbox for a little while. Mastery doesn't have an expiration date and humans can have a growth mindset until they die. One day at a time, you will start to see your confidence reemerge.

Diane Flynn, fifty-five, worked at the Boston Consulting Group, attended Harvard Business School, and spent a decade working at Electronic Arts in a senior marketing role, and she had no intention of ever pausing her career. She was energized, focused, and felt positively challenged in her work. But she also had two toddlers at home and enough stress to result in chronic sinus infections. She finally decided something had to give, and it wasn't going to be her family. So she did what she said she'd never do. She paused her career. That pause turned into sixteen years and a third child. Just to clarify, she paused only her paycheck, not something everyone can do. Diane was lucky she had the financial support of her husband, which allowed her to work tirelessly in volunteer roles, serving on boards and advising at Stanford Children's Hospital. She had a great deal of flexibility and could make it to all of her kids' dance recitals and soccer games.

In 2014, she had the chance to return to the workplace. Her initial instinct was not to return full-time, so she committed to twenty-five hours per week. After a month, she realized how thrilling it was to put on a starched, ironed shirt, get out of the house, and have meaningful work challenges to contemplate. She also enjoyed working with younger people who kept her current and reminded her of being around her adult children who had now left the house. Diane's tech skills flourished and she enjoyed the paycheck. But she also realized she was woefully unprepared for a workplace that looked very different from the one she had left sixteen years before.

Diane shared with me that, despite having both a background and strong interest in tech, she felt ill-equipped and underskilled, especially when it came to all the workplace technology tools that didn't exist when she paused her career—LinkedIn, social media, collaborative tools (Google Suite), presentation graphics, video technologies (Zoom, Google Hangouts, Skype, WebEx), and commonly used communication tools like Slack and Telegram. "I was encouraged by how quickly I did get up to speed," she recalls, "but I also sensed an overwhelming interest from peers in my community to return to paid work, either because of financial need, intellectual stimulation, or social connections. This made me think there's an opportunity to help women interested in reentering the workforce." Fortunately, there were four equally passionate women who felt the same way Diane did, and together, they founded ReBoot Accel.

ReBoot Accel offers a suite of programs to get women current, connected, and confident to return to the workforce or pursue new goals. At the time of writing, it has served over one thousand women in Silicon Valley, Chicago, Seattle, Boston, Atlanta, Detroit, Houston, New York, and Los Angeles and is spreading across the country. ReBoot also taps into a huge and growing pool of talent that has been largely overlooked. According to a study published by the Center for Talent Innovation in 2010, 43 percent of women pause their career and 90 percent want back in. That's 3.3 million women per year in the US alone.

Diane concludes, "The main challenge is that these experienced women in ReBoot Accel—most of whom have graduate degrees—have so much to offer yet have very low self-confidence. What they don't realize is that their experience (whether paid or unpaid), connections and soft skills are immensely valuable to employers. Unlike many newly minted college grads, they are able to work autonomously, bring a certain degree of gravitas to the table, and are master multitaskers. In addition, they have wisdom, maturity, solid communication and persuasion skills, and they are loyal, committed, and often have higher job retention."

Martin Ewings is in the business of spotting talent as part of the global recruitment consultancy Experis. He says more and more employers are tapping into a fresh talent pool of "boomerang" workers, who've retired and then later decide to seek new employment elsewhere, and "alumni" of companies who realize, once they've been retired or left the organization for another company, that they would still like to help out at the company on occasion.

These older workers, who've taken a pause, provide a valuable means of upskilling and mentoring the existing workforce and tend to be strong on "loyalty and commitment." But Ewings also shoots down the assumption that older workers cannot learn new skills. Instead he believes they are too often pigeonholed based on past work experience when, in reality, an equally important consideration is their inherent personality traits. He says, "There are a variety of almost unteachable capabilities that have more to do with the person than their age: drive, adaptability, resilience, and curiosity or a willingness to learn new things. These capabilities are not age-specific and they're far harder to recruit for than experience, but we are starting to see organizations are becoming more open to the idea of searching for candidates who have proven they're masters at these four capabilities." He told me the best way to determine if a candidate has these qualities is to ask them to describe a time when they were presented with a challenge or problem that was outside of their comfort zone, what they did to come up with a solution—and ultimately what they learned from that.

Ewings also told me that while older workers are often considered to have out-of-date skills, even college students who learn a coding language in their first year of college may find it out of favor by the time they graduate. Digital transformation is not new, but the pace of change is like nothing we've ever seen, so those who will succeed are those who are constantly learning. And adaptable learning is not a skill exclusive to youth.

Do age-friendly employers exist out there? Yes, and you can find some of them at RetirementJobs.com where they provide peer-to-peer reviews from employees who are over fifty years old in companies as diverse as Amazon, Home Depot, Marriott International, and Aetna. The site also has certified age-friendly employer programs that have met a rigorous vetting process. Some of the companies that meet that standard include AT&T, CVS Pharmacy, Fidelity Investments, and Wells Fargo.

Even with the most age-friendly employers, however, be prepared to answer the following questions if applicable to you: "Why are you changing fields or industries at this point in your career?" or "Are you sure you want to work again?" or "It looks like you've been an entrepreneur before but it may not have worked out. How can we be sure you're truly committed to us if we hire you?"

And be prepared with your own questions to ask too. Here's a question Facebook COO Sheryl Sandberg says was the most impressive one an interviewee ever asked her: "What's the biggest challenge you're working on and how can I help solve it for you?" Remember Peter Kent from the end of chapter 3? He turned his job interview with three-decades-younger founder and CEO Joanna Riley into an opportunity to teach *her* something even though he was the one looking for a job. Even in a job interview, Modern Elders let their wisdom speak for itself.

QUESTIONS TO CONSIDER:

1. What resources exist that can help you rebuild your confidence if you've been out of the workforce for a while?
2. How can you sketch your life story in a way that shows a potential employer you've developed mastery in your life based upon both your résumé as well as other life experiences?
3. How can you help the person interviewing you realize you're there to help them solve a vexing problem based upon your history of experience?

RECONSIDERING A GAP YEAR

In her 2010 book, *Composing a Further Life: The Age of Active Wisdom,* Mary Catherine Bateson writes, "What would it take to offer large numbers of adults a year off (or even two) somewhere around age fifty or fifty-five, a year that would challenge them to rethink their lives and return to their jobs with renewed energy and motivation?" Hence, her metaphor of the midlife atrium from earlier in this chapter.

Adult life can feel a bit like a run-on sentence that goes on too long without some punctuation. Selling my hotel company in the trough of the Great Recession, on the precipice of my fiftieth birthday, wasn't part of my business or life plan. But it was clear, as evidenced by my heart failure mentioned at the start of this chapter, that it was time for me to take a time-out to create some space to breathe in my life.

I take inspiration from the Australians, who have long enjoyed their wanderlust. Rather remote in the world, Australian culture is known for its global walkabouts both early and later in life. In fact, the Australian government mandates Long Service Leave (LSL) that is typically two months of additional vacation for every ten years of continuous service to an employer. The Aussies have proven you don't have to be college- or graduate-school-bound to take an extended break.

When kids take a break before or after college, we call it a "gap year." But why should eighteen- or twenty-two-year-olds be the only ones entitled to some punctuation, when they've barely even begun writing the run-on sentence of adult life? What about fully baked adults who just need a little space to pause, to hit refresh, or to rewire? Luckily, as more and more people are liberating themselves from the three-stage model of life that we talked about in chapter 3, the idea of a lengthy sabbatical in midlife is gaining currency. As Holly Bull, the president of the Center for Interim Programs in Princeton, New Jersey, the first and longest-running gap year consulting service in the United States, says in a *New York Times* article, "We mainly work with students, but we see an increasing number of older adults who aren't completely retired. They're looking for a new direction and asking themselves what they want to do for the rest of their lives."

Yet almost all the resources associated with helping people plan and execute their gap years are still directed toward young adults who want to apprentice in a craft, experience voluntourism, or just travel like a global nomad (possibly staying in a few affordable Airbnb homes along the way). Furthermore, only 12 percent of US employers offer unpaid sabbatical leaves, so the only opportunity midlifers often have to take this time is in between employment.

As I was writing this book, and talking with friends my age about how they planned to spend their next few decades, I was amazed by both the level of angst that exists around how to finance retirement, and the sense of bewilderment about how to feel relevant again pre-retirement. As one person said, "In my early forties, my employer implicitly told me to 'butt out' of decision-making because my knowledge was too old-school. That 'bummed' me out. Then, I felt progressively 'burned out' because I was working hard but not feeling engaged. Then, my employer 'bought me out' with severance during a bad year for the company. And, now, I'm ready to 'bust out' to figure out what's next for me. I wish there was a place I could go to figure this out. I'm so wired, I'm tired."

Butt out, bum out, burn out, buy out, bust out . . . what about bliss out? Epiphany. What if I created a Modern Elder Academy, the first of its kind in the world, where people mostly forty-five to sixty-five could experience a rite of passage and initiation into this new era? A place where midlife caterpillars turned into Modern Elder butterflies. A place where people could experience the JODO (Joy of Dropping Out) instead of the FOMO (Fear of Missing Out). A place where people could share stories of what brought them to this midlife atrium along with their dreams for where to go next. A place where new skills could be cultivated—with classes and lectures on everything from starting a new business, to self-esteem and self-care techniques, to understanding technology better, to just getting clearer on what gives meaning to this stage of life. Never underestimate the value of wisdom and curiosity, especially when it's offered in a safe crucible of people with shared experience.

The first Modern Elder Academy opened in beta mode in January 2018 in El Pescadero, Baja Sur California, just one hour north of Cabo San Lucas, Mexico. The foundational pillars of the program derive from this book: evolve, learn, collaborate, counsel. Attendees receive a certificate in "Mindset Management," which includes skills that can be meaningful at any juncture in life, particularly this one. The Academy's mission is to inspire the ability to reframe a lifetime of experience and recognize one's mastery, relevance, and value in the modern workplace. More information is available at www.modernelderacademy.org.

You can probably imagine a trip in your car that takes one tank of gas. The model of a three-stage life taught us that this is a one-tank journey, so we can find ourselves running on fumes as we realize it takes two tanks of fuel to propel us to a fulfilling lifelong journey. Especially as we're going to live a decade or two longer than expected. The Academy is meant to be a refueling pit stop where you just might experience a "Baja-Aha!" as well as an architectural blueprint for how to create your own midlife atrium. Whether you can make it to the Modern Elder Academy or not, creating a community of like-minded people your age—who can share their stories, fears, dreams, and plans—is one of the most effective means you have for rebuilding your confidence and finding your joy as you embark on this next chapter of your life and career.

QUESTIONS TO CONSIDER:

1. Does your career feel like a run-on sentence? Or even a jail sentence? How could you take a pause to consider your options and connect with a community of people who get what you're going through and can support your continued learning and growth?
2. Can you create a community of people who want to experience the shared "Joy of Dropping Out" and help one another get clearer about what really matters at this time in their lives?

REWIRING MEANS RECONNECTING

If this chapter has taught you anything, it's that you have multiple options but those rewiring options require reconnecting with yourself, with others, and definitely with those younger than you. If you're looking to stay relevant as a Modern Elder, you'll need to know where mastery is firmly embedded in your toolbox. You'll need to connect with others whether it's like Ben Davis tapping into his collaboration skills to create one-of-a-kind pieces of public art, or like Diane Flynn, who's helping women coming back into the workplace to learn from one another. Whether it's connecting with new people facing the same circumstances or reconnecting with those you've known since childhood, you have likely already amassed quite a network of relationships to support you. But you have to be willing to call on it.

And, let's not forget, you'll also likely need to reconnect with those younger than you—a group that may include your next boss. It's time for us to overcome the generational biases against things like younger colleagues' lingo, tattoos, clothing, or hairstyles. A lot of us over fifty are still very "square" (a favorite old boomer term) about this kind of stuff. Just remember that people of your parents' generation probably made unfair assumptions about you, too, and that you can be a cultural anthropologist in a new habitat by turning fear and judgment into curiosity and growth.

Imagine yourself at age one hundred looking back on your life to right now. Imagine you're blessed with 20/20 vision for the last few decades of your life. You can see the forks in the road and the choices you've made. In hindsight, it may seem obvious where you should have explored a little more, when you might have said a wholehearted yes to that path that scared you.

But, now at one hundred, you don't have the opportunity for a "do-over" and that leads to a little (or more than a little) regret. Two of the saddest words in the English language are "if only." Author Frederic M. Hudson says our middle age is the time between foolishness and wisdom, without much character on its own. And yet, this is the time when your character, your mastery, your sense of legacy are all forged for the second half of your journey.

Albert Schweitzer didn't live till one hundred, but he came close: when he died, in 1965, he was ninety years old. He's a person who evolved, or rewired, many times in his life. He was a concert organist who became a pastor and theological scholar. At thirty, he decided to study medicine and surgery so that he could become a medical missionary in Africa. And he gave numerous organ concerts in Europe to finance the hospital he built in French Equatorial Africa, now known as Gabon. All the while, he was a philosopher in spirit and contended in his books (yes, he was an author as well) that modern civilization was in decay because it lacked the will to love. His philosophy became defined as the "reverence for life," or embracing compassion in any way you can. He earned the Nobel Peace Prize at age seventy-seven.

Schweitzer offers some midlife advice to you: "The tragedy of life is what dies inside a man while he lives." And further, "In everyone's life, at some time, our inner fire goes out. It is then burst into flame by an encounter with another human being. We should all be thankful for those people who rekindle the inner spirit." Who or what will you connect with that will rekindle your inner flame?

[9]

The Experience Dividend: Embracing Modern Elders in Organizations

"The values of youth are about possession, consumption, expression and individuality; the values that underpin dignity in age and death are about relationships, connectedness, sharing and participation—far more powerful drivers for social change."
—BRITISH AUTHOR CHARLES LEADBEATER

―――――

"But is she a culture fit?"

Not long ago, a younger male friend from another tech company asked me this loaded question when I recommended a woman in her late forties for a job. While I believe his intention—to determine whether she would effectively fit in with their unique company culture—was sincere, he could just as easily have asked, "Is she the kind of 'bro' you want to grab a beer with?" In the past decade, hundreds of leadership books have extolled the virtues of investing in corporate culture, so it's not surprising that this seemingly harmless question sneaks its way into recruiting interviews and corporate recruiting processes all over the world. But, perhaps too often, it's code for, "We hire people like me." So, whether it's gender, race, or age, it's a form of unconscious bias that can lead to homogenous cultures—which is why we've done our best to strike it from the conversation about recruitment candidates at Airbnb.

Fortunately, given the well-publicized cultural meltdowns of too many young tech companies, this has become a forbidden question or comment in framing a candidate's prospects for joining many companies. More often, today, the question is whether the person might be a "culture add" or a "core values fit"—a decided improvement assuming the values don't carry any unconscious bias in them.

PricewaterhouseCoopers (PwC) used to bill itself as "the place to work for millennials" with a "strikingly young" workforce. The firm's unabashedly direct appeal for youth landed them in court with a class action lawsuit. In the relentless pursuit of the young that helps them feel like they're shoring up their DQ (digital intelligence), many companies have put themselves at risk not just of lawsuits, but of creating exclusionary workplaces that marginalize women, minorities, and, yes, middle-aged workers.

Many companies have admirably focused resources on becoming more diverse and inclusive when it comes to gender and race, but too many are laggards when it comes to age. In a 2015 survey of global CEOs, PwC found that 64 percent of companies have a formal diversity and inclusiveness strategy and 85 percent of CEOs think it's improved their bottom line. However, only 8 percent of the 64 percent include age as a dimension of their strategy. At a time when labor shortages are emerging, due in part to new restrictive immigration policies, while there simultaneously exists a demographically aging workforce that declares they want to delay retirement, it's shocking to see so few company leaders think expansively age-wise about how they can attract and retain both the smartest and the wisest.

Equally puzzling is that most companies don't have a longevity strategy, a comprehensive plan that makes them a model employer for the fastest-growing demographic in the workplace population: employees fifty and above. But, mark my words, just like the Industrial Revolution led to the creation of a whole new set of workplace laws and standards more than a hundred years ago, the Longevity Revolution—that is the phenomenon of more and more people living to one hundred—will usher in a new set of age-agnostic laws and principles that will define the twenty-first-century workplace. The companies that will flourish will be those that proactively create this new Modern-Elder-friendly workplace before their competitors.

But unfortunately, too many employers are as ambivalent about older workers as Bert Jacobs was about me outing myself as a Modern Elder at the start of this book. Their ambivalence is often the result of a series of myths and stereotypes with little evidence behind them. So much of our thinking about productivity is stuck in an industrial-era model. As in, companies calculate how many widgets a worker can produce in an eight-hour shift, for the least amount of labor cost, without factoring in the positive spillover effects of the "invisible productivity" that a dollop of wisdom offers the workplace.

Organizations need to build job descriptions for Modern Elders that take into account this "Experience Dividend": the holistic positive effect that experienced leaders can have on those in their orbit. This book has thus far outlined the value and virtues of diverse cultures and how pairing wise Modern Elders with smart and ambitious millennials can lead to symbiotic results. This chapter is for the CEOs, HR leaders, and others who help write the recipe book for recruiting in their company who want to reap the myriad benefits of a multigenerational workforce.

If you are one of them, the ball is in your court.

DEBUNKING AGEIST STEREOTYPES

Before we talk about how managers and companies can create the kinds of policies and organizational cultures in which Modern Elders can thrive, let's explode a few of the myths and stereotypes about older workers, which are getting in the way of them being hired or retained. The following is based on the extensive research of academics Richard Posthuma and Michael Campion and others.

1. **Poor Performers and Less Engaged:** *Older workers have lower abilities, especially with technology, are less motivated, work more slowly, and are less productive than younger workers.* A variety of research indicates this is false for two reasons: (a) Job performance doesn't often decline with age. In fact, it often improves, especially if you measure it holistically with respect to the effect on teams; (b) There is much more variation in performance between employees based on differences in skill or health than across age. Additionally, data from Aon Hewitt and Gallup indicate that workers who are fifty-five and older are more engaged and motivated than younger workers, with 65 percent of workers in this demographic scoring high on measures of engagement, compared to 60 percent of workers overall. In fact, no other age group has as high a level of engagement as older workers. (The study defines engagement as consistently speaking positively about the employer, having an intense desire to be part of the organization, and exerting an extra effort to contribute to business success. You want workers like these, right?)

2. **Resistant to Change:** *Older workers are harder to train, less adaptable, less flexible, and more resistant to change. As a result, older workers will provide a lower return on investment on things such as training and will not adapt well to shifts in procedure or management.* Researchers Posthuma and Campion found no compelling evidence that this was the case. In fact, the study by Zenger and Folkman cited in chapter 4

found that older workers feel more confident and therefore are more open to feedback. Some of this perceived resistance to change is a self-fulfilling prophecy, since many corporate training programs exclude longtime employees or older workers, as their focus is more on the new hires and the young.

3. **Less Able to Learn:** *Older workers are slower and have a lower ability to learn—particularly when it comes to technology— and, therefore, less potential for professional development.* Research is mixed on the validity of this stereotype, but there is reliable evidence that older workers learn new information somewhat more slowly than younger workers partly because they already have more knowledge in their brains. There is some compelling evidence that older workers might learn better from different training methods than those used with younger workers. The key is to evaluate learning agility or the capacity to learn and be open to new concepts, which is essential in a constantly changing environment. What's irrefutable is that with age, the brain's two hemispheres become more in sync, facilitating "lateral thinking"—our ability to synthesize and make connections between far-flung ideas, which can help with problem solving.

4. **Shorter Tenure:** *Older workers won't "last" as long (due to health issues or voluntary retirement) and therefore provide fewer years during which the employer can reap the benefits of recruiting and training investments.* Research indicates this is false. Older workers are less likely to quit than younger workers and therefore actually have similar job tenures. Aon Hewitt's database revealed that nearly half of employees under fifty say they would consider another job offer or are actively looking. In contrast, fewer than three in ten workers over fifty say they're job hunting or open to offers. With the cost of turn-

over estimated to be $8K to $30K per employee, hiring and retaining older workers can benefit a company's bottom line.

5. **More Costly:** *Older workers cost more because they receive higher wages, use health benefits more, and are closer to retirement.* There is no compelling research on validity, but there is some indication that older workers do have slightly higher wages though it's correlated more with experience in the job—and therefore value to the employer—than age. But the money-saving effect of their lower rates of absenteeism helps offset this. Plus, some older workers actually prefer to move to part-time status at a lower level of compensation if their employer allows this flextime benefit. And in the tech industry, data shows that earnings peak at age forty-five and go down from there.

6. **Less Trusting:** *Older workers are less willing/able to trust coworkers and instigate more conflicts than younger workers.* False. A wealth of research shows that young and old workers demonstrate the same willingness to trust, but older workers are actually better able to regulate their emotions and resolve interpersonal problems more effectively. But surveys have shown older workers care more about fairness so, as an employer, you may need to show more transparency.

7. **Less Healthy:** *Older workers are less healthy than younger workers, and they therefore are less productive, more likely to take sick days, and more likely to incur higher health-care costs.* False. Older and younger workers are equally healthy (both physically and psychologically), at least day to day. And, in fact, on average, older workers take less time off than younger workers. And, because health-care costs are substantially affected by the number of dependents on the family insurance policy, an older single worker or "empty nest" couple may have lower

health-care costs than a young family. Plus, for those working later in life, Medicare can cover workers at age sixty-five.

8. **Work-Family Imbalance:** *Older workers have a harder time balancing work and personal life and therefore are more likely to prioritize family over work.* False. Older and younger workers experience the same amount of push and pull between work and family and report similar levels of balance.

What's troubling is that older adults actually endorse these ageist stereotypes more than younger adults. So how can we banish these misconceptions both in ourselves and in our workplaces? First, we simply need to be aware of our biases and recognize when they are bubbling to the surface. Here, even small semantic shifts can help; if I'd changed each of those stereotypes listed above to "Experienced workers" instead of "Older workers," it might have altered one's perception of their bias. The truth is, *Older* workers are typically more *Experienced* workers.

Second, those in positions of leadership need to adopt and model practices to educate employees—of all ages—on the value of older workers and create a culture of respect and inclusion, instead of ageism. As the management professor Peter Cappelli and coauthor of the book *Managing the Older Worker* says, "Every aspect of job performance gets better as we age. I thought the picture might be more mixed, but it isn't. The juxtaposition between the superior performance of older workers and the discrimination against them in the workplace just really makes no sense." Other academics may quarrel with the word "Every" at the start of this quote, but there's a growing sentiment among researchers that we've undervalued the experience of older workers the past few decades.

If employers can reverse their ageist practices and create a workplace where older workers are celebrated rather than sidelined, this mixture of experience and youth can foster higher productivity, profits, and innovation. In return, older workers will have to let go of their attachment to status and, at times, start thinking of themselves as an intern as much as a mentor. Remember, wisdom is most powerful when it is exchanged freely across the generations.

TOP 10 PRACTICES FOR BECOMING AN AGE-FRIENDLY EMPLOYER

Drumroll, please. I'm going to offer you my countdown of employer practices that can create a competitive advantage for you in attracting and retaining experienced employees. We start with some of the easier practices and move toward those that are more impactful as we zero in on number one.

10. BECOME DATA-CENTRIC WHEN IT COMES TO UNDERSTANDING YOUR WORKFORCE

If you are like most employers, you likely keep data (usually private) about the various demographics of your workforce. But what do you do with that data? And what additional information might be helpful to understanding the state of mind (or body) of the various age segments of your workers? Have you examined health and absentee data across age groups in order to proactively support good health strategies? Have you looked at the extent to which your company is or isn't diverse when it comes to age? Sometimes, racial and gender diversity issues are more obvious because the visual evidence is more easily discernible. But no one wears a pin on his or her shirt that states their age, so age profile data may be necessary to help you explore demographic challenges.

San Francisco–based team collaboration software company Atlassian is in the business of helping companies understand the value of demographic diversity on company effectiveness. They've shown that team performance can increase by 58 percent with the introduction of a diverse team member, and yet, they realized, their own company diversity reports didn't cover subjects like age diversity—nor did they analyze the actual level of collaboration that happens at a team level. So Atlassian chose to sing from its own hymnal and release data not just on companywide age diversity, but also on how those belonging to underrepresented groups were spread across the company's teams. In 2016, they released data that shows how many women, people over forty, and members of racial or ethnic minorities were on each team within the company.

Another issue worth exploring through data is in the area of employee satisfaction. Some companies have found that while they are struggling to fill the recruiting pipeline with younger employees, their experienced, long-tenured employees are feeling neglected. Smart companies work to prevent this by slicing and dicing their annual or quarterly employee satisfaction data to determine engagement, happiness, and risk of departure among their various age cohorts. The more enlightened companies ask their employees about how flextime policies or staged retirement plans might meet the needs of their more experienced workers. But truly great companies move beyond the data-gathering exercise to create meaningful change. What we measure matters only to the extent it helps leaders to set benchmarks that can be embedded in future corporate goals. The more you communicate those goals externally—say by posting them on the company website—it shows how publicly committed you are to creating a more diverse and inclusive workplace. Consider taking the Mercer Age Ready Checklist test to determine how many different age-friendly programs you currently offer, and how that stacks up against other companies: https://survey.mercer.com/Survey.aspx?s =2c381537060843c3a66bdc5f1647d537.

9. CREATE AN INTERNAL AFFINITY GROUP BASED ON AGE

In her midsixties, Gretchen Addi was surrounded by fellow employees the age of her own children at the celebrated global design firm IDEO. Gretchen already stood out among her youthful colleagues when she joined the company in her late forties and then went through a series of life experiences that many of her coworkers didn't necessarily understand, like taking care of her elderly parents, which seemed only to distance her further. She felt respected by the company, which was enlightened enough to allow her to bring on board ninety-year-old designer Barbara Beskind for a series of projects focused on creating tech products for older people. And yet, Gretchen acknowledged that at times she felt lonely and a little isolated because she had no formal venue for sharing her experiences of being an older worker in the "land of the young."

Gretchen is not alone. I've heard stories like these again and again, from friends, former colleagues, and readers. At Airbnb alone I've had private conversations with at least a dozen employees over the age of forty who enjoyed working in the company but felt like social outcasts because their idea of bonding with teammates wasn't going out after work for karaoke night. Fortunately, these conversations inspired two of my colleagues—Elizabeth Bohannon and Desirree Madison-Biggs—to take a bold step in creating one of the first age-based Employee Resource Groups (ERGs) at a sizable Silicon Valley tech firm. The group, called Wisdom@Airbnb, is open to any employees over the age of forty—plus anyone else committed to the goal of an age-friendly workplace.

Groups like these can be an invaluable source of mutual support and mentorship that improves quality of life for this demographic of workers. And, in helping to make those workers feel more valued and included, these groups can have a huge positive effect on the overall culture of the company. And yet, while 90 percent of Fortune 500 companies have ERGs, only a tiny fraction have an affinity group serving their older demographic. Kudos to MasterCard for their Workers With Accumulated Value Experience (WWAVE) group, Aetna for their BoomERGroup, American Express for their Generations Employee Network, and Bank of America/Merrill Lynch for their Intergenerational Network. And hats off to our fellow tech companies who have followed suit with ERGs like Uber Sage and Google Greyglers.

For such a group to be effective, it generally needs to: (a) connect the mission to a business challenge so the group doesn't feel frivolous or extraneous; (b) offer a tangible benefit to the employees to attract and retain members; (c) create clear goals and a clear definition of success; and (d) include senior leaders as sponsors to show the company is serious in its commitment. With Wisdom@Airbnb, one of the first things we did was issue a mission statement. It was: "to raise awareness of the value of cross-generational connection at work and throughout our community (including the Airbnb host and guest community). We will help Airbnb become a model organization for the 21st century where age is embraced like any other diversity, and mature employees feel valued for their experience, wisdom, knowledge, and guidance."

You can easily replicate this model in virtually any organization, and you may be surprised by how easy it is to get buy-in from your colleagues. When Wisdom@Airbnb was first introduced companywide in the summer of 2017, it was expected that maybe twenty to forty employees would sign up, but within a couple of months there were over a hundred, making it one of the largest ERGs in the company. How about creating a Wisdom@ group in your company? I've created a Wisdom@ affinity group tool kit you can download at www .WisdomAtWorkBook.com.

8. STUDY BEST PRACTICES OF OTHER EMPLOYERS

You don't have to reinvent the wheel. There are a variety of sources of great information for what other companies are doing to create a workplace full of intergenerational reciprocity. Ruth Finkelstein is the dynamo and driving force behind Columbia University's Age Boom Academy and directs the Age Smart Employer Awards program. You can review the annual winners of these New York City–focused awards to create a checklist of age-friendly policy options to consider: whether it's providing support for employees caring for aging relatives or setting up older worker apprentice programs or creating specific training for skill gaps for long-term workers.

Peter Cappelli and Bill Novelli's book, *Managing the Older Worker*, is full of best practices from diverse companies, like CVS Pharmacy's "snowbirding" program, which offers part-time older workers from the Northeast the opportunity to work winter jobs in Florida (when there's more need for staff due to the vacation area being inundated with visitors). The Conference Board's Mature Workforce Initiative offers a database of best practices on topics like succession planning for older workers, how to train young line managers to manage long-time employees, and age-friendly approaches to recruiting.

7. HAVE YOUR CEO HIGHLIGHT THE IMPORTANCE OF AGE DIVERSITY

Aaron Levie, thirty-one, is the cofounder and CEO of the enterprise cloud company Box and one of the more high-profile millennial leaders of a company worth more than $1 billion. At Salesforce's large annual conference, Dreamforce, Levie took a public stance on age diversity when he said onstage that mixing younger and more experienced employees creates a healthy, effective dynamic. "You always want to be able to have that kind of tension, where you have people that have seen it before and you have some new and fresh ideas, and you're trying to blend those two together—that's when you get real disruptive innovation."

Levie recognizes that Box benefits from having some grayhairs on staff—people who used to be employed at companies like Oracle and thus understand the legacy sales process of enterprise customers— but he pairs them with young idealists. Levie continues, "What's really important for the experienced individuals is to understand that the reason they're joining a start-up is to do it differently. In our case, as we were going in and disrupting the content management software industry, we have hired a handful of leaders that had experience in that market, but understood that it was being reinvented for the cloud and mobile." Much like what I needed to remember as a longtime hotel exec at Airbnb.

UK's Oxford University spinout Animal Dynamics is run by cofounder and CEO Alex Caccia, who is quick to note how much he loves the fact that nearly a quarter of their engineers and consultants are sixty-five or older, which creates a more relaxed and mature working environment. He cites an engineer who was turning seventy and remembered a paper he'd read from the 1950s that had an analogous design issue. Alex told me, "It's so inspiring for younger engineers to see those a few decades older who are still curious and turned on by interesting questions and puzzles. It helps you realize this work can be a calling, not just a way to make a quick buck from an IPO."

Airbnb CEO Brian Chesky has been publicly vocal about the fact that our most effective home-sharing hosts happen to be single women over the age of sixty, which is a bit of a surprise for a company that symbolizes the new millennial sharing economy. He also was a big supporter of the idea of bringing Michael and Debbie Campbell, crowned the "Senior Nomads" by the *New York Times* for having been guests at so many various Airbnb's around the world, to our headquarters for a ten-week senior internship on the "voice of the customer." When senior leaders in a company, especially younger tech CEOs, embrace age diversity internally and externally, it sends a positive contagion into the world that encourages other leaders to do the same.

6. CREATE THE CONDITIONS FOR MENTORING AND REVERSE MENTORING TO FLOURISH

Intergenerational alliance is at the heart of a culture that prizes its Modern Elders. It requires switching up the physics so that wisdom flows in both directions—sometimes from old to young, and sometimes uphill from young to old. Quite often, as you read in earlier chapters, this uphill transfer of wisdom means helping digital natives to educate those forty and older about how to use their smartphone more effectively, or the ins and outs of new social media sites. "Millennials, after all, grew up with computers, and they are 'natural consultants,'" said Debra Arbit, chief executive of BridgeWorks, which helps companies deal with generational differences. In the *New York Times*, she was quoted as saying, "America's younger workers have already been personal technology consultants in their own families, so it's a role they're very comfortable playing."

Sometimes companies formalize these programs as Jack Welch did when General Electric became the first company to publicize its reverse mentoring programs nearly two decades ago. The Hartford insurance company's Reverse Mentoring Initiative is so successful that it led to two patents being written and filed due to this multigenerational collaboration. Barclays Bank in the UK created its Bolder Apprenticeship program for workers over fifty who want to be retrained in newer technologies by those younger than them. Huntington Ingalls Industries, the largest military shipbuilding company in the country, offers intergenerational mentoring programs for its age-diverse workforce (38 percent of its 22,000 employees are baby boomers, 40 percent are millennials, and 20 percent are Generation

Xers), and admits employees of any age into its accredited Apprentice School. And after IBM recently identified areas of the company where massive attrition could happen due to retirements, the company's response was to create "mentoring pools" for six-month relationships to help accelerate the process of deepening institutional wisdom.

From my perspective, bridge building between generations is most effective when it's informal and baked into the company's values and culture, as it feels more organic and less like an arranged marriage. I've found that mutual mentoring—where I'm learning from a millennial about one topic and they're learning from me on a different one—creates a more dynamic and interesting relationship. My strength may be their weakness and vice versa. One of the ways companies can foster this kind of relationship is by connecting those just joining the company with "new hire buddies"—and encouraging new hires to choose a buddy who is likely to be from a different generation. Given that those who volunteer to be a buddy in the first place are likely to have a growth or learning mindset, this is likely to result in ripe connections that could last years. Liz Wiseman writes in her book *Rookie Smarts: Why Learning Beats Knowing in the New Game of Work* that Intel has created an intranet to provide mentoring matchmaking options across state lines and national boundaries based upon the shared interests of the participants.

5. HELP EMPLOYEES ACHIEVE A FINANCIALLY SECURE RETIREMENT

Do you prepare your employees for the financial and social implications of retirement? Very few companies have adapted their employee education to meet the evolving needs of an aging workforce. In a Transamerica Center for Retirement Studies annual review of employer plans and employee needs published in August 2017, 81 percent of companies say they support their employees working past age sixty-five, and 69 percent of employers know their employees have to work past sixty-five because they haven't saved enough to meet retirement needs. Yet only 31 percent of these companies offer full- to part-time flexibility as an option. And only 27 percent encourage employees to participate in succession planning for how they can financially ease into retirement. Many employers don't extend 401(k) benefits to part-time employees. Clearly there's a mismatch between what employers know and what they offer their employees, even though employers see longtime workers as a great source of training and part-time peak demand support for the company. This is particularly true of smaller companies who are three times less likely than larger companies to feel any responsibility for helping their employees achieve a financially secure retirement.

Luckily, there is a win-win path here: a gradual withdrawal from the workplace is often the best solution, financially and emotionally, for loyal, longtime employees, and a flexible work arrangement is usually at the top of the list of what preretirees want from their employer. It's also a great way for an employer to ensure longtime institutionalized knowledge isn't walking out the door each month based upon traditional "cold turkey" retirement. There are a wide variety of best practices to solve this: whether sponsoring innovative preretirement programs that help retirees know they can be an "alumni" worker during seasonal peak periods; or, as employers like Steelcase and Scripps Healthcare have done, create intentionally phased-retirement plans that manage retirement funds to effectively allow a part-time worker to earn a full salary and benefits; or give employees the option of transitioning into programs like Encore.org that allow them to earn money and apply their mastery at nonprofits and social enterprises.

4. DEVELOP PROGRAMS TO HIRE OLDER WORKERS

For those looking for an alarming demographic window into the future, study Japan, where their unemployment rate is below 3 percent and companies have had to reduce operating hours, services offered, or delayed expansion as a result of their labor shortages. Faced with high employee turnover and not enough qualified candidates to hire, a growing number of companies are prioritizing experience and older workers' skills in hiring and promotions and shifting some of their college recruitment investment to programs that target the fifty-plus crowd. There are also recruitment agencies that are starting to specialize in older workers. The advantages accrued are many: more efficient recruiting since applicants are more likely to accept an offer (because they are actually interested in the job and aren't just "floating" their résumés), a larger pool of educated workers who aren't looking for greener pastures, emotionally intelligent team members (sometimes with strong leadership and advisory skills), an abundance of mentors and role models, and openness to flexibility in schedule during slower times. And these are just a few of a myriad of positives for a company.

Many companies are also actively recruiting retirees or semi-retirees for part-time or seasonal work, and this goes well beyond roles like museum guide or crossing guard that one might stereotypically associate with older workers. For example, as America's most dominant online retailer, Amazon often faces significant staffing shortages during seasonal and holiday peaks. With approximately one-third of the company's business occurring in the fourth quarter, their staffing needs were far outstripping their steady manpower, so about ten years ago, the company developed a clever initiative called "CamperForce" (profiled in a September 14, 2017, article in *Wired* magazine) that taps into the nomadic retiree population who travel America by RV. These mobile RVers perfectly suited the on-demand needs of Amazon, so CamperForce recruiters went on scouting missions in more than a dozen states, setting up recruiting tables at popular RV destinations like Yellowstone National Park and the motor home mecca of Quartzsite, Arizona, where tens of thousands of RVers camp in the desert each winter.

Other companies, like Michelin, create "Retire and Rehire" programs that offer longtime employees (typically after the age of sixty-five) the opportunity to take on some seasonal work after retirement, and there exist a number of job banks like Seniorbank.org that match employers with part-time (and full-time) workers in their fifties, sixties, and seventies.

Pitney Bowes, the mail systems company headquartered in Connecticut, hires full-time workers year-round, not seasonally, and nearly 20 percent of them are over the age of fifty. For all of the reasons I've outlined in the book, Pitney Bowes has targeted older workers as a ripe recruiting demographic. As outlined in the book *Managing the Older Worker*, the company has a "My Next Phase" program to help workers think about their transitions, and their Retirement Education Assistance Program helps those over forty-five pay for classes on retirement planning. Pitney Bowes doesn't do this to win awards from organizations like the AARP Foundation, even though they have. They do it because it's smart business.

3. RETHINK YOUR DEFINITION OF PRODUCTIVITY AND CREATE 20 PERCENT TIME FOR MODERN ELDERS

We still have an industrial-era mentality toward productivity: how many quality widgets an employee can produce quickly for the lowest potential overhead cost. In some companies, this penalizes loyal, experienced workers who've accumulated many salary increases over a long period of time. Yet their impact on productivity may well be far more comprehensive than the number of "widgets" they are producing. There's growing data showing that the presence of older workers increases productivity of younger workers *and* reduces their likely turnover, due to the elders' advice and guidance. And (unsurprisingly given their capacity for collaboration) in surveys of a wide range of employees, older workers tend to answer yes more often to the question "Did you help anybody at work today?" as compared to younger workers. So it's time for us to find a metric to capture the value-add of experienced workers.

While it's difficult to develop productivity measurement tools that capture these effects, there are some proxies that consider the collateral team benefits of older workers. For one, your employee satisfaction surveys might ask questions about which team members were most valuable for team performance. Some companies ask their employees to stack-rank their team members from most collaborative to least and you could even use employee surveys to help identify Modern Elders who've become informal counselors by asking something like "Who in the company—outside of your direct boss or a team member—do you look to for helpful advice?" or "Who in the company is a role model for wisdom?"

Due to the positive spillover effects of Modern Elders on their younger coworkers, I think it's time we take a page out of Google's playbook, specifically their now-legendary 20 percent rule. Given the engineering-driven culture of the company, and the fact that innovations often happen when an engineer explores a passion project in the context of their work, Google popularized the idea of providing approved technical staff to dedicate 20 percent of their time on exploratory projects of their choosing. Why not offer qualified Modern Elders in your organization 20 percent time to dedicate to the role of being an adviser to younger leaders, helping to guide their growth and effectiveness? In some cases, an in-house coach who understands the unique company dynamics and is there every workday may be far more effective than a coach who only comes to the office every other week or once a month. *Training Magazine* reported that corporate coaching and mentoring was cited by HR leaders as being the most effective of twenty-one different training modalities offered in most larger companies. But external coaches also represent more than $1 billion in annual corporate spending. Could you shave your budget a little while also providing a new, enriched career path for some of your more experienced leaders?

Of course, all kinds of details need to be considered here and you will need to provide training and tools to set these internal coaches up for success, but the chances are that many of these workers are performing a part-time nonofficial advisory role already. Upon reflection, let me just say, I would likely have stayed longer in a full-time capacity at Airbnb if my workload had been reduced 20 percent to take into account the role I outlined in chapter 7 as the company librarian and confidant.

2. ADAPT TO AN AGING WORKFORCE

The numbers don't lie. In 2002, 24.6 percent of the US workforce was fifty or older. That grew to 32.3 percent by 2012. It will likely be at 35.4 percent by 2022 and probably closer to 40 percent one decade later, as more workers are staying full-time employed longer and a growing number of workers expect to work part-time into their seventies. What are you doing as an employer to adapt to this trend by ensuring that your workplace is conducive and comfortable to older people? And, with 40 percent of US employers reporting difficulty in filling jobs, how are you evolving your existing workforce in ways that make you less reliant on new hires while also allowing you to take advantage of this growing pool of experienced workers? Have you considered job rotation or shadowing programs that allow your current employees to ease into new positions?

For inspiration, we can look to other countries like Germany who've had to adapt sooner than the US due to the accelerated aging of their workforce. In 2007, the managers of a BMW plant in Southern Bavaria faced the fact that the projected average age of their workforce would increase from thirty-nine to forty-seven over the next decade. So these BMW leaders decided to test how a 2017 production line would operate a decade into the future; everything from mixing teams to ensure generational diversity to installing a collection of ergonomics better addressing older worker needs: better seats and workbenches, brighter lights, more of a cushioned flooring, and easier-to-read computer screens. They also offered workshops giving the older workers the opportunity to explain what was most important to them and what conditions would facilitate their best work. This led to a 7 percent productivity improvement, fewer defects, and healthier workers just through adaptation of workspaces, more training on health and safety, and improved relations within teams.

Similarly, the Swiss retailer Migros—which employs one in every one hundred people as the country's largest retailer—retrains employees for jobs that better suit their age. For example, rather than firing a warehouse worker in her midsixties who has trouble exerting herself physically as the job requires—Migros might simply move her into a more stationary customer service relations position that doesn't require as much standing up. Similarly, Marriott's Flex Options for Hourly Workers program helps older workers transition out of physically taxing roles by teaching them new skills on the job.

Finally, as documented in multiple places in this book, one of the fundamental ways employers can adapt to the changing demographics of their workplace is by formalizing the role of coach or mentor. For example, my friend Karen Wickre tells me about a longtime senior executive assistant (EA) who became a paid mentor and advocate for a large group of EAs in one sizable company. And apprenticeship programs not only offer Modern Elders a way to pass their skills, wisdom, and institutional knowledge on to the next generation, they also ensure that wisdom and knowledge will continue to live on in the company once that person does retire.

The future is here. It's time to create positions that give you an even higher ROI on Modern Elders' mastery by allowing them to share it with others.

1. CREATE A LONGEVITY STRATEGY FOR YOUR EMPLOYEES AND CUSTOMERS

Let me be blunt. Most companies are stuck in the twentieth century when it comes to thinking about their workforce or customer life cycles. As mentioned earlier in the chapter, only 8 percent of companies that have a diversity and inclusion strategy have developed that strategy more expansively beyond gender and race/ethnic demographics to include age. Clearly, these companies haven't read this book yet. But you have. And it's time for you to create a comprehensive corporate longevity strategy.

What's a longevity strategy? Think of another burgeoning business opportunity, like the growing middle class in Asia. If you're a global company and you haven't developed an Asian strategy, you'd be considered foolish. Similarly, when it comes to the fact that an extra decade of living means workers staying in their jobs longer and customers spending money on midlife purchases later in their life, what innovations can you offer to older employees or customers that set you apart from your competitors?

Developing a plan to offer a graceful exit for your experienced workers isn't enough. Recruitment, retention, and engagement can move from the tactical to the strategic for your HR team. This book is full of examples of practices and programs you could incorporate into your plan. According to a 2014 Society for Human Resource Management survey of HR professionals, only 6 percent say they have

actually implemented comprehensive policies and practices associated with an aging workforce. Yet 73 percent of HR professionals see
the retirement or departure of older workers as a "crisis," "problem,"
or "potential problem" in the next decade or two.

Moreover, how is your marketing team rethinking the lifetime
value of your core customers if they're going to live a decade or two
longer than past generations? No doubt, older employees understand
older customers. I saw it at Airbnb when some millennial designers suggested that "no one uses laptops anymore" so we should only
design for a mobile format, but I knew our older hosts live and die by
their laptop and desktop computers because the font size on mobile
can be daunting. I'm proud that Airbnb, considered to be a millennial
poster child as a company, has thought through our relationship with
hosts and guests so much so that it's influenced how we market to *all*
of them—not just those under forty. And we're proud that our most
effective hosts globally are those over the age of fifty.

The bottom line is: your longevity strategy isn't just a feel-good
measure; it's good business strategy.

IS AGING YOUR COMPANY'S BLIND SPOT?

I spent my thirties worried about my growing bald spot. Unfortunately, many millennial business leaders may be more focused on
their own bald spots than on their company's blind spot. Young
founders and leaders don't think about their older workers all that
often. Maybe it's because they're a reminder of their parents. Or their
mortality. Maybe it's because they don't have any context for understanding midlife or beyond. Maybe it's because when diversity comes
up as a topic, it's so much cooler and politically correct to champion
gender or racial diversity first. It only seems fair; I mean, let's be
honest, older people got their shot when they were younger and yet,

women and people of color have rarely been part of the ruling class. Plus, ageism is a relatively new phenomenon so let's get those other two institutional biases solved first.

This is zero-sum thinking. Unconscious bias, left unchecked in any form, can multiply and spread like a cancer. When people have the narrow point of view that "I want to work with and sell to people like me," it's a slippery slope from a well-meaning "Is she a culture fit?" to systemic exclusion and discrimination. Unless you plan to have just one employee—yourself—then you and your company need to be more expansive in your inclusive thinking. I'm hoping, now that you've read this chapter, you realize that the "Experience Dividend" is real and available to you. So what are you waiting for?

[10]

The Age of the Sage

"I am still every age that I have been. Because I was once a child, I am always a child. Because I was once a searching adolescent, given to moods and ecstasies, these are still part of me, and always will be. Because I was once a rebellious student, there is and always will be in me the student crying out for reform. This does not mean that I ought to be trapped or enclosed in any of these ages, but that they are in me to be drawn on; to forget is a form of suicide; my past is part of what makes the present Madeleine and must not be denied or rejected or forgotten."

—MADELEINE L'ENGLE

———

"Does this beard age me?"

"No, darling, it sages you," was my friend Vanda's response after seeing me for the first time with a face full of Hemingway-like gray whiskers. It was the summer of 2016, not long after my Tulum speech, and I'd moved from full-time to part-time with Airbnb. Feeling both younger and wiser than I'd felt in years, I was just back from a couple of weeks in Baja where I had been starting to mentally compost what it means to be a Modern Elder. I'd always tried to hide my gray—maybe from myself as much as anyone else—but now, I was owning it. Maybe a little gray hair is the Modern Elder's way of announcing their earned wisdom to the world. We age in public, but our true gifts are often private, deeply concealed in our heart and soul.

I write books and give speeches primarily because both help me to make sense of my life. Only then can I (hopefully) impart whatever wisdom is gleaned to others. I had no idea that my Airbnb sojourn would lead to a book. But, just a few years into my tenure, I became "pregnant" with the idea that a new role is emerging for Modern Elders in the workplace . . . and not a moment too soon. During my early days with the company, I was both fascinated and perplexed by what I was witnessing and encountering as a "mentern" at Airbnb—I was a jumble of feelings in search of a coherent thought. But I soon started crystallizing all I had learned, felt, and experienced, and I knew it should be shared. So I guess this book is my own way of contributing to the "sharing economy." Now, after serving up all that practical advice about how to harness and reap the benefits of wisdom at work, I want to leave you with something more heartfelt.

If you're my age, chances are you may live another thirty or forty years. And, if you're anything like me, you likely want to live a life that is as rich and meaningful as it is long. One thing I have learned is that living richly is less about the net worth on your bank statement and more about the value of the lessons you offer those who want to learn from you.

I love this delicate African proverb: "When an elder dies, it's like a library has burned down." Many indigenous communities couldn't conceive of their cultural survival without elders, much in the same way we might have a hard time imagining life without books or music or movies. In the digital era, libraries—and elders—aren't quite as popular as they used to be. But both are critical conduits for wisdom across the ages. If you keep your wisdom to yourself, it dies with you. But if you can lend your gifts of age to the next generation, that wisdom will never grow old.

The longer you've been on this planet, the more you have the opportunity to leave something behind. If we choose to be, we are all elders in the making.

WISDOM NEVER GROWS OLD

"As I listened to people's stories, I heard their yearning for reciprocity. As teachers and learners, they wanted to establish relationships of mutual benefit, of give and take. They dispensed wisdom and experience to the next generation and expected youthful insight and perspective in return."

—SARA LAWRENCE-LIGHTFOOT

It is often said that youth is wasted on the young. Does that mean wisdom is wasted on the old? It all depends on how we choose to experience the second half of life: Do we practice gratitude, or pursue gratification? Grow into our individuality, or confine ourselves to stereotypes or social norms? Strive to attain and share knowledge, or to accumulate material rewards?

"Ancora Imparo"—"I'm still learning"—was written above Michelangelo's studio door in the ninth decade of his life. We all need this reminder, don't we? Successful Wall Street trader Eli Scheier experienced his at age forty-six. With no criminal record, he ended up in a rural jail cell for twenty-four hours due to a drug possession offense and experienced a dark night of the soul. He realized he was always chasing something and yet had nothing lasting to show for it.

Eli left his big New York job and moved to Israel to tap into his inner wisdom. He tended three hundred sheep as a shepherd, studied the Kabbalah, and reconnected with what nature meant to him. Upon moving back to the US, he created an organic vegetable farm in upstate New York. He became known as "The Gardener" and he now plants seeds in people, as a yoga teacher and clinical psychologist with a specialty in spirituality for mind and body. But what sets Eli apart is the knowledge that everything the seed will become is already within it. The gardener simply creates the atmosphere for the seed to live up to its potential. Eli helps people see that there's a seed of wisdom in each one of us.

Through some fortuitous circumstances, Eli ended up moving to Tulum and attended that first talk I gave on being a Modern Elder in 2016. Nearing his midfifties, Eli could not be more content. As both a mentor and a mensch, he embodies what I talked about at the end of chapter 8: someone who helps to rekindle the inner spirit of others by tapping into his own wisdom. All of Eli's emails end with this Mayan phrase: "In Lak'ech hala Kiin" ("I am the other you"). He tells me, "Every person I meet was some person like myself at some point in my life," which reflects another hallmark of the Modern Elder . . . empathy.

Psychologist Viktor Frankl wrote, "Between stimulus and response there is a space. In that space is your power to choose your response. In your response lies your growth and your freedom." Wisdom is lodged in that space where elders can step back from the moment in order to improve their perspective. But the true power is unleashed when they choose to share that perspective with others.

Most of us come to the realization that the older we are, the less we have to prove, and the freer we are from the shackles of convention. With this freedom comes life-giving energy, an unconquerable generosity of spirit, and a profound desire to give back.

Author Allan Chinen writes that those in the second half of life are "taking the transcendental inspirations of later life and using them to help the next generation." At this age, an elder grows a metaphorical third set of teeth—the teeth of an editor who can separate the extraneous from the soul of all matters—becoming a sage who can instantly distinguish between the meaningful and the meaningless. In our daily behavior as elders, we embody the abstract truths of spirituality, let go of the petty grievances, and focus on being grateful for the inspirations in our life. This is why your voice, your spirit, and, yes, your teeth (assuming you still have them . . . chuckle, chuckle) are needed more than ever before.

DOES GREATER LONGEVITY HAVE A PURPOSE?

"Our longevity exists, has meaning, and creates value because it provides human beings with a mechanism for improving the lives of all ages. That mechanism is a pattern of reciprocal relationships that unite the generations. Far from being society's expensive leftovers, elders and the elderhood they inhabit are crucial to the well-being of all."

—Gerontologist Dr. Bill Thomas

Author Jared Diamond says that the way a society treats its elders speaks to their perceived usefulness. That is, the more useful they are, the more they're respected and woven into the fabric of society. Historically, elders' usefulness had to do with their ability to recognize patterns in the crops and weather, sourcing and cooking food, trading acumen with other tribes, telling stories to the village children and caring for the village grandchildren, and the fine art of basket weaving.

Most of these skills are no longer valued in the West. But, no doubt, there are many children who could use more love, more gardens in need of tending, more stories waiting to be passed down. Old age doesn't need to be synonymous with uselessness. Developmental psychologist Erik Erikson believed the second half of life is the time when one weaves one's life experiences together in a revelatory way and offers this gift of wholeness to those younger. Modern Elders may not be basket weavers, but we are life weavers and, in a time when the young search ever more for meaning, our gift is of even greater value to society. Carl Jung suggested, "Man cannot stand to live a meaningless existence." With the second half of life extending decades longer than it did just a century ago, it's time we explore the purpose and meaning of longevity to the modern world.

In a 2016 *New York Times* op-ed column, H.H. the Dalai Lama (with Arthur Brooks) highlighted one experiment in which researchers found that older people who didn't feel useful to others were nearly three times as likely to die prematurely as those who did. "This speaks to a broader human truth," the Dalai Lama concluded. "We all need to be needed."

In their book, *The Joy of Old*, John S. Murphy and Frederic M. Hudson suggest there are three peaks in life: physical, which happens in one's early twenties; economic, which may happen in one's forties or fifties; and human, which happens later in life. During our physical peak, we are our bodies; during our economic peak, we are our work; and during our human peak, we are ourselves. Society often judges people in the second half of life based on a standard that venerates youthful bodies and high-octane, high-earning careers. But the true value of elders is in their humanity; and how they enhance the humanity of those who surround them.

Apple CEO Tim Cook was the commencement speaker at MIT's graduation ceremony in 2017 where he offered the following wisdom: "I'm not worried about artificial intelligence giving computers the ability to think like humans. I'm more concerned about people thinking like computers without values or compassion, without concern for consequences." Modern Elders can bring humanity to a world increasingly ruled by technology. Murphy and Hudson surmise, "In youth we seek perfection. In elderhood, wholeness." And, in role modeling that wholeness, we create a more integrated, fulfilled community that comes to realize it can "live more fully, then die more willingly."

SURVIVAL OF THE WISEST

"What is left once you have left the stage is an idiosyncratic image, especially the one presented in later years. . . . One's remaining image, that unique way of being and doing, left in the minds of others, continues to act upon them—in anecdote, reminiscence, dream; as exemplar, mentoring voice, ancestor—a potent force working in those with lives to live."

—JAMES HILLMAN

"I am what survives of me," famously wrote Erik Erikson in describing the war between "generativity and stagnation" at this later stage in our lives. We are generative when we move beyond our selfish needs and into serving something bigger than ourselves—whether it's your children, the quality of your friendships, the health of a religious institution or charity to which you've been devoted, or the young leaders you've incubated. And it is often our wisdom—in whatever forms it emerges—that survives us like a lasting fragrance that lingers long beyond our time.

Academic Else Frenkel-Brunswik found that we grow more selfless—and more giving to humankind in general with the passage of time. She was a student of Erik Erikson and helped give evidence to the "widening social radius" we experience as we grow older.

A young tree grows stronger when it's planted in an area with older trees, as the roots of the young tree are able to follow the pathways created by those of older trees. Over time, the roots of many trees graft themselves to one another, creating an intricate, interdependent foundation hidden below the surface and the forest becomes healthier and more resilient. The same is true for people; we are stronger when we are all connected. So how do we create a healthier "forest" in our later life? We become intentional about the pathways we carve for those we leave behind. While it may be fairly clear how we can do this in our families, how can we do it at work . . . where we spend most of our waking hours? It's plausible that the number one role of an effective leader is to create more effective leaders, right?

Dr. Marshall Goldsmith is one of the best-known executive coaches in the world and the author of a number of best sellers. At sixty-eight, after a lifetime of being a wise mentor and librarian, he became more intentional about how he will be survived. As Marshall pondered his heroes later in life, they were people like Peter Drucker and Frances Hesselbein, both of whom had been so generous in all that they had taught him, without asking for compensation of any kind. So he decided to "adopt" one hundred high-potential coaches, academics, and leaders to whom he could impart his wisdom, completely free of charge, with one condition: that they pay it forward when they themselves became elders. He calls this legacy plan "The Marshall Goldsmith 100 Coaches," a.k.a. the MG100, and it has been shortlisted by Thinkers50 as one of the most innovative ideas of the year in the business world. Marshall told me, "I don't have a big fortune I can give away like Bill Gates or Warren Buffett. But I can give away my knowledge."

Bill Plotkin, founder of Animas Valley Institute, is a depth psychologist, author, and agent of cultural evolution. Bill has guided thousands of adults on a variety of nature-based soul initiation journeys, including a contemporary Western adaptation of the pancultural vision quest in nature at his Animas Valley Institute. Wilderness and soul are fierce and ruthless, yet generous teachers—and fountains of untold wisdom. Faced with these survival challenges to one's self-image and worldview, it's amazing the kinds of epiphanies his participants experience. He writes eloquently of the role of the sage in the complicated, modern world, "When we are with a Sage, we're more likely to intuit a coherent and meaningful pattern in life, something we are part of, a feeling that things ultimately make sense even if we can't begin to articulate it. We are regenerated and strengthened by the living presence of a Sage, who renders our world less confusing, ambiguous, chaotic, and daunting." Although Bill's idea of the journey of soul initiation may be too extreme for some, how can you create a teachable moment to pass on your learning to a young sapling (sage-ling?) and keep your wisdom alive?

There's an unspoken pact that lies between the generations, touching everything from genes to values. We are like a conduit to the future, but are we conscious of how we're shaping that future? Every life is rooted in our ancestors and you and I aren't just elders-in-training, we're also ancestors-in-training. What gifts will we leave our descendants?

In his book, *Boomer Reinvention,* author John Tarnoff offers an eloquent metaphor from Carl Jung: "Imagine that you are standing outside on a sunny day. Think of yourself as a sundial. In the morning, as the sun rises, you cast a long shadow in one direction. As the morning continues, your shadow gets shorter and shorter until, at noon, you cast no shadow at all, with the sun being directly overhead." What Jung meant by this is that by midlife we can completely lose the sense of who we are because we may be trying to live someone else's image of us. But in the afternoon of life, according to Jung, something new happens. We begin to cast a shadow again. Tarnoff writes, "The key difference is that the shadow is lengthening away from us in a different, opposite direction from the one it took during the morning." He says that we can follow that shadow as it extends out into new territory, redefining us in a new way, expanding us in a profound, fresh direction. "By the time the sun sets, and we cease to cast a shadow and merge into the night, we have extended ourselves fully, creating a complete life that reflects our transformation from learner and experimenter into explorer and discoverer."

That beautifully expresses my shift from CEO of Joie de Vivre to Modern Elder at Airbnb and reminds me how psychologist G. Stanley Hall describes these elder years, "We rarely come to anything like a masterly grip till the shadows begin to slant eastward, and for a season, which varies greatly with individuals, our powers increase as the shadows lengthen."

HAS BEEN TO WILL BE

"The afternoon knows what the morning never suspected."

—SWEDISH PROVERB

We don't lament the lovely imperfections that start to appear over time on great architectural wonders. We don't worry about the cosmetic wrinkles that emerge at the hands of Mother Nature on aging natural landmarks, like the fissures in seaside cliffs or the knots in towering trees in the forest. Nor are we distressed when a comfortable leather chair grows a well-worn, lovable patina. So why do we get so wrapped about our own age spots and blemishes? Your patina could be as intriguing and exquisite as the façade of a crumbling Mayan temple, or the crags of the Canadian glaciers. Yes, these physical markers are a sign we've left our youth behind. But, as we get older, we must take everything in stride, including the passage of time.

When I was a teenager, the difference between a thirteen- and a nineteen-year-old seemed a divide as unbreachable as the Grand Canyon. Yet half a dozen years between two Modern Elders in their fifties is a rounding error. At this age, the small differences no longer seem so alienating and actually make us feel more connected.

I've been called a "perennial millennial" because I'm constantly focused on what's next. I don't mind walking into the unknown—whether it's a roomful of young strangers or the back alley of some city—as I don't see danger, I see serendipity. Maybe it's divine intervention, or an attuned skill, or merely a near-religious belief that the past has prepared me for the future. Whatever the case, I always create an empty and uncharted space in my life for Serendipity to have her way with me, like she did in my post–Joie de Vivre years. This is a radical change for the guy who used to believe that a full calendar was the mark of a worthy person.

Who among us hasn't looked longingly over our shoulder at the past? It's natural to reflect back once in a while. But too much nostalgic reflection and yearning for the familiar can foster an unhealthy love affair with what "Has Been." The challenge is to transcend our sense of history and self-importance and transplant ourselves into a habitat where a listening audience wants to receive the wisdom from our past, but where we can also look ahead, with optimism and anticipation, to falling in love with the future. While our body may get a little creaky, our soul can still dance wildly in a wider universe. Or, as Ingrid Bergman suggested, "Getting old is like climbing a mountain; you get a little out of breath, but the view is much better!"

At the peak of that mountain, you have the perspective to see not just what "Has Been," but what "Will Be." But only if you "Will It." And surround yourself with others with a "Will Be" mindset. Author Terry Jones suggests in *Elder: A Spiritual Alternative to Being Elderly* that we all have a "box of unlived life," almost like a time capsule from the future that we're meant to open later in life. Who can help you explore that box of unlived life waiting to be opened?

If you're a parent, the obvious answer is your children. And, if you're lucky, this gives you a second youth later in life (plus maybe some assistance in your last few years). At seventy-five, Rebecca Danigelis felt like a Has-Been. After fifty years of devotion in the hospitality industry, during which she'd never missed a day of work, she was unceremoniously fired. Rebecca had raised two sons as a single mother on her small salary made in hotel housekeeping operations and management. Her son, Sian-Pierre (SP) Regis, knew his mother wasn't a Has-Been. But she'd spent her life dedicated to her sons and to her work and thus never had time to dream about what Will Be. Upon losing her job, SP, an entertainment and millennial issues contributor for CNN, encouraged his mother to go on a "bucket list" adventure to check off all the things she'd always wanted to do . . . like milking a cow in Vermont, skydiving in Hawaii, reuniting with her daughter, and joining Instagram—where she now has 70,000 followers, a good bit more than her social-media-savvy son.

SP and Rebecca created a successful Kickstarter campaign to fund this bucket list journey, which soon became a reality. Their short video outlining their tour has already amassed nearly forty million views on Facebook, and their documentary called *Duty Free* will make the film festival circuit in 2019. I can't wait to see the film as the themes are so well aligned with this book: the sharing of wisdom between a Modern Elder and a millennial; perspective on the second half of life that is full of hope and anticipation for the future; the reality that anyone can rewire themselves for a successful "second act"—and one that's helping to create some financial security in a society that has seriously trimmed the safety net for its aging members.

Modern Elders like Rebecca come to realize that life is a series of thresholds, transitions, and reinventions. We essentially die and are reborn multiple times in this life. Or as the Japanese say, fall down seven times, get up eight.

If you live to ninety-five, you will take approximately 798,912,000 breaths. How many have truly been conscious? How would you live differently if you knew you'd just surpassed 798,900,000 and only have 12,000 more? The less time you have, the less you sweat all those past breaths. As we move to the finish line, we think less about time gone by and more about time well spent. And we even imagine what

"Will Be" written on our tombstone. I want mine to read, "Passionately lived his life with grace and grit . . . in that order." What about you?

"YOU KNOW IT WHEN YOU SEE IT"

"Leadership is like beauty—it's hard to define but you know it when you see it."

—WARREN BENNIS

Living half-time in Baja, I get to read a lot, which was very instructive for the writing of this book. I read an academic tome, the *Handbook of Wisdom*, while on a beach—an unlikely pairing of sand, ocean, and scholarly debate on the various definitions of wisdom. Of course, there's no single, clear-cut definition, but I appreciated one academic who suggested wisdom could be defined in the same language famously used by the Supreme Court in 1964 to define obscenity or pornography: "you know it when you see it." A Modern Elder's wisdom may be somewhat intangible, but we recognize it when we see it.

Part of being a Modern Elder is recognizing the burgeoning wisdom in the young when we see it. During my tenure at Airbnb, Nick D'Aloisio, nineteen, and possibly the world's youngest-funded venture capital entrepreneur, joined the company for a few months as an "entrepreneur-in-residence." Record labels seek out talented teenagers with silky voices, and NBA teams look for young basketball players with poised jump shots. But there isn't much of a history of this in the business world. Yet it wasn't hard to see the potential in Nick, and not just because he sold his first company to Yahoo at seventeen, was awarded the "Innovator of the Year" by the *Wall Street Journal*, and was honored by *TIME* magazine in the "Time 100" issue as one of the most influential teenagers in the world.

Socrates saw the definition of wisdom as being able to recognize the limits of one's own knowledge, which is difficult for many young entrepreneurs to understand especially if they've only experienced success in their twenties or thirties (or, in Nick's case, even younger). Arrogance and ignorance sound the same and, in many young tech companies, they can look the same as well. But I could see right away that this was not the case with Nick.

Nick was so much wiser than his years, perhaps partly due to the fact that he was studying both computer science *and* philosophy. It's easy as a Modern Elder to bemoan the fact that power will continue cascading to youth as our society becomes more and more reliant upon technology. Yet in my brief couple of one-on-ones with Nick, I felt more encouraged about our future generation of leaders than ever. Here was a young man who knew so much more than I did about all kinds of subjects, despite his age. And yet he was hungry for and appreciated the intangible wisdom I could offer. Nick and I hung on each other's words.

In some African tribal societies, the word "youth" is translated to "that which is still moist," raw and untested, yet pliable and full of potential. You could say a Modern Elder's legacy, particularly in the workplace, lies in how they help this "moist" generation achieve the fullness of their potential.

So what was my legacy at Airbnb? Coincidentally, my last day as an official Airbnb employee, nearly four years after I began my journey, coincided with our biannual gathering of all employees in San Francisco. We call this internal love-fest "One Airbnb." On January 19, 2017, on the very last night of this three-day tribal gathering, I was offered the opportunity to share twenty minutes of parting words to nearly three thousand employees from twenty-two offices from around the globe. We, as a company, had come so far in just four years—when we had just four hundred employees.

Brian introduced me and poignantly expressed the impact I'd

had on him as a leader; it seemed that as much as we had grown as a company in the time since I'd joined, Brian himself had grown more. Then he invited me onstage and, to my surprise, a spontaneous standing ovation erupted. Because my heart was overflowing in that moment, rather than sticking to my script, I began my parting words with a quote from Kahlil Gibran (from *The Prophet*), "Work is love made visible." Then, feeling the overwhelming responsibility to be the voice of the elder, I spoke about how our "little tech company that could" needed to "stay hospitable, stay human" as that's what truly differentiated us in the data-centric Valley and the transaction-focused online travel industry.

Ironically, I gave a commencement-like speech and yet, as Brian suggested in his introduction that night, I was the one graduating. It felt like giving the speech was the perfect ritual for receiving a new kind of degree—the Modern Elder diploma.

Being a Modern Elder is all about reciprocity. Giving *and* receiving. Teaching *and* learning. Speaking *and* listening. Everyone gets *older*, but not everyone gets *elder*. The first just happens (if you're lucky and healthy). The other you have to earn. By investing your time in reading this book, you've taken the first step to earn—but also to embrace and celebrate—your role as a Modern Elder.

An ending foreshadows a beginning, so I will offer this wise poem as my last gift to you in this coming new era of your life.

FOR A NEW BEGINNING

—JOHN O'DONOHUE

In out-of-the-way places of the heart,
Where your thoughts never think to wander,
This beginning has been quietly forming,
Waiting until you were ready to emerge.

For a long time it has watched your desire,
Feeling the emptiness growing inside you,
Noticing how you willed yourself on,
Still unable to leave what you had outgrown.
It watched you play with the seduction of safety
And the gray promises that sameness whispered,
Heard the waves of turmoil rise and relent,
Wondered would you always live like this.
Then the delight, when your courage kindled,
And out you stepped onto new ground,
Your eyes young again with energy and dream,
A path of plenitude opening before you.
Though your destination is not yet clear
You can trust the promise of this opening;
Unfurl yourself into the grace of beginning
That is at one with your life's desire.
Awaken your spirit to adventure;
Hold nothing back, learn to find ease in risk;
Soon you will be home in a new rhythm,
For your soul senses the world that awaits you.

Appendix

1. PERSONALITY TYPING TOOLS
(as referenced in the ModEl Practices section of chapter 6)

I believe that the success of any wise leader is largely a result of their ability to understand personalities. Here I've compiled a list of tools that I've found particularly useful. But, while understanding personalities is exceptionally valuable for self-awareness and collaboration, be careful in using these modalities as a blunt tool in labeling others. Your intention may be pure, but for the person who feels labeled, you come across as an amateur psychologist or first-class know-it-all and this could have the effect of reducing rather than building trust and understanding.

- Myers-Briggs Type Indicator (MBTI): This psychological self-analysis feels a little clinical for some, but it's probably the most prevalent methodology used and there are a variety of resources and books that can help you interpret results. www.myersbriggs.org

- Strengthfinders: Tom Rath's popular book, with follow-ups called 2.0, is core to some of the thinking behind the Gallup organization's work. It's a helpful approach to understanding the best words and descriptors to define yourself to others. www.strengthsquest.com

- Hogan Assessments: This more in-depth personality analysis focuses on three areas: Values (core values and motivators for leadership roles), Potential (strengths and competencies for leadership), and Challenges (derailers and personality-based performance risks). www.hoganassessments.com

- DISC: Along with MBTI, this is one of the more popular assessment tools because it's simple and nonthreatening. It's particularly helpful for new groups to encourage collaboration. www.discprofile.com

- Color Code or True Colors: There are a variety of tools that distill personalities down to four colors. I find these a little too basic and more like a parlor game, but they have been effective ways for people to learn about varying personality styles if they have no experience with this. www.colorcode.com. www.true-colors.com

- Enneagram: My fondness for the Enneagram is because it feels less specific to surface personality and more about the underlying influences. While the Riso-Hudson Enneagram Type Indicator (RHETI) is the best-known tool (www.enneagraminstitute.com), there are two others that address the nine personality types in the context of organizations in a more focused way: The Enneagram in Business: http://theenneagram inbusiness.com/ and Integrative 9: https://www.integrative9.com/

2. MY 10 FAVORITES

I want you to think of this book as a resource you will use for years to come. In each of the following sections, I list my ten favorites for each category. And I want you to think of me as that "Modern Elder" friend of yours whom you occasionally turn to for some sage advice, whether it be an inspirational quote; a book full of wisdom; an informative article; a snackable video; some web wisdom in the form of enjoyable blogs, newsletters, resource sites, and even a "Wisdom Scorecard"; some brainy academic studies and resources; and great organizations providing helpful services. Consider me your friend and "librarian" and know that in future editions of this book, this list will evolve (just like we do), so I'm always open to your suggestions as well, which you can send to info@wisdom@work.com.

QUOTES

What a relief to know that some of my favorite quotes that didn't quite fit in the chapters could find their way to inspire you here. I like to imagine an elder-only dinner party with James Baldwin, Winston Churchill, Gray Panthers founder Maggie Kuhn, Mark Twain, Lillian Hellman, and Socrates: a bon mot bonanza! And if I were so lucky to attend, here's one from me that might resonate with you: "My wrinkles represent tributaries from the wise river of life. My crow's feet embody all I've seen and understood. My forehead lines mark the stresses of the past that have been solved. My cheek hollows signify my valleys and redemptions. My laugh lines represent the number of times I've smiled in my life. My face is full of badges, not Botox."

1. "Any real change implies the breakup of the world as one has always known it, the loss of all that gave one identity, the end of safety. And at such a moment, unable to see and not daring to imagine what the future will now bring forth, one clings to what one knew, or thought one knew; to what one possessed or dreamed that one possessed. Yet it is only when man is able, without bitterness or self-pity, to surrender a dream he has long cherished, or a privilege he has long possessed, that he is set free—that he has set himself free—for higher dreams, for great privileges."—James Baldwin

2. "We are all happier in many ways when we are old than when we are young. The young sow wild oats. The old grow sage."—Winston Churchill

3. "We are not 'senior citizens' or 'golden-agers.' We are the elders, the experienced ones; we are maturing, growing adults responsible for the survival of our society. We are not wrinkled babies, succumbing to trivial, purposeless waste of our years and our time. We are a new breed of old people."—Maggie Kuhn

4. "I am making the case for elderhood, not for easy agedness. I'm doing so mostly by wondering what happened. Because something happened. Something happened to ancestors and elders and honour. There's work to be done, and there's an old wisdom to be learned where there used to be the wisdom of old, and you can't fix what you don't understand. That's where we're headed: to grievous wisdom. Let us see if we can bear the sound, the particular sound, of no hand clapping. This is a plea and a plot for elders in training."—Stephen Jenkinson

5. "Old paint on a canvas, as it ages, sometimes becomes transparent. When that happens it is possible, in some pictures, to see the original lines: a tree will show through a woman's dress, a child makes way for a dog, a large boat is no longer on an open sea. That is called pentimento because the painter 'repented,' changed his mind. Perhaps it would be as well to say that the old conception, replaced by a later choice, is a way of seeing and then seeing again. That is all I mean about the people in this book. The paint has aged and I wanted to see what was there for me once, what is there for me now."—Lillian Hellman

6. "I enjoy talking with very old people. They have gone before us on a road by which we, too, may have to travel, and I think we do well to learn from them what it is like."—Socrates

7. "When the cold front of demographics meets the warm front of unrealized dreams, the result will be a thunderstorm of purpose the likes of which the world has never seen."—Dan Pink

8. "In speaking of our growth potential, why do I use the verb 'to elder'? Eldering for me is a process word, a verb that connotes change and movement. It doesn't connote the unchanging frozen state of a noun. When we call someone a 'senior,' for example, this noun points to a static, lifeless condition. It's as if a state called 'senior' had been attained and all further organic growth had ceased. But when I refer to someone as 'eldering,' the 'ing' of the word refers to a state of growth and evolution, a process with endless possibilities. Eldering implies that we take active responsibility for our destiny in old age, living by conscious choice rather than social expectations."—Zalman Schachter-Shalomi and Ronald S. Miller

9. "A man is not old until regrets take the place of dreams."—John Barrymore

10. "The man who works and is never bored is never old. Work and interest in worthwhile things are the best remedy for age."—Pablo Casals, regarded by many as the greatest cellist of all time, who wrote an autobiography at ninety-three called *Joys and Sorrows*

Honorable Mention: Early in chapter 1, I paid homage to Gloria Steinem's quote, "One day I woke up and there was a seventy-year-old woman in my bed" as well as Bernard Baruch's quote, "To me, old age is always fifteen years older than I am."

BOOKS

In my research for writing *Wisdom@Work*, I read nearly 150 books, so I wish this list could be longer. The first four (1–4) gave a strong intellectual framework for some of my thinking. The middle three (5–7) provided a sprinkling of spirituality to the premise of the elder. And the final three (8–10) are great personal stories that demonstrate the value of an elder in today's world.

1. *The 100-Year Life: Living and Working in an Age of Longevity* (Lynda Gratton and Andrew Scott)

2. *The Big Shift: Navigating the New Stage Beyond Midlife* (Marc Freedman)

3. *The Adult Years: Mastering the Art of Self-Renewal* (Frederic M. Hudson)

4. *The Third Chapter: Passion, Risk, and Adventure in the 25 Years After 50* (Sara Lawrence-Lightfoot)

5. *Elder: A Spiritual Alternative to Being Elderly* (Terry Jones)

6. *From Age-ing to Sage-ing: A Revolutionary Approach to Growing Older* (Zalman Schachter-Shalomi and Ronald S. Miller)

7. *Mentoring: The Tao of Giving and Receiving Wisdom* (Chungliang Al Huang and Jerry Lynch)

8. *The Monk and the Riddle: The Education of a Silicon Valley Entrepreneur* (Randy Komisar with Kent Lineback)

9. *Life Reimagined: The Science, Art, and Opportunity of Midlife* (Barbara Bradley Hagerty)

10. *The New Old Me: My Late-Life Reinvention* (Meredith Maran)

ARTICLES

When, a year into my tenure at Airbnb, *Fast Company* wrote an article chronicling my mentor role with Brian (https://www.fastcompany.com/3027107/punk-meet-rock-airbnb-brian-chesky-chip-conley), I was amazed at how many emails I received from boomers who were similarly offering their wisdom to a millennial. A poignant article can be a source of validation and inspiration. Many of these were called out in the book, but I'd like to highlight a few: the first article is the long-form *Fast Company* piece about Paul Critchlow, the Pfizer senior intern. You read some of his story in chapter 4, but pay close attention to the short video embedded halfway through that gives you a hint of why senior internships might become more popular. The second article is a practical guide to understanding the most natural transitions from one industry or job classification to another; and the third article by Betty Friedan is worth noting because her 1993 book, *The Fountain of Age*, was meant to be a rallying cry for the over-fifty crowd, just as *The Feminine Mystique* was such a literary catalyst for the women's movement three decades earlier. This article is her passionate, smart synopsis of *The Fountain of Age* as captured in *TIME* magazine. The fourth article is a treasure trove of research and references about generational differences at work. The fifth article applies design thinking to career reinvention, through the story of a lawyer who switched careers to become a pastry chef then went on to get a master's in psychology. Honorable mention is *The New Yorker* article about Bill Campbell, the Coach, mentioned in chapter 2.

1. "Why a 70-Year-Old Retiree Went Back to Work—As an Intern." *Fast Company*, David Zax (September 20, 2016) https://www.fastcompany .com/3062378/senior-citizen-intern#

2. "Switching Careers Doesn't Have to Be Hard: Charting Jobs That Are Similar to Yours." *New York Times*, Claire Cain Miller and Quoctrung Bui (July 27, 2017) https://www.nytimes.com/2017/07/27/upshot/ switching-careers-is-hard-it-doesnt-have-to-be.html?_r=0

3. "My Quest for the Fountain of Age." *TIME*, Betty Friedan (September 6, 1993) http://faculty.randolphcollege.edu/bbullock/pdf/friedan.pdf

4. "A Complete Guide to Handshakes, Memeing, and How to Bridge the Generation Gap at Work." *Quartz at Work*, Prudential (October 6, 2017) https://work.qz.com/1095822/a-complete-guide-to-handshakes -memeing-and-how-to-bridge-the-generation-gap-at-work/

5. "I Used Design Thinking to Reinvent My Career—Here's Why It Worked." *Fast Company*, Paula Davis-Laack (October 16, 2017) https://www.fastcompany.com/40481175/i-used-design-thinking-to -reinvent-my-career-heres-why-it-worked

6. "What to Call the Time of Life Between Work and Old Age?" *The Economist* (July 6, 2017) https://www.economist.com/news/leaders/ 21724814-get-most-out-longer-lives-new-age-category-needed-what -call-time-life

7. https://www.washingtonpost.com/lifestyle/magazine/the-midlife -doldrums-are-a-social-crisis-now-theres-momentum-for-some -radical-fixes/2018/04/10/c5674db8-2e96-11e8-8688-e053ba58f1e4 _story.html?noredirect=on&utm_term=.8379a0e62470

8. "The Brutal Ageism of Tech." *New Republic*, Noam Scheider (March 23, 2014) https://newrepublic.com/article/117088/silicons-valleys-brutal-ageism

9. "Surviving as an Old in the Tech World." *Wired*, Karen Wickre (August 2, 2017) https://www.wired.com/story/surviving-as-an-old-in-the-tech-world

10. "What Could I Possibly Learn from a Mentor Half My Age? Plenty." *New York Times*, Phyllis Korkki (September 10, 2016) https://www.nytimes.com/2016/09/11/business/what-could-i-possibly-learn-from-a-mentor-half-my-age.html?emc=eta1&_r=2

Honorable Mentions: "Postscript: Bill Campbell, 1940–2016." *The New Yorker*, Ken Auletta (April 19, 2016) http://www.newyorker.com/business/currency/postscript-bill-campbell-1940-2016 and "Low Unemployment Healing US Job Market's Ugly Secret." Bloomberg, Craig Torres, and Catarina Saraiva (November 14, 2017) https://www.bloomberg.com/news/articles/2017-11-15/low-unemployment-healing-u-s-job-market-s-ugly-secret-age-bias

FILMS

This is a diverse list, but—of course—is topped off by *The Intern*. Three documentaries on this list capture the way older people find their passion later in life: Jiro, the world's best-known sushi chef; Wendy Whelan, still a famous ballet dancer at forty-seven in *Restless Creature*; and legendary jazz musician Clark Terry, who taught Quincy Jones and mentored Miles Davis, becoming the mentor of a blind twenty-three-year-old pianist in *Keep On Keepin' On*. Keep an eye on AARP's annual list of "Movies for Grown-Ups," which includes an awards ceremony.

1. *The Intern*
2. *Jiro Dreams of Sushi*
3. *Restless Creature*
4. *Keep On Keepin' On*
5. *Harold and Maude*
6. *The Best Exotic Marigold Hotel*
7. *The Curious Case of Benjamin Button*
8. *About Schmidt*

9. *While We're Young*
10. *Faces Places*

Honorable Mention: *Duty Free* (documentary scheduled to release in 2019 and mentioned in chapter 10)

VIDEOS/SPEECHES

If you want a short, hilarious depiction of the millennial-boomer generation gap, watch the first video. The second video is also short and compelling as it dispels the myth that as we get older we're less inclined to take feedback and evolve. The third through seventh videos are TED or TEDx talks. Pay particular attention to numbers 3 and 4 as these two women— Ashton Applewhite and Elizabeth White—are fierce and courageous in their depictions of the challenges of an ageist society.

1. "A Millennial Boss Interviewing a Boomer Candidate for a Job" (Hilarious and brief!) https://www.youtube.com/watch?v=Ed-5Zzdbx0E

2. "How Confidence and Willingness to Change Are Related" (*Harvard Business Review*) https://hbr.org/video/4793534579001/how-confidence-and-willingness-to-change-are-related

3. "Let's End Ageism," Ashton Applewhite (TED talk) https://www.ted.com/talks/ashton_applewhite_let_s_end_ageism

4. "Fifty-Five, Unemployed, Faking Normal," Elizabeth White (TEDx VCU) https://www.youtube.com/watch?v=hFpQ5N_ttNQ

5. "Choosing Conscious Elderhood," Larry Gray (TEDx Whitehorse) https://www.youtube.com/watch?v=gDrBtTYJ0G4

6. "Elderhood Rising: The Dawn of a New World Age," Dr. Bill Thomas (TEDx San Francisco) https://www.youtube.com/watch?v=ijbgcX3vIWs/

7. "How I Became an Entrepreneur at Sixty-Six," Paul Tasner (TED talk) https://www.ted.com/talks/paul_tasner_how_i_became_an_entrepreneur_at_66?utm_campaign=social&utm_medium=referral&utm_source=facebook.com&utm_content=talk&utm_term=business

8. "How to Design Moments That Help You Live (almost) Forever," John Coyle (TEDx Naperville talk) https://www.youtube.com/watch?v=kNhyOYv2ejw

9. "Re-Visioning Retirement," Ken Dychtwald https://www.merrilledge .com/article/video-revisioning-retirement-7-life-priorities

10. "10 Rules of Mentorship" https://www.youtube.com/watch?v=0qAbsgFjRW4

Honorable Mention: You may remember the heroic emergency landing by pilot Chesley "Sully" Sullenberger, hero of the *Miracle on the Hudson*, in New York of a US Airways plane carrying 155 passengers in January 2009. This inspiring story is certainly one of great courage under fire, yet there was another, less-talked-about attribute that also factored into his accomplishment. His ability to consider so many different things at once under such stressful conditions can be explained by a brain phenomenon known as bihemispheric processing. I mentioned this earlier in the book in association with psychiatrist Gene Cohen's findings that older people move to an "all-wheel drive" brain functioning due to a bridge of tissue that develops around age fifty between the left and right hemispheres of our brains. In this *60 Minutes* TV interview with Katie Couric, Sully says, "I think in many ways, as it turned out, my entire life up to that moment had been a preparation to handle that particular moment. . . . One way of looking at this might be that for forty-two years, I've been making small, regular deposits in this bank of experience, education, and train- ing. And on January 15, the balance was sufficient so that I could make a very large withdrawal." If you want to be inspired about how your life has prepared you for your future, watch this video. https://www.youtube.com/ watch?v=rZ5HnyEQg7M

WEB WISDOM

There are so many fascinating and fun references on the web, it's hard to distill this down to just ten. Next Avenue is probably one of the best sources for interesting articles about life after fifty. Retirement Jobs helps you find a job after fifty. And International Living and Ageist are beautiful sites that provide eye candy and beautiful stories about how life gets better after fifty.

1. Next Avenue http://www.nextavenue.org/
2. Retirement Jobs http://www.retirementjobs.com/
3. International Living https://internationalliving.com/
4. Ageist http://www.agei.st/
5. AARP Disrupt Aging Stories http://www.aarp.org/disrupt-aging/ stories/?intcmp-DISAGING-HDR-STORIES/

6. This Chair Rocks https://thischairrocks.com/
7. *New York Times*'s "Wisdom Scorecard" http://www.nytimes.com/ref/magazine/20070430_WISDOM.html
8. Pfizer's "Get Old" https://www.getold.com/
9. Gap Year After Sixty http://gapyearaftersixty.com
10. When to Start Receiving Retirement Benefits https://www.ssa.gov/pubs/EN-05-10147.pdf

ACADEMIC STUDIES AND RESOURCES

I'm a nerd when I'm writing a book, so I pored over dozens of academic studies that helped create some intellectual ballast for *Wisdom@Work*. The first half of this list includes some of those studies while the second half includes some of the institutions that help create some of the most cutting-edge research on the subject of longevity and aging today.

1. "Making Fast Strategic Decisions in High-Velocity Environments" (Kathleen M. Eisenhardt, *The Academy of Management Journal*, September 1989) http://www.edtgestion.hec.ulg.ac.be/upload/qualitatif%20-%20eisenhardt-amj-1989-high%20velocity.pdf

2. "Age Stereotypes in the Workplace: Common Stereotypes, Moderators, and Future Research Directions" (Richard A. Posthuma and Michael A. Campion, *Journal of Management*, October 26, 2007) http://journals.sagepub.com/doi/abs/10.1177/0149206308318617

3. "Reconsidering the Trade-off Between Expertise and Flexibility: A Cognitive Entrenchment Perspective" (Erik Dane, *The Academy of Management Review*, October 2010) http://amr.aom.org/content/35/4/579.short

4. "How BMW Is Planning for an Aging Workforce" (David Champion, March 11, 2009) https://hbr.org/2009/03/bmw-and-the-older-worker

5. "The Truth About Ageism in the Tech Industry" (Visier Insights Report) https://www.visier.com/wp-content/uploads/2017/09/Visier-Insights-AgeismInTech-Sept2017.pdf

6. The Conference Board Mature Worker Initiative (many studies) https://www.conference-board.org/matureworker/

7. Stanford Center for Longevity (many publications) http://longevity.stanford.edu/

8. MIT Age Lab (many publications) http://agelab.mit.edu/

9. Milken Institute for the Future of Aging (many publications) http://
   aging.milkeninstitute.org/

10. HowWeGather.org's "Care of Souls" https://www.howwegather.org/

ORGANIZATIONS PROVIDING SERVICES

These organizations are doing phenomenal work and often don't get enough attention. Special appreciation to Encore, which is building a movement to tap the skills and experience of those in midlife and beyond to improve communities and the world. Marc Freedman, who runs Encore, has been one of my biggest supporters and intellectual guides as I went from knowing nothing about aging to becoming one of the thought leaders in the space. He's been my Modern Elder.

1. Encore https://encore.org/
2. Bridgeworks http://www.generations.com/
3. Center for Conscious Eldering www.centerforconsciouseldering.com/
4. SCORE (Service Corps of Retired Executives) https://www.score.org/
5. Opportunity@Work http://www.opportunityatwork.org/
6. Institute for Career Transitions http://www.ictransitions.org/
7. The Transition Network https://thetransitionnetwork.org/
8. My Next Season https://mynextseason.com/
9. Generations United http://www.gu.org/
10. AARP http://www.aarp.org/

3. EIGHT STEPS TO BECOMING A MODERN ELDER

Movements always start with the personal. Momentum is gained when a collection of isolated individuals compare hearts and minds and a social connection is formed. Out of this social connection can emerge a new community and a new language along with the power of naming this community. Finally, this community makes the case for solving its needs, which often means righting an injustice. The rights of women, African Americans, the disabled, and LGBTQ people have all followed this arc. The rise of the value of the Modern Elder to society might follow this same path.

Here are eight steps you can take—from the personal to the movement-driven—to secure your own rise in value:

1. After reading *Wisdom@Work* a first time, go through it a second time using the exercises in chapters 4–8 as a guide for understanding whether the Modern Elder persona suits you.

2. Create a book club with a small group of friends who share some of the same challenges you face. Start by reading and talking about *Wisdom@Work* as well as some of the other books mentioned in it, especially the ten listed as my favorites in the Appendix.

3. Research and dive deeper into the resources in the Appendix listed under "Web Wisdom," "Academic Studies and Resources," and "Organizations Providing Services." You might also take the *New York Times*'s "Wisdom Scorecard" listed under "Web Wisdom."

4. Explore the idea of creating a Wisdom@ ERG (Employee Resource Group) at your company. As mentioned in chapter 9, for such a group to be effective, it often needs the following attributes: (a) connect the mission to a business challenge so the group doesn't feel frivolous or extraneous; (b) offer a tangible benefit to the employees in order to attract and retain members; (c) create clear goals and a clear definition of success; and (d) include senior leaders as sponsors in order to show that the company is serious in its commitment. And this ERG can hold the company accountable for the Top 10 Practices for Becoming an Age-Friendly Employer.

5. Spend some time reviewing the *Wisdom@Work* website, including my blog. Follow me on Twitter to keep abreast of webinars, workshops, and events for the Modern Elder.

6. Explore applying to the Modern Elder Academy and/or beginning your own "gap year."

7. If you attend and enjoy the Academy, consider becoming a Master Elder so that you can help train others. Becoming a Master Elder is only available to those who've graduated from the Academy.

8. Tap into the growing anti-ageism movement. Take a look at listings 4, 5, and 6 in the "Web Wisdom" section of the Appendix: Age.ist,

site. Over the next few years, while the movement may not be televised, you will hear more and more of its forming on websites like these. Our strength isn't just in our massive numbers as a Modern Elder population, but it's also in our resolve and, no doubt, many of us have roots in political activism that go back to our childhood. It's time to dust off the protest signs and put on our comfy shoes. "The times they are a changin'."

Acknowledgments

We all deserve to have a few wise people in our lives. Longtime friend and evolutionary astrologer Steven Forrest is one of mine, as he always seems to know what new spirit is gestating in me long before I do. In 2012, Steven told me to "embrace your wizard," which was jarring to hear as I was barely age fifty. But, lo and behold, one year later I was embedded in the high-tech land of the young. And in 2015, before I defined my role at Airbnb as that of a Modern Elder, or imagined this book, he planted another soulful seed suggesting that I would go on to offer my elder wisdom to a much larger audience.

The process of writing a book has often been compared to a pregnancy, although being a man I have little authority to suggest this metaphor. For me, I just start to feel different, almost like something is forming in my head, heart, and gut. Then serendipity kicks in and all kinds of thought leaders come into my life to guide me. In this case, Dr. Katy Fike and Stephen Johnston invited me to speak at their Aging2.0 conference—a few years before I had any real connection to the aging/longevity world. And Soren Gordhamer asked me to speak at his Wisdom 2.0 conference before I'd even written a book proposal. Sometimes others see in us what we can't yet see in ourselves. The world was mentoring me.

In the literary world, I have a primary source embedded in Manhattan, my agent, Richard Pine. Although he wasn't convinced about this idea when I first proposed it, like any good mentor, he challenged me to an intellectual joust and suggested some homework. My confidant, "story gardener," and thought partner for over a dozen years, Debra Amador DeLaRosa brought her editorial and creative midwifery to help me birth the book and all things Modern Elder. (Big thanks to Deb and Jennifer Raiser for helping me arrive at the title, *Wisdom@Work*, after I'd been myopically fixated on another name.)

With our more compelling book proposal in hand, Richard made the connection to the phenomenal crew at Crown/Currency. The universe gave me an extra nod with Talia Krohn (pronounced just like "crone," the archetypal wise woman) as my editor and the perfect teammate to test the book's boomer/millennial premise. It's the "Talia's" of the world who are helping to keep the publishing industry relevant. *Wisdom@Work* wouldn't have been half as good without her. And the Crown/Currency team, including Vice President and Publisher Tina Constable, Associate Publisher Campbell Wharton, Nicole McArdle in marketing, Owen Haney and Megan Schumann in publicity, and Erin Little in editorial have been champions in so many ways and a true delight to partner with.

Once I got the green light, I sat at the feet of aging/longevity community luminaries who taught me so much, including Marc Freedman, Dr. Ken Dychtwald, Dr. Laura Carstensen, Paul Irving, Ashton Applewhite, Keith Yamashita, Dr. Bill Thomas, and AARP CEO Jo Ann Jenkins and her colleague Karen Chong. And a variety of academics from Bob Sutton to Adam Grant helped guide me through the troves of research on wisdom in the workplace and intergenerational collaboration.

One hallmark of wisdom is the ability to forecast some of the costs and collateral benefits of the decisions we make. It took quite a bit of time to interview nearly one hundred fifty people for the book (some as many as four times), but the collateral benefits were the inspiration and education I received. Many of these folks made it within these pages. I wanted to thank everyone, so I've added a comprehensive list in the Acknowledgments section of the book's website at www.WisdomAtWorkBook.com. Extra appreciation to the following folks mentioned in the book: John Q. Smith, Michael and Debbie Campbell, Luther Kitahata, Joanna Riley and Peter Kent, Andrew Scott, Elizabeth White, Diane Flynn, Liz Wiseman, Fred Reid, Paul Critchlow, Jack Kenny, Bert Jacobs, Randy Komisar, Marianna Leuschel, and Karen Wickre.

More than two hundred wise women and men read early and later versions of the manuscript and the following gave me particularly valuable feedback: Dr. Carla O'Dell, Andrew Greenberg, Leslie Copeland and Mark Cooper, Dr. Prasad Kaipa, Evan Frank, Drew Banks, Craig Jacobs, Jeff Davis, Kiran Mani, Alpa Agarwal, Katherine Makinney, Neel Sharma, Lex Bayer, Alan Webber, Ruth Stergiou, Mattias Knaur, Fred MacDonald, Radha Agarwal, Pat Whitty, Amy Curtis McIntyre, Jonathan Mildenhall, Mark Levy, Tom Kelley, Kyrié Carpenter, Fred MacDonald, Jan Black, and Jeff Hamaoui.

Huge thanks to Nicki Dugan Pogue and her team at OutCast for leading the work on brand marketing strategy, website, and publicity. Perennial thanks to Peter Jacobs and his CAA team who support my speaking efforts. And my presentations wouldn't be nearly as compelling without alimat's Alison Macondray and Matt Clark.

This goes without saying, but I'll write it anyway: There would be no book had there been no introduction to Airbnb. Natalie Tucci, you've got quite an intuition. As the in-house "hospitality guru," I got to witness first class, new wave hospitality from teammates like Dave O'Neill, Jenna Cushner, Markus Vitulli, Laura Hughes, Clement Marcelet, Jessica Semaan, Lisa Dubost, Sarah Goodnow, and my extra special EA, Sarah Zoucha. The founders and Estaff created the perfect crucible for my beta test in the making of a Modern Elder. And a huge thanks to Beth Axelrod, Dessirree Madison-Biggs, Elizabeth Bohannon, and James Lynch for helping to provide the runway for my takeoff and landing.

No person stands alone. This culmination of my life's work (so far) has sprouted from an epic support network including Peggy Arent, Zain Elmarouk, MeiMei Fox, Ping Fu, Ben Davis, Wanda Whitaker, Lisa Keating, Frank Ostaseski, Gabriel Galluccio, and Mike Rielly. My emotional, spiritual, and Modern Elder life wouldn't be complete without the phenomenal advice and support I receive from Vanessa Inn, whose gifted talent helped elevate Ben Davis mentioned in chapter 8, as well as thousands of clients over three decades. And the Modern Elder Academy that grew from this book wouldn't exist without Oren Bronstein (the best friend one can imagine), Saul Kuperstein, Karla Caro, Tony Peralta, Barak Gaon, Lynda Malone, and our awesome director Christine Sperber.

My muse, coach, and spiritual sister Vanda Marlow has been my "Chip-whisperer" for nearly two decades, and I'm not just a better writer and teacher because of her support, I'm a better human as well.

Although my sweat and tears helped, this book wouldn't have happened without my blood. My parents, Fran and Steve, are my Modern Elders. My siblings, Cathy and Anne, and their loved ones, Bill and Nathalie and their kids, provide a humility ballast by reminding me of the many times in my life when I was far from a Modern Elder. Special shout-out to Anne, who's worked with me for more than twenty-five years and is now my business manager. There's no way I could be the whirling dervish I am without her steady, consistent support. And finally, my chosen family, Laura and Susan, and our two young boys, Eli and Ethan. We all want to leave a legacy, whether it's through our children, writing books, or serving the world as a Modern Elder. I hope this book brings my legacy to life for Eli and Ethan—who won't even be my current age a half-century from now—with the message that the future is bright for anyone, at any age, in our increasingly diverse society.

Finally, and somewhat awkwardly, I want to acknowledge the challenges and odds against writing a book. Thoreau wisely wrote, "The cost of something is measured by how much life you have to give of yourself." Writing a book extracts a cost. And when you've written before, there's always a frightened voice inside your head that questions whether your best work is behind you. This is my fifth published book (my eighth if you include the two I wrote at Stanford and the one I self-published at age fifty for my friends). Yet I feel—down to my toes—that this may be my best. And it might have the most lasting impact. If I'm right, then it's one more piece of evidence that your best years, dear reader, may still be ahead of you. I hope so.

And, just remember the wise words of Mark Twain: "Age is an issue of mind over matter. If you don't mind, it doesn't matter."

Index

About the Author

Bestselling author, hospitality entrepreneur, disruptive business rebel, and social change agent, Chip Conley is a leader at the forefront of the sharing economy. At age twenty-six, the founder of Joie de Vivre Hospitality took an inner-city motel and turned it into the second largest boutique hotel brand in the world.

In 2013, after being CEO of his innovative company for twenty-four years, he accepted an invitation from the founders of Airbnb to help transform a promising home-sharing start-up into what is today the world's largest hospitality brand. As head of Global Hospitality and Strategy, Chip taught his award-winning methods to hundreds of thousands of Airbnb hosts in nearly two hundred countries, and created the Airbnb Open that brings thousands together in a global festival of belonging (he transitioned to a part-time role as Strategic Adviser for Hospitality and Leadership in January 2017).

Chip founded Fest300 in 2013 to share his passion for travel and the world's best festivals (the company merged with Everfest in 2016, where he is part-time Chief Strategy Officer). He serves on the boards of the Burning Man Project and the Esalen Institute, and has received hospitality's highest honor, the Pioneer Award. He is the founder of the Celebrity Pool Toss, which has raised millions for the Tenderloin neighborhood where he opened his first hotel, and San Francisco's Hotel Hero Awards that shine a light on the unsung heroes serving hotel guests every day.

Inspired by psychologists Maslow and Frankl, Chip's books, *Peak* and the *New York Times* bestseller *Emotional Equations,* share his own theories on transformation and meaning in business and life. Chip holds a BA and MBA from Stanford University, and an honorary doctorate in psychology from Saybrook University.